S(p)lasher Flicks

S(p)lasher Flicks

The Swimming Pool in Horror Cinema

Cullen Wade

McFarland & Company, Inc., Publishers
Jefferson, North Carolina

Author's Statement: This book is 100 percent the product of human effort. No generative artificial intelligence played any part in the conception, composition or editing of this text.

LIBRARY OF CONGRESS CATALOGING-IN-PUBLICATION DATA

Names: Wade, Cullen author
Title: S(p)lasher flicks : the swimming pool in horror cinema / Cullen Wade.
Description: Jefferson, North Carolina : McFarland & Company, Inc., Publishers, 2026. | Includes bibliographical references and index.
Identifiers: LCCN 2025037779 | ISBN 9781476698151 paperback ∞
ISBN 9781476656120 ebook
Subjects: LCSH: Horror films—History and criticism | Swimming pools in motion pictures | Water in motion pictures | BISAC: PERFORMING ARTS / Film / Genres / Horror | LCGFT: Film criticism
Classification: LCC PN1995.9.H6 W244 2025 | DDC 791.43/6164—dc23/eng/20250903
LC record available at https://lccn.loc.gov/2025037779

ISBN (print) 978-1-4766-9815-1
ISBN (ebook) 978-1-4766-5612-0

© 2026 Cullen Wade. All rights reserved

No part of this book may be reproduced or transmitted in any form or by any means, electronic or mechanical, including photocopying or recording, or by any information storage and retrieval system, without permission in writing from the publisher.

Front cover image: Megan Fox in the 2009 film *Jennifer's Body* (20th Century-Fox/Photofest)

Printed in the United States of America

*McFarland & Company, Inc., Publishers
Box 611, Jefferson, North Carolina 28640
www.mcfarlandpub.com*

To my dad,
for letting me
show off all my tricks

Table of Contents

Acknowledgments ix

Preface 1

Part I—Something in the Water: The Pool as a Site of Secrets

Introduction 6

1. Buoyant Spirits: Haunted Houses and Their Pools 9
2. Beach Entry: The Natural and the Unnatural 19
3. Synchronized Swimmers: Narcissus and the Mirror Self 30

Part II—Adult Swim: The Pool as a Site of Sexuality

Introduction 44

4. The Changing Room: Atavism, Contagion and Transforming Women 48
5. The Back Stroke: Aquatic Female Vengeance 63
6. The Sunken Sorceress: Pools, Witchcraft and Youth 77
7. Matching Two-Piece: Queer Femme Awakenings Poolside 91
8. Fish Out of Water: Challenging Masculinity 104
9. Night Swimming Prohibited: Queer Vampires at the Pool 114
10. Skinny Dipping: Misogyny in Slashers and Gialli 122

Part III—A Dip in the Labor Pool: The Pool as a Site of Social Segregation

Introduction 140

11. Swimming Pools, Movie Stars: Los Angeles and Secret Societies 145
12. Suburbed, Othered, Submerged: Outsider Status in the Teen Horror Film 155

13. The Stepford Dives: Manufactured Perfection at the Pool — 171
14. Skimming the Gene Pool: The Ghost of Eugenics — 181
15. Life Guards: Interlopers and Home Invasions — 191
16. Underwater Mortgage: Housing and Class Struggle — 203
17. Pool, A/C, Cable TV: Travel for the Leisure Class — 213

Postscript — 225
Filmography — 229
Chapter Notes — 233
Bibliography — 245
Index — 247

Acknowledgments

First-time authors get a little latitude for effusive acknowledgments pages, right? Every few years, when I'd pull out my sixth grade yearbook and see my teacher Carol Horn's inscription asking me to send her a copy of my first book, it was a reminder that I should write a book at some point. Much love to Wo Chan, who is my best writer friend, both in the sense that they are my best friend who is a writer and the best writer who is my friend. I couldn't let them be the only one with a book out. Another friend partially to blame for this book is Tod Gorman, who gassed me up by assuring me my film critique was valid even though I didn't go to school for it. Jillian Hatch doesn't know it, but her couch where I crashed the summer I was homeless was also where this book idea was hatched and the first notes jotted.

I've learned more about film writing and analysis from my Letterboxd circle than from any book I've read or course I've taken. Writers like Sally Jane Black, pd187, Nathaxnne Walker, andread, and Marna Larsen showed me the way to a kind of film critique I could put my whole self into, while the platform gave me a space to sharpen my writing and document my winding journey through movieland. Special shout-out to Letterboxders Cait Cibs and miau, who showed unsolicited enthusiasm for this project. Offline friends whose appreciation of my film writing kept me motivated include Raven, Jeremy, Sabr and Tim (RIP), as well as my students Jack, Rain and Richie.

Research is a cinch when you are fortunate enough to live in a town with two splendid library systems; I am especially grateful that I can still use the University of Virginia library, even though I dropped out of grad school more than a decade ago. Sorry about that interlibrary loan I requested and then decided I didn't need. My colleague Tim Klobuchar and Scarecrow Video in Seattle were also helpful with sourcing materials.

Thanks to Stan Stepanic for guidance, feedback on sample chapters, and generosity with providing outlets for my writing. The Live Poets Society of Charlottesville was the first group of people to read and/or hear any portion of this book, and they helped quiet my misgivings about prose style. I am also grateful to my employer, Monticello High School, for not monitoring too closely what gets printed in the copy room.

I've been reading books published by McFarland for 20 years, so it's an honor to have one with my name on it. Thanks to the editors for deciding I have something to offer. Thanks more broadly to the entire ecosystem of horror scholarship and critique. I'm privileged to offer a small addition to our passionate niche.

Thanks to Laura Jane Grace for opening her concert with "The Swimming Pool Song" and giving me the opportunity to stage-dive three days after I signed the contract to publish this book.

My wife Emma deserves more credit than I can express for tolerance of my hyper-focus, movie-watching companionship, and encouragement every time I worried this book was stupid. Emma is my most steadfast champion, and I am proud to be hers.

Preface

> I am a haunted swimming pool, I am emptied out and drained, my capacity remains unchanged.
> —Laura Jane Grace, "The Swimming Pool Song"

The idea for this book came to me in summer 2014, after nearly back-to-back viewings of *House* (1985) and *Gremlins* (1984) got me intrigued about how these two '80s monster comedies used the symbol of the swimming pool. One presented a residential pool on the grounds of a stately mansion as a portal to the past, a site of reckoning with submerged memories and shaking off the shackles of guilt. The other film turned a public pool into a manifestation of the Reagan "'80s" xenophobia, a place where "undesirables" multiply out of control and threaten quaint small-town values. If the same, rather mundane image—a concrete pit full of chemically treated water—could do such different kinds of work in two superficially similar films, what else was hiding in the deep end?

The thought excited me. I started jotting notes, brain-dumping every horror film I could think of with a pool scene, and sorting them into rough categories—thematically as well as by subgenre, by era, and by type of pool (public pools, private pools, residential pools, school pools, empty pools, neglected pools, above-ground pools, etc.). The following year I started keeping a running Letterboxd list called "Horror Films Featuring Swimming Pools." At the time of this writing, it has 230 entries. This text is the product of a decade's worth of thinking about what makes the swimming pool such a potent image in horror cinema.

My earliest exposures to swimming pool horror were not movies, nor any kind of narrative fiction at all. A public service announcement by the Partnership for a Drug-Free America, launched in 1989, when I was four, featured a woman diving into what the closing shot revealed was an empty swimming pool.[1] I remember the uproar in 1995 when champion diver Greg Louganis revealed himself to be HIV-positive, and while the public panicked over whether he could have infected others by bleeding in the pool after hitting his head on a diving board during the 1988 Olympics, the news looped slow-motion footage of the accident, over and over.[2] Around the same time, a bully at YMCA day camp repeatedly gave me aggressive wedgies in the pool. I don't remember the kid's name or what he looked like, but I remember the abrasion from nylon swim trunks yanked into the crack of my ass.

I didn't quite grasp the quasi-sexual nature of this violation, but it was not lost on my father. Speaking of my father, he was an attorney who had done personal injury work, and he continually cautioned me about all the horrific accidents that can accompany the sport of diving. Of course, if I had been a Black American, you could have added generational trauma from being excluded from public swimming pools, and various harmful stereotypes around Black people and swimming in general.

So my childhood experience of pools was a mixture of the fun and the dreadful, and I suspect it is the same for a lot of people. A 2008 Gallup study found that 46 percent of participants reported being afraid of the deep end of a pool.[3] Annually nearly 400 children drown in swimming pools,[4] and diving boards send about 6500 people to the emergency room.[5] But bicycles kill about 1000 people a year,[6] and the horror genre isn't brimming with movies about deadly bicycles. So why are swimming pool scenes in horror so numerous?

From an artistic standpoint, the pool presents interesting visual opportunities: tile mosaics in blue, dancing ripples reflected on walls, the way water distorts what's beneath it. The cool, sometimes sickly colors of pool lighting; the otherworldliness of underwater photography that turns humans into floating apparitions; and the perennial concern of the horror artist: the look of blood when it mixes with water. The pool also offers sound design possibilities: hollow indoor pool reverb, lapping and splashing echoes on concrete, tile and steel.

From a production standpoint, a lot of filmmaking happens in Southern California, a region known for its abundance of pools. Smart filmmakers—especially those working on low budgets as horror projects often are—tend to use every available part of a location. If there is a pool, it will likely find its way into the movie. Rob Zombie said of the empty-pool climax of *Halloween* (2007), "The swimming pool idea came much later, it wasn't in the script originally, because when I was location scouting and found the Myers house, I saw this giant swimming pool in the backyard. I was like, 'Great!'"[7] Last but not least, exploitation-minded filmmakers might use a pool scene as an excuse to photograph their attractive casts in revealing swimsuits.

But I don't think such prosaic reasons fully explain the preponderance of pool scenes in horror. In undertaking this work, I've come to realize that people are drawn to pools for many of the same reasons we are drawn to horror. They touch something primal. They have a quality of danger and the forbidden. They are nostalgic. They make us aware of our bodies. They are artificial: Horror movies let us experience peril from a safe distance, and swimming pools give us some of the benefits of a natural body of water with less risk. The swimming pool's in-betweenness makes it perfect for representing borders between the familiar and the strange, the natural and the wild, the human and the non-human. Theorist Barbara Creed, drawing on Julia Kristeva's notion of the abject, writes:

> The concept of a border is central to the construction of the monstrous in the horror film. …Although the specific nature of the border changes from film to film, the function of the

Serendipity: Director Rob Zombie (background) and cinematographer Phil Parmet stumble upon what would become the Myers pool while location scouting for *Halloween* (2007). Source: *Michael Lives: The Making of* Halloween (2008).

monstrous remains the same—to bring about an encounter between the symbolic order and that which threatens its stability.

"Most horror films," Creed goes on, "construct a border between what Kristeva refers to as 'the clean and proper body' and the abject body ... which has lost its form and integrity."[8] We will return to this concept throughout the book, as we learn about the swimming pool's associations with hygiene (clean body) and fitness (proper body). Often we can tell what side of Kristeva's border a character is on by where they are in relation to the pool.

The swimming pool has been one of the genre's most enduring and versatile symbols. I've divided this text into three parts for the three overlapping symbolic territories that the swimming pool occupies. (These umbrella categories were among the first things I wrote down when I began this work back in 2014, and they have proven surprisingly durable.) Part I discusses the pool as a site of secrets, from the primal fear of what lurks in deep water to the shame and trauma we conceal beneath a placid surface. Part II is about the pool as a site of sexuality, of bodies on display, and the use of water symbolism for femininity. In Part III, I'll talk about the pool as a site of social segregation, a symbol of inequality and control. Along the way, we'll learn some swimming pool history and take detours through psychology, mythology, eugenics, virology, economics, motherhood, moral panics, ecology, social media and a whole lot of politics. We'll learn why Southern California has so many cults, why American teen culture would not exist without the suburbs, and why real estate agents are usually women. If you don't see what any of those things have to do with swimming pools or horror movies, please read on.

Although there are 14 countries represented, the overwhelming majority of the films in this book are from the United States. Most of the history and politics I'll discuss will pertain to the U.S. as well. It is the country where I have lived most of my life and the national cinema I have the most exposure to, but I've taken care to indicate when I am writing about an idea or a trend that is specifically American rather than trying to paint it as universal. Speaking of acknowledging bias, my critical lenses tend to be cultural, feminist, queer, and Marxist. I will also use psychoanalytic and disability lenses here and there. I have avoided delving into the people behind the films themselves, or the circumstances of their production. The only name I'll use is that of the director, whom I refer to as the author of a film. This is not meant to dismiss the contributions of screenwriters and other personnel, but merely for simplicity's sake. I will refer to the films by the titles under which I first encountered them, but original-language titles, as well as significant alternate titles, are listed in the Filmography.

Most of the films I'll discuss will fit into more than one of the three overarching categories. My reading of any particular film may lean more in one direction for the sake of taxonomy, but I had to do something to keep this thing organized. I am confining my analysis to feature-length films—no shorts or TV episodes (with two exceptions). Made-for-TV movies and direct-to-video releases are eligible. This is not meant to be an exhaustive list of swimming pool horror movies. It's a survey of approximately 100 films that I think are significant. If your favorite movie isn't included, it's either because I couldn't think of anything interesting to say about it, or I haven't seen it. I will give only as much synopsis as is necessary to make my point, so the amount of detail will vary by the movie, and any plot surprises will probably, but not definitely, be spoiled. Some readers will no doubt take issue with my categorizing a few of the films here as belonging to the horror genre, to which I reply, in the spirit of Lloyd Kaufman: Write your own damn book.

Before we proceed, I'd like to revisit what I described above as my earliest encounters with swimming pool horror: the drug PSA, the bully at the Y, and Greg Louganis. It occurs to me that these three memories map nicely onto my three categories. Something terrible hiding below a pleasant exterior (Part I), a physical violation when partially nude (Part II), and a person of marginalized status causing panic by simply being in a pool (Part III). I guess I learned everything I know about swimming pool horror before the age of ten. I just finally got around to writing it all down.

Now, if you're the kind of reader I am, you will be grateful that I resisted the temptation to end this introduction with a corny pool-related pun. So whatever we do, let's *not* dive in.

PART I
Something in the Water
The Pool as a Site of Secrets

Introduction

> The perfect pool is bright,
> but it has no colour—
> —John Tranter, "The Pool"

It's the first sentence of the first chapter, and I am going to break my own rule and talk about a TV episode, because to my best recollection it's the first swimming pool horror film I saw—at least, the first to make an impression. Directed by D.J. MacHale, "The Tale of the Dead Man's Float," a 1995 episode of the Canadian kids' anthology show *Are You Afraid of the Dark?*, tells the story of two tweens who discover a hidden, disused swimming pool in their school and manage to get it reopened, only to discover the reason it was bricked up in the first place: It's haunted by a grotesque undead creature. The school's caretaker tells the students the pool was built atop a graveyard (more on this trope later) and the creature is a dead body animated by a vengeful ghost. The caretaker lives with guilt from having let a child drown when he was a lifeguard. Despite the pool having been sealed up for decades, the spirit's appetite for vengeance is still not sated.[1]

The films in Part I exploit the fundamental human fear of the unknown—the root of our uneasiness about dark places, strange people and bodies of water. You want to believe that if someone or something is in your personal space, you will know about it. To imagine otherwise is deeply unnerving. All other things being equal, people feel more vulnerable in the water than they do on land. The ocean in particular is an alien and only partially understood place. Its size and power are difficult for humans to grasp. Some amount of our fear and awe of natural bodies of water is carried over to swimming pools—after all, your brain knows that you are in a human-made and controlled environment, but your body doesn't. You know your chance of being eaten by a shark in your friend's pool is zero, but that doesn't stop it from being a surprisingly common fear. This tension between natural and artificial bodies of water is fertile for exploring the horrors of both.

Water hides things, but so do people. We submerge memories, sublimate urges and suppress unwanted thoughts. No matter what sits at a pool's bottom, the surface will remain perfectly flat and tranquil—a handy metaphor for the turmoil we can hide under a placid exterior.

The pool in "The Tale of the Dead Man's Float" is hidden in more ways than one. Its physical concealment behind a wall in the locker room puts the story in the realm of the gothic, where buildings hide passageways and characters hide their motives. As we'll see, the gothic mode is common in pool horror: spaces are bigger on the inside than they look on the outside—or to put it in our terms, have hidden depths. By hiding away the pool, the school administration is also hiding the memory of what happened there. The films we'll examine commonly depict conflict between those who want the past to stay buried and those who want to expose it, thereby neutralizing the pernicious effects of secret-keeping. In most of these tales, the latter group wins. The kids of "Dead Man's Float" reopen the pool and reckon with its past, while the caretaker rescues a child to make up for the one he didn't save.

A similar dynamic—the elders wishing to sink the past and the kids to dredge it up—is at the heart of the *Nightmare on Elm Street* franchise. Samuel Bayer's series reboot from 2010 jettisons the coy suggestiveness of the '80s films and makes it canonically clear that Freddy Krueger was a child molester. The Springwood kids, rather than just being the children of the mob who killed Freddy, are the victims of his sexual assault. The assaults happened when the children were in pre-school, too young to have more than vague memories of them, and their parents have made efforts to keep the kids in the dark about what happened. "I didn't want you to go through your life with this memory," says the mother of Final Girl Nancy. "I wanted you to forget."

On the other hand, Freddy—who is now a spirit with the ability to enter the teenagers' dreams, where he tortures and murders them—wants them to remember. After killing all but two of the kids, he attacks Quentin when he passes out during swim practice. Here is a trope we'll return to plenty: the pool as portal. Quentin is pulled through the swimming pool's bottom and surfaces in a pit of dirty water in the industrial area where Freddy was killed. The scene of Freddy's extrajudicial

In *A Nightmare on Elm Street* (2010), Quentin (Kyle Gallner) is transported from swim practice into Freddy Krueger's backstory.

murder at the hands of the parents' mob is replayed while Quentin, wet and shivering in his swimsuit, watches.[2]

By pulling him through the school's institutional pool and into a concrete cistern, Freddy is symbolically pulling Quentin through the layer of denial the parents have placed on top of the ugly truth. Was it right of the parents to try to make their children forget? It spared them some pain in the short term, but in the long run it denied them the knowledge of what they faced. The kids were unprepared for Freddy when he began targeting them. Freddy wants Quentin to bear witness to his suffering, but by pulling him out of the pool, he inadvertently gives Quentin and Nancy the tools to defeat him.

At its most basic, the swimming pool is a hole in the ground. The classic pool shape, the rectangle, is identical to that of a grave. It is filled not with earth but with water, making it easy to deposit bodies, and equally easy for those bodies to resurface. In the words of Dick Hebdige, "The pool in contemporary popular culture is, more often than not, the scene of disquiet and ugly catharsis: the exposed location where intimations of mortality and looming crisis suddenly intrude out of the blue."[3] As we'll see, that looming crisis can be personal, global, or at any scale in between. The films in Part I all deal with pools that conceal things: creatures, secrets, forbidden knowledge, or truths we refuse to admit even to ourselves.

CHAPTER 1

Buoyant Spirits

Haunted Houses and Their Pools

> Sharp government spending cuts have forced contentious choices on local authorities, perhaps none more so than one council's decision to heat a community swimming pool with energy diverted from a crematory.
> —John F. Burns, "Britain: Crematory to Heat Swimming Pool,"
> *The New York Times*, February 9, 2011

> I remember everything, things I can't forget,
>   swimming pools of butterflies that slipped right through the net.
> —John Prine, "I Remember Everything"

I'm going to begin this section with two films that are, in a way, bookends: the film that first got me thinking about the topic for this book, 1985's *House*; and a film from the current year of this writing, *Night Swim* (2024). As it happens, they share some key themes and end up pairing nicely. *House*, directed by Steve Miner, tells its story in a deceptively complex, non-linear narrative, where the past constantly intrudes on the present as flashbacks and ghostly apparitions. I'm reminded of what memoirist Lidia Yuknavitch calls "the chronology of water":

> Events don't have cause and effect relationships the way you wish they did. It's all a series of fragments and repetitions and pattern formations. Language and water have this in common. All the events of my life swim in and out between each other.[1]

To an observer, horror novelist Roger Cobb's life may seem charmed, but on the inside, things are falling apart. He is grieving the disappearance of his young son Jimmy, and the divorce that resulted from its fallout. His aunt, who raised him, just committed suicide. The good will from his last bestseller has almost run dry, and his agent is demanding a new book. He wants—he says *needs*—to write a memoir of his experience in the Vietnam War, but suffers from serious writer's block. Amidst all this, he moves back into his aunt's house, the site of both her suicide and Jimmy's disappearance. Ostensibly the move is meant to kickstart his new book, but perhaps subconsciously, Roger needs to confront the ghosts of his past. Nobody told him those ghosts would be so literal.

The property's irregularly shaped swimming pool, made to look like a natural pond, triggers Roger's memory of Jimmy's disappearance. He believes he last saw Jimmy struggling in the water, but when he dove in to save him, the boy was not there, and indeed hasn't been seen since. This isn't the only memory that tortures Roger; he also has flashbacks to his time in Vietnam, when his failure to perform a mercy killing on his wounded buddy Big Ben resulted in Ben being captured by the Viet Cong and tortured for days. Implied to suffer from post-traumatic stress disorder, Roger relives the war, donning his G.I. uniform complete with helmet and goggles for an anticipated ghost encounter. Convinced after several spectral disturbances that Jimmy is somewhere in the house, Roger breaks the bathroom mirror and climbs through it into a black void. He falls into a seemingly bottomless body of water which transforms into the wetlands of Vietnam, and finds Jimmy in a POW cage, presumably like the one where Ben was kept. He frees the boy, leaps with him into the water, and surfaces back in the house's swimming pool. It turns out that Ben's vindictive spirit has kidnapped the boy to punish Roger for letting him suffer. It's not until he confronts Ben directly that he can declare that his memories no longer have any power over him. By reckoning with his painful past, Roger is able to recover his child and reunite with his ex-wife (and presumably write his book).[2]

House's swimming pool serves a similar function to *A Nightmare on Elm Street*'s: the act of going through and emerging from the pool represents crossing the boundary between the characters and the truths of their pasts. This haunted house distorts not just time, but space as well, concealing irrational gulfs behind mundane surfaces—the world beyond the looking-glass. Like the house, Roger is bigger on the inside than he is on the outside, and he struggles to integrate the disparate parts of his identity. His war memories—of being sent across the world to fight in an unpopular conflict, derided as a killer by those at home and made to feel like a coward by his colleagues for not killing enough—have him at the mercy of forces more powerful than he is. By breaking the mirror, he rejects his surface reflection and determines to go deeper. This action is echoed when he breaks the swimming pool's surface and emerges with his rescued son. The image of the pool links two bodies of water that played host to Roger's two most traumatic experiences: losing his son and losing Big Ben. The haunted house is a site of psychic residue, a place where the past refuses to let go. But it is also the place where Roger must go to vanquish his demons, first by looking them in the eye, and finally with cleansing fire.

In the tradition of Stephen King's reading of *The Amityville Horror* as a parable about the stress of buying a house you can't afford,[3] many a modern-day haunted house tale is seasoned with economic precarity. The haunted pool in Bryce McGuire's *Night Swim* does double duty as a symbol of the historicity of place, like *House*'s pool, and a reminder of the financial hole so many Americans live uncomfortably close to. In *Night Swim*, big-league baseball player Ray Waller has his career stopped short by an aggressive case of multiple sclerosis. Thus the family finds themselves with enough financial reserves to buy a suburban house with a pool, but without a safety net for medical expenses. For a while, things look good. Hydrotherapy in

Roger (William Katt) rushes to save his son from the pool in *House* (1985).

the pool seems to have a miraculous effect on Ray's MS, to the point where he dares to hope of returning to the baseball diamond. The healing, though, comes at a price, as his wife Eve learns when she discovers that the former occupant of the house sacrificed her healthy daughter for the salvation of her sick son.[4]

Therapeutic immersion in healing waters is an old idea. During the Victorian era, people of means flocked to spas and seasides to "take the water cure."[5] The original pitch to establish public swimming pools was a salutary one. As Jeff Wiltse discusses in *Contested Waters: A Social History of Swimming Pools*, before the widespread acceptance of germ theory, it was thought that immersion in water of any kind was healthful for the populace. Public pools were touted as a remedy for the diseased condition of the unwashed masses.[6]

So historically, swimming pool salubrity has been associated with both the very rich and the very poor. The Wallers are somewhere in between. They have savings, but Eve reveals that she had to take a job as a public school office associate in order to get health insurance. I worked for three years as a public school office associate and—not to demean the work—I know that it's a very low-paying job. The lurking threat symbolized by the haunted pool is twofold: the Damocles sword of illness that could take a turn for the worse at any time, and the grim reality of how many Americans are one health crisis away from insolvency.[7] Twenty million Americans live with medical debt they never expect to repay.[8]

Night Swim's haunted pool, like *House*'s, opens at times into what might be an endless gulf, complete with underwater shots looking up at a tiny blue rectangle of sky in the midst of black, cosmic cold. But unlike in *House*, this pool's secrets do not lose their power when exposed. There is a suggestion similar to the conceit of Stephen King's *Pet Sematary*, that the pool, fed by a natural spring, was built atop a

Eve (Kelly Condon) and Elliot (Gavin Warren) swim desperately to escape the stygian gulf beneath their backyard pool in *Night Swim* (2024).

place of power that had been used for magic since time immemorial.[9] This reinforces the symbolism of precarity, both financial and medical—the idea of being perched over a yawning chasm, one uncaring and little-understood. Like disease; like the economic forces we're all at the mercy of; like a backyard swimming pool when you can't see the bottom.

Night Swim's view of the long now, and its concern with what lies underneath its haunted house, bring us to the most well-regarded and influential modern haunted house film: Tobe Hooper's *Poltergeist* (1982). The Freeling family lives in a suburban subdivision called Cuesta Verde, where Steve Freeling sells houses for the developer who built it. The first family to move into the development, the Freelings have watched the neighborhood grow up around them. Steve's wife Diane is a stay-at-home mom who looks after their three children, including five-year-old Carol Anne, who was born in the house. A series of inexplicable disturbances seems to focus on Carol Anne, culminating in her abduction by the ghosts through a portal in the closet. With the help of parapsychologist Dr. Lesh and a medium named Tangina, the family is able to rescue Carol Anne. The spirits renew their assault on the house in a final volley that sees corpses arising from the property's unfinished swimming pool.[10]

While it's far from a rip-off, *House* certainly got a lot of its moves from *Poltergeist*, from the slam-bang effects-heavy climax—a far cry from the subtlety of classic haunted house movies—to the image of a parent tying a rope around themself before entering extradimensional space to rescue their child. But whereas Roger in *House* is haunted by his personal traumas, the *Poltergeist* characters seem to have no pasts at all. There are no flashbacks, and the only reference to anyone's childhood is a sleepwalking story Diane tells in the opening ten minutes. For all the background we are given, these people's lives may as well have started the day they moved to Cuesta Verde. But this absence of backstory is not a flaw in *Poltergeist*'s storytelling—it is the point. If *A Nightmare on Elm Street* indicts those who want to bury the past, and *House* cautions those who can't make peace with it, *Poltergeist* criticizes those who never seek to know in the first place.

Steve thinks of himself and his family as Cuesta Verde's first citizens, the pioneers. This is obviously not true. *Poltergeist* satirizes American ignorance of the land's original occupants. "Hooper's movies have always concerned the fear and ugliness of death," writes John Kenneth Muir. "The suburbs, even with all their luxuries, do not elevate humanity beyond the level where it must fear death."[11] In the U.S., to confront the history of the land is to reckon with death and displacement. In response to Steve's misgivings about relocating a cemetery to build a new development, his boss Mr. Teague jokes, "It's not ancient tribal burial ground. It's just people." The line dehumanizes Native Americans as something other than "just people," and also indicates that Teague does not know or care about the history of the land before Europeans came along. What little concern he has is for the white people buried there, and that concern is merely a matter of optics. After he reveals that Cuesta Verde too was built atop a displaced graveyard, he adds, "It's not the sort of thing one goes around advertising on a billboard." Teague knows that reminding customers of the land's history—or that the land even *has* a history—would be bad for business. For the most part, Steve's customers—and until recently, Steve himself—are content not to know.

When Cuesta Verde's long-ignored past finally explodes into the present, it does so through the bottom of the swimming pool. We'll talk more about the pool as a status symbol in Part III of this book, but for now, suffice it to say that Steve is not just selling houses, he is selling the American dream. Tellingly, in the same early scene where Diane makes the only mention of her life before Cuesta Verde, she also voices anxiety about the pool: She worries Carol Anne might fall in while sleepwalking. Steve quickly defuses the thought; his business forbids him to mention death and bourgeois luxuries in the same breath.

Metaphorically speaking, Diane's sleepwalking episodes did not end after childhood. She's spent her time in Cuesta Verde walking around dreaming that American dream, eyes closed to the realities beneath her. She, not Carol Anne, is the one who sleepwalks into the pool. As it happens, Teague's business calculations didn't stop at covering up the cemetery's existence. It was also a lot cheaper to move the headstones and leave the bodies. If the unfinished pool excavation resembles the empty grave of Teague's sales pitch, it's only because they didn't dig deep enough. Those bodies erupt from the soil at the climax, one of them inside a casket that juts up like a middle finger to Tangina's declaration "This house is clean." Maybe Diane and the others can learn to integrate their modern lives with respect for the land they inhabit, but not without acknowledgment of what happened there, and recognition that this house can never be truly clean.

The second *Poltergeist* movie addressed Native American topics more directly (if problematically) but is pool-less. *Poltergeist III* (1988), directed by Gary Sherman, marks the swimming pool's return to the franchise, albeit a different kind of pool, and a different approach. Where *Poltergeist* dealt with history, *Poltergeist III* is about perception. Everything in the film centers on the act of seeing, from the opening shot of Carol Anne's distorted image slowly clearing as a window washer squeegees the glass in the skyscraper where she now lives. *Poltergeist III* operates on a mirror motif. With ghosts that can access our world through reflective surfaces, the film asks us to consider what we are really seeing when we look at a reflection.

Carol Anne, the spirit-sensitive youngest Freeling child, has been sent to live with her aunt Pat, Pat's new husband Bruce, and Bruce's teenage daughter Donna in Chicago. Their home is the John Hancock Center, a wealthy high-rise where Bruce is the building manager. She goes to a special school for "gifted children with emotional problems," in the words of Dr. Seaton, who runs the place. As her psychotherapy and hypnosis sessions with Dr. Seaton stir up memories, the ghost of the psychotic preacher Kane, *Poltergeist II*'s antagonist, regains enough strength to enter our world and attempts to take Carol Anne back with him.[12]

The greater visibility of teenagers in *Poltergeist III* may have to do with the *Nightmare on Elm Street* series' runaway success. After all, the 1980s was the era of what Roger Ebert derisively called the Dead Teenager Movie,[13] which also popularized the "rubber reality" style that is a key part of *Poltergeist III*'s aesthetic.[14] The teenagers' subplot revolves around the John Hancock Center's swimming pool. While Kane chases Carol Anne around, Donna, armed with her father's master key and knowledge of the security system, sneaks her friends into the pool and teaches them how to avoid the security cameras. She enters the security office, turns off the pool camera, and switches the monitor to playback. When the security guard returns, he will think he is seeing a live image, but he'll actually be watching a recording of an empty pool from hours ago. This episode encapsulates the film's themes of mediated perception: We don't always know what we're looking at, especially when we are looking indirectly. In between the seer and the thing being seen is a vast gray area of interpretation.

We first meet Dr. Seaton as he watches Carol Anne through a window. The next time we see him, he is observing her through a two-way mirror. As she stares seemingly through the mirror directly at him, Seaton explains his theory: Carol Anne has the ability—not supernatural, but heretofore unexplained—to manipulate people into seeing things. He posits that the events of *Poltergeist* were a mass hallucination that she caused. Tangina, the medium from the previous movies, insists the ghosts are real and that Carol Anne is in contact with them. Bruce believes that Carol Anne is a normal child, and that the Cuesta Verde incident involved nothing more exotic than cheaply built houses and a bad land deal. These perspectives on Carol Anne come into direct conflict when the three adults all converge at the skyscraper. Amid the chaos, Pat asks Bruce if this is really happening, to which he replies, with gestures toward Tangina and Seaton, "Depends on who you want to believe." In other words, it's a matter of perspective.

Chapter 1. Buoyant Spirits 15

The mediated gaze: pranking Donna's friends through the skyscraper's security system during their illicit pool party in *Poltergeist III* (1988).

Early in the film, Bruce references the myth of Narcissus which, in addition to being a cautionary tale about vanity, also warns us against making assumptions about what we see. (More on Narcissus in a later chapter.) *Poltergeist III*'s characters suffer when they believe the evidence of their eyes. Evil spirits under Kane's command lure Seaton and others to their deaths by inhabiting doppelgängers of Donna, Scott and Carol Anne. We learn that Donna and Scott are not really Donna and Scott when we notice that the text on their clothing is backwards. In this film, our reflections are twins with wills of their own.

Like in the first movie, *Poltergeist III*'s pool is a site of secrets. The teenagers want to keep the pool excursion secret from their parents. The secret world on the other side of the mirror lurks beneath the glassy water. Visual trickery is another kind of secret-keeping. Pool water bends light, so when we see something beneath the surface, we are not looking directly at it, but rather just off to the side. The act of seeing through things—water, glass, television cameras, other people's interpretations—is fraught with potential deception. We get another instance of pool as portal, when Scott bursts through the suddenly frozen-over pool surface on his way back from the other side. But was the pool really frozen? Was it really Scott? "Depends on who you want to believe."

In some ways, *Poltergeist III* plays like a declawed sequel. The original film's satirical edge is gone. The movie does not problematize Bruce's involvement with the hi-tech skyscraper's bourgeois extravagance, and it preaches an old-fashioned love and family values moral. What's more, Tangina's assertion that Seaton caused this spirit intrusion by making Carol Anne dredge up the past directly contradicts the message of the first movie, that we ignore the past at our peril. To its credit, the film leaves room for a viewer to interrogate these assumptions. The suburban family home and the city high-rise occupy different kinds of psychic space. Where the meaning of *Poltergeist*'s pool is literally grounded, *Poltergeist III*'s is "up in the air," and its soapy windows invite us to contemplate the slipperiness of any one perception of reality.

Dan Curtis' *Burnt Offerings* (1976) is from the older, pre–*Poltergeist* haunted house tradition. With minimal special effects and almost no visible supernatural manifestations, the film relies on the power of suggestion and the commitment of its cast. Middle-class family Ben and Marian Rolf with their tween son Davey are in the market for a summer rental. Despite Ben's misgivings, they accept a too-good-to-be-true offer on a huge but weedy country mansion owned by the eccentric Allardyce siblings. The Rolfs are told they have just one responsibility: to leave food at the bedroom door for the reclusive unseen matriarch Mrs. Allardyce. Also moving into the house is Elizabeth, Ben's septuagenarian aunt.

The Rolfs quickly restore and begin using the property's swimming pool. One day, roughhouse play between Ben and Davey in the pool escalates until Ben appears to be trying to drown Davey. The following night, Ben and Marian go swimming and he makes sexual advances. She is not interested, he doesn't want to take no for an answer, and he comes very close to raping her. After this incident, Marian becomes increasingly withdrawn, less interested in her family and more interested in the house. Her clothing, hairstyles and speech become old-fashioned. Ben has recurring visions of a creepy hearse driver from a distant memory, which culminate in the figure appearing in Aunt Elizabeth's room when she is at the point of death. After every incident or accident the house rejuvenates itself, drawing from the family's energy. Ben tries to escape with Davey, but an accident incapacitates him. Back at the pool, the water begins to roil like a storm-tossed sea, threatening to drown the boy while Ben tries in vain to reach him. In the final sequence, Ben finds Marian in Mrs. Allardyce's room, preternaturally aged with gray hair and glassy eyes, before the house ejects him through the window and Davey is crushed by a falling chimney. The final shot shows framed photos of Ben, Davey and Elizabeth, the house's three most recent victims, while Marian has presumably taken her place as the new Mrs. Allardyce.[15]

Burnt Offerings plays with the fear of a supernatural force that amplifies the worst impulses already existing in us. Even scarier than a ghost making us do things is the idea of a ghost making us do things that, deep inside, we know we *are* capable of. Ben Rolf is stodgy and somewhat humorless. Even when being jovial, he laughs a bit too loud and forcefully. He carries the look of a man wracked by internal struggles. He is the first one to have his vitality siphoned by the house: After he cuts his finger on a champagne bottle, a lightbulb which was previously shown to be broken suddenly works. The cause of his erratic behavior at the pool—assaulting his son and almost raping his wife—is left ambiguous. Is the house making him behave this way, or is he just that kind of guy? After almost drowning Davey, a remorseful Ben tells

Summer fun turns frightful as Ben (Oliver Reed) approaches his son with menace in *Burnt Offerings* (1976).

Marian, "I wanted to hurt him." The next night, as he begins to force himself on his wife, a look of guilt comes over him and he collapses. At the last instant, he has mustered enough self-control to suppress the violence within him—on the lawn next to the pool, that symbolic hiding place for things we don't want others to see.

The film's focus then shifts to Marian and the way the house is changing her. This is the house she fought for, despite her husband's concerns—that its size would make it a nightmare to keep clean, that looking after an elderly stranger would be too much responsibility, that the low rent was too good to be true. "Does it really mean that much to you?" Ben asks during the first-act debate, to which Marian replies, "You know it does." Her desire for a stately house full of antiques—symbols of status but also of domesticity—takes a turn for the macabre as she puts the house before family, even skipping Aunt Elizabeth's funeral, and cries instead over shards of a broken crystal bowl. This fixation on materialism, which the film implies always lurked within her, eventually becomes so serious that it prevents her from leaving the house at all.

Burnt Offerings also exploits the fear of aging. The house, like a vampire that feeds on the living to stay young, seems to self-repair with the fuel of human suffering. It accelerates their aging while reversing its own decay. Elizabeth sickens and dies after a short time in the house, and in the last scene Marian appears to have aged 40 years overnight. The shades-wearing hearse driver of Ben's vision is an embodiment of death, with mocking youthful smile and sunglasses that evoke a skull's empty sockets. The swimming pool, with its connotations of health and exercise, symbolizes our fruitless attempts to beat back death's approach. Early in the film, Aunt Elizabeth stands on the deck begging Ben to stop playing so rough with Davey, her delicate physicality preventing her from intervening. The scene is mirrored later, when the incapacitated Ben watches helplessly as the churning pool itself tries to drag Davey under. Ben has aged into Elizabeth's place, just as Marian becomes the new Mrs. Allardyce, and Davey, for all his youthful vigor, is swimming hopelessly against the current.

The pools in this chapter stand in for larger forces that hold characters at their mercy. These systems make them fight in unwinnable wars, live in fear of worsening medical conditions, or measure their worth by how much they can sell, even if the product is horrible. *Burnt Offerings* zooms in on the unsavory elements of each individual's personality, and on weaknesses for the house to exploit—and then confronts the only universal truth: At the bottom of the pool, death awaits us all.

Chapter 2

Beach Entry

The Natural and the Unnatural

> Well her pool's real cool,
>   but it hasn't got ten-foot waves.
>   —The Fantastic Baggys, "Tell 'Em I'm Surfin'"

> People will swim in the ocean, even though there are definitely many corpses in it. People will not swim in a pool with a corpse in it. Humans all have a corpse:water ratio that is acceptable for them to swim in.
>   —JollyTraveler, r/ShowerThoughts subreddit

The movies in this section deal with the pool and its relationship to natural bodies of water. Some use pools as an analog for open water, imparting some of its characteristics on them. Others deliberately contrast the pool with natural water, usually the ocean, drawing attention to its artificiality. These films, most of which involve wildlife, recognize the ocean as an alien, forbidding place, and laugh at our feeble attempts to conquer it. We'll meet authority figures who embody that hubris, trying to contain the uncontainable. The pools in these films are monuments to denial, to the illusion that civilized humanity is separate from the natural world. It is a position both of privilege and of safety ... until something extreme happens and we are caught unprepared to handle it.

Fear of the ocean is called thalassophobia, though the word doesn't seem to be used as much in clinical applications as it does in popular culture. As of this writing, the subreddit r/thalassophobia has 1.6 million subscribers who gleefully share and comment on pictures and videos that capture the ocean's incomprehensible vastness.[1] Presumably, few of these people have true, debilitating phobias—I think the best term is *awe*, that mixture of fascination and fear when we can't wrap our heads around the scale or alienness of something we encounter. It's in this space of awe that horror films come to play.

We'll start with a survey of "creatures in the pool" movies. While the premise may seem far-fetched to non-pool owners, wildlife is, of course, attracted to water. Depending on where they live, people with outdoor pools can reasonably expect to remove (both living and dead) insects, birds, snakes, rodents, raccoons, lizards and/

or frogs on a regular basis.[2] It's not uncommon for larger predators like bears and cougars to find their way into pools.[3] Not to mention the ones that are put there on purpose, like Albert, a 750-pound alligator who lived in his owner's swimming pool in Hamburg, New York, for 34 years.[4]

As human industry and climate change continue to disrupt habitats and natural cycles, wildlife is increasingly driven into unaccustomed spaces. In the world of speculative fiction, "cli-fi" that deals with water-related topics has been a booming subgenre since at least the mid-2010s.[5] Where the subconscious is concerned, psychologist Kelly Bulkeley writes in *Psychology Today*, "It seems likely that dreams will accurately reflect people's rising anxieties in both directions, from too little and too much water."[6] As everybody knows, wherever nightmares go, horror movies can't be far behind.

Discussing 1954's *Creature from the Black Lagoon*, filmmaker David Cronenberg sums up the fascination of cinematic waters: "The Black Lagoon is the dark pool of the unconscious and of course there are creatures within it."[7] Beyond being eco-conscious, whether implicitly or explicitly, "creatures in the pool" movies play with the notion of the cinematic swimming pool as an in-between place, where the natural meets the artificial, and the slippages and transgressions that can occur across these boundaries. They are the most literal expression of the primal fear of unknown predators in our personal space.

Joe Dante's *Piranha* (1978) starts at a swimming pool before the action moves to open water. In the first scene, two young lovers trespass into a gated government facility to skinny-dip in its pool. It turns out that the pool is home to a population of super-piranha, genetically engineered by military mad scientists for use in Vietnam. After the couple disappears, a skip tracer named Maggie teams up with a mountain drunk named Paul to find them. It's only after they drain the pool, releasing the piranha into the river, that they learn the secret and race to stop the fish from wreaking havoc on a downriver summer camp and newly opened resort.[8]

Piranha carefully depicts the tension between pool and river. Dr. Hoak, the military scientist who provides exposition about the fish, panics when he sees Maggie draining the pool. In the pool, the monsters are contained. In the river, they can go anywhere—including, we later learn, the ocean, since they are genetically engineered to survive in both salt water and fresh. Paul's daughter Suzie attends the imperiled summer camp. Suzie's counselor asks her why she is afraid to go in the river, pointing out the short distance she has to swim: "You've probably swum twice that far in a pool." Suzie replies that the river is different because she is afraid of "things" in the water. Fear of unseen creatures is common among aquaphobia sufferers. Although Suzie makes a distinction between pools and open water, many aquaphobics transpose the fear of "something getting" them to deep pool water as well.[9] In a bit of dramatic irony, the viewer knows that even as the counselor reassures her, Suzie does indeed have something to fear. In another ironic touch, she later shows

Bones are disclosed after Maggie (Heather Menzies) and Paul (Bradford Dillman) drain the pool in *Piranha* (1978).

bravery when it matters and gets into the water with a raft to save that same counselor from piranha attack.

Here, as in *House*, we are fighting Vietnam again, but instead of traumatized veterans, the characters are put in the shoes of the Viet Cong, facing the same biological weapons designed to kill and destabilize the ecosystems of North Vietnamese rivers. Like the V.C., the humans in this movie face a foreign invasion and stiff odds, but they ultimately prevail thanks to their knowledge of the environment. Paul used to work for a smelting plant that got shut down because they were "killing too many fish." The land now belongs to the resort, but Paul uses the defunct waste facility to intercept the piranha. In the finale, military scientist Dr. Mengers reassures the news cameras that the threat is neutralized, which recalls the U.S. government's attempts to spin the outcome of Vietnam as something other than a shameful defeat.

The film portrays another Vietnam-era anxiety: the looming military-industrial complex. Hoak is an academic who considers his employment by the army to be "pure research." Both the mountaintop testing facility and the smelting operation are former commercial enterprises that were bought by the army. The latter was sold to the resort developer, but as shown by the collusion between the resort owner and Colonel Waxman to keep the deadly piranha under wraps, the military is still involved. The piranhas' pool is a former fish hatchery, and its position at the film's start is somewhere between private and public, between open and sealed, between natural and engineered. Commercial and military interests are like salt water and fresh: They mix at the estuary, and the killer fish move freely through both.

The slimy, corner-cutting resort owner Buck Gardner represents another key theme: the interconnectedness of environmental degradation, government overreach, and the bourgeois leisure industry. Gardner differs from his obvious model, the mayor from *Jaws* (1975), in an important way. Whereas the mayor is merely willing to risk losing bathers to the monster to avoid disrupting his town's tourist trade,[10] Gardner is implicated in the misdeeds that brought the monster in the first place.

This theme is echoed in a much later film to come out under the *Piranha* name: 2012's *Piranha 3DD*. In the film, directed by John Gulager, college student Maddy returns to her hometown to find that her stepfather Chet has rebranded the water park they co-own with a suggestive ad campaign and a clothing-optional adults-only section. Worse, it turns out that Chet dug an illegal well, pumping water from a subterranean river into the park to avoid paying for municipal water. The piranha find their way into the underground river, setting the stage for their attack on the water park's opening day celebration.[11]

With Chet bribing a local cop to overlook his illicit well, we have the familiar dynamic of private industry conspiring with public authorities to commit and cover up ecological crimes. Although it is more concerned with juvenile humor, *Piranha 3DD* pays tribute to its progenitor by directly addressing the environmental costs of the leisure industry as it sows the seeds of its own destruction.

John Sayles, screenwriter of the original *Piranha*, wrote another killer animal movie with a key pool scene: 1980's *Alligator*, directed by Lewis Teague. *Alligator* works with themes we've already examined: the encroachment of wildlife upon human habitation, and capitalist ecological meddling with the complicity of local government—here in the form of a pharmaceutical company dumping the bodies from their illegal animal testing into sewers. The film sees Chicago homicide detective David Madison teaming with reptile expert Marisa Kendall to find a killer alligator that has grown to unnatural size in the city's sewer system. After the gator bursts from the sewer and starts attacking people aboveground, Dr. Kendall advises, "It'll go for water." This is followed by helicopter shots of the city's residential areas, dotted with blue rectangles, and a closeup of the alligator lurking in someone's backyard swimming pool. It all pays off in a night scene at a kids' party where a boy playing pirate dress-up with his friends is forced to "walk the plank," i.e., is pushed off the darkened pool's diving board. At the last moment, Mom turns on the outdoor lights, revealing the gigantic alligator in the pool, but it's too late to save the boy as he falls into the water and disappears in a blooming cloud of red.[12]

Although Sayles' scripts for *Piranha* and *Alligator* have a lot in common, the latter ditches the earlier film's rustic setting for fully urban terrain, inspired by apocrypha about baby alligators purchased as pets and flushed into urban sewer systems.[13] Central to the film's horror is the essential wrongness of an alligator running amok in a modern American city. The film assumes a stark line between natural and human environments. But the city has everything an alligator needs: water, nesting places and a food supply. The pool scenario is both abject and absurd, with the kids' pirate game invoking the ocean while reminding us that we are definitely not

Chapter 2. Beach Entry

there. This swimming pool should be a place of security, where the kids are able to play-act the terrors of the ocean with the knowledge that they are safe from them. Of course, that might be generally true in Chicago, but in Florida it's always wise to check your pool before you dive in. The Florida Fish and Wildlife Conservation Commission, which operates a "Nuisance Alligator Program," publishes a pamphlet called "A Guide to Living with Alligators," which includes a photo of a gator having fun in someone's backyard pool.[14]

Like any animal attack movie post–1975, *Piranha* and *Alligator* are both riffs on *Jaws*. But there is an important difference: The shark in *Jaws* carries an element of mystery. Why it starts indiscriminately attacking people, and why it follows and menaces the *Orca*, is unknown.[15] Its behavior is strange for its species, which the film remarks on but never explains. There is a quality of the mythical about the shark's aggression and preternatural intelligence. By contrast, there is nothing unexplained about the aquatic menaces of *Piranha* and *Alligator*, nor are they to blame for the havoc they cause. Ideologically, these films are more in line with 1950s mad scientist yarns, where human meddling with nature, symbolized by the uncanny image of wildlife in the swimming pool, yields disastrous results. Though mutated thanks to human interference, these films' animals are doing what they do; it is the *people* who create the problems and put themselves in harm's way.

Ping Lumpraploeng's 2018 crocodile survival thriller *The Pool* unfolds along similar lines. Protagonist Day is a production assistant on a music video shoot in a deep, disused swimming pool. After a long day's work, he falls asleep on a raft while the pool is draining. By the time he awakes, the water level is too low for him to climb out. With his dog Lucky chained on the pool deck, his cell phone waterlogged and no way to reach the outside world, he has no choice but to wait until the pool finishes draining. The plan is complicated by the arrival of two other players: his girlfriend Koi, who injures herself on the way into the pool, and a crocodile that recently escaped from a nearby flooded farm. Trapped together in the empty pool with no food, it's only a matter of time before Day and Koi clash with the crocodile in a fight for survival.[16]

If a film like *Alligator* gives us humans the home field advantage, and a film like *47 Meters Down* (which we'll get to later) pits us against wildlife on the beasts' home turf, *The Pool* takes a third option, setting its confrontation in a place where neither species really belongs. The title character, after all, is neither the crocodile nor the human protagonist; the film is named after the battlefield, and it frames the pool as an eerie midground between the natural and artificial.

In his book *The Weird and the Eerie*, theorist Mark Fisher defines the title concepts thus:

> The weird is constituted by a presence—the presence of *that which does not belong*. …The eerie, by contrast, is constituted by a *failure of absence* or by a *failure of presence*. The sensation of the eerie occurs either when there is something present where there should be nothing, or there is nothing present when there should be something.[17]

Day (Theeradej Wongpuapan) must protect the injured Koi (Ratnamon Ratchiratham) from the crocodile with whom they share *The Pool* (2018).

By this rubric, an empty swimming pool is a potent example of the eerie, hence Raymond Chandler: "Nothing ever looks emptier than an empty swimming pool."[18] We've already seen empty pools in *Poltergeist* and *Piranha*, both of which divulge secret bodies, and we'll return to them several times more. The presence of the crocodile, foreign to *The Pool*'s setting, is an injection of the weird, but it's not the only one. Day does not belong here either. It is not his pool. No one knows that he, Koi and Lucky are there, so no one is coming to rescue them. When he learns that Koi is pregnant, he muses that he is too poor to be a father. Day is aware of his class status, and knows his predicament is partly caused by his play-acting, pretending to be someone who can afford a luxurious pool of his own. The film features a symbol of this class disparity in the form of a prop from the music video: a sumptuous red sofa that sits at the pool's bottom, another intrusion of the weird.

In this scenario, the humans and the crocodile are both disadvantaged in different ways. The croc is faster and more agile in water than on land, but all the water drains away soon after the croc falls in. The crafty humans lose their edge too: Day's cell phone is useless as soon as it hits the water, and they have no tools other than what they can fashion from their clothes, jewelry and various bits of detritus at the pool's bottom. The playing field thus leveled, all three are trapped together in the pool, competing for the same resources.

As mentioned above, this crocodile behaves like a real animal rather than a bloodthirsty monster. In fact, it spends most of its screen time napping. Not only is this realistic, it also adds suspense: The viewer and the characters know that even while the crocodile is not being aggressive, it's only a matter of time before it gets hungry enough to attack. Day and Koi can only hope it happens before their own hunger renders them too weak to fight back.

The Pool also shows us another side of the swimming pool: as a place of entrapment. We'll return to this trope throughout the book, and though we've already seen it in *Poltergeist* (Diane sliding down the crumbling excavation, unable to climb out) and *Burnt Offerings* (Davey overpowered by supernaturally surging water), *The Pool* makes it a basic premise. There is an inherent claustrophobia in this trope, even when the pool is open to the sky—perhaps more so, because escape seems frustratingly close and yet unattainable.

Another non-human, non-crocodile character whose in-between status mirrors that of the swimming pool is Lucky the dog. Lucky is neither wild nor civilized, but in the middle. Chained to the pool deck, he is neither trapped in the pool nor able to roam free. He is able to alert Day to the presence of others, but his barking is also what attracts the crocodile. In an ending bemoaned by pet lovers everywhere, Day sacrifices Lucky to save himself, Koi and their unborn child. He beckons Lucky to leap over the pool coping while still chained by the neck, hanging himself to death from the pool's edge but giving Day the opportunity to use his body to climb out. In so doing, Lucky becomes a makeshift ladder, part of the eerie scenery, caught between worlds.

We end our survey of pools and crocodilians with 2019's *Crawl*, directed by Alexandre Aja. Climate change has been on the periphery of many of this section's films, but *Crawl* forefronts it. Although never addressing the issue directly, the film deals with the present-day reality of increasingly severe storm seasons and wildlife habitat displacement on the Florida coast. In fact, eight days before the film's theatrical release, the decomposed body of a 16-year-old boy was found surrounded by alligators in a lake not far from where some of the film's exteriors were shot.[19]

Crawl opens in a swimming pool at the University of Florida (home of the Gators), where protagonist Haley is a competitive swimmer. As a category 5 hurricane approaches, Haley travels to check on her estranged father Dave, who lives alone in Tampa and whom she has been unable to reach by phone. She finds him injured in the crawlspace of their flooded family home, trapped by alligators blocking the exit. Haley and her father battle rising flood waters as well as increasingly aggressive gators to get to safety.[20]

The swimming pool does not play a major role in *Crawl*, but it does serve as the film's opening image, and the sport of competitive swimming is a significant theme. The film's title has a triple meaning: "crawl" refers to the way alligators move, the crawlspace where the characters are trapped, and the most common swimming stroke. The film's pool imagery calls attention to the artificiality of human aquatic endeavors, and the competitive swimming motif emerges as a symbol of hubris.

Although humans have swum for at least 10,000 years, the sport of competitive swimming did not flourish until after the creation of the indoor swimming pool. The ability to standardize conditions—control water temperature and quality, eliminate

Apex predator: In *Crawl* (2019), competitive swimmer protagonist Haley (Kaya Scodelario, with her arms above her head) gets in the zone.

weather as a factor—meant that results would be valid and meaningful across competitions.²¹ *Crawl*'s opening pool doesn't just mock humanity's presumed dominion over nature, but also reminds us that swimming as a sport, with its stopwatches and photo finishes and regulation attire, is irremediably artificial.

Dave was Haley's first swim coach, and we learn that his pushing her too hard is part of the reason for their estrangement. But she still uses the affirmation he taught her, calling herself an "apex predator." Although she intones it victoriously after outswimming some gators, the film's context proves the statement untrue. Yes, Haley and Dave survive, but only after leaving behind the trappings of human civilization: cell phones, radios, cars, boats, the house itself, and even a human arm are sacrificed on the way to freedom. As a species, we might be able to survive the changes that climate disaster will wreak, but not without giving up a lot of things we believe make us who we are. If being an apex predator means domination of our habitat, we have no claim to that title. What we are, says the film, is sprawling, shortsighted, clay-footed emperors. It's easy to claim "apex predator" when you're safe in your swimming pool with roped-off lanes, rather than sharing water with the animals whose homes you destroyed. We might make it, but only if we can learn to live in harmony with them. After all, as *Crawl*'s tagline reminds us, "They Were Here First."

Like *Crawl* and *Piranha*, Johannes Roberts' *47 Meters Down* (2017) opens in a swimming pool before moving to more dangerous waters. The camera starts on the ocean floor as the opening credits play. It begins to travel upward, pointed at the seafloor until it is lost in distance, and then the blue blur resolves into a rectangle of sky and an inflatable pool raft. Through an invisible cut, we have gone from moving toward the ocean's surface looking down, to traveling from the bottom of a swimming pool looking up. Foreshadowing a shark attack, Kate, one of the main characters, swims up from beneath to scare her sister Lisa off the raft. The sisters are in a swimming pool on vacation at a Mexican hotel, and we learn that Lisa's boyfriend has recently left her. They meet two local men who convince them to go cage diving

Chapter 2. Beach Entry   27

with great white sharks, although Lisa has no scuba experience. During their dive, the boat's winch breaks and the sisters fall 47 meters to the ocean bottom. Trapped and surrounded by sharks, running out of air, with the threats of decompression sickness and nitrogen narcosis preventing them from swimming directly up, they must survive until they are rescued.[22]

By opening at a swimming pool, the film is again contrasting the pool's safety with the ocean's dangers. But here that contrast is only one element in a larger point about the nature of foreignness. The film's first act is full of implicit xenophobia. When Kate suggests they go dancing and Lisa asks where they can go in the middle of the night, Kate responds, "This is Mexico!" and claiming that they are the only ones *not* enjoying the nightlife. The statement is absurd—as if nobody in the whole country needs to work in the morning—but it betrays the tourist tendency to exoticize the foreign places they visit. The line "This is Mexico!" is repeated later by one of the local men when Lisa asks if she needs a diving certification. His reply suggests that Mexico is a country where people play fast and loose with the rules and, to quote an old exploitation movie tagline, "life is cheap."[23] Upon seeing the roughshod boat and its crew, Lisa tells Kate about her misgivings, having heard "horror stories" about tourists who fall victim to "shady trips" not approved by the hotel concierge. All of these touches reinforce the sisters' perception of Mexico as a backwards, twilight place—a little scary but also a little thrilling—a place where they can break the rules and go back to their respectable lives, instead of a country where a hundred million people live as normal humans with jobs and families.

As soon as Roberts' camera dips into the ocean, everything changes. Here is a world that is truly alien—where we need compressed air and regulators and wetsuits to survive longer than a few minutes; where our eyes play tricks on us; where just 47 meters (a bit over half a football field) is too far for a radio signal to travel. Every shot of tiny humans against the blue-black vastness reinforces the fact that we simply don't belong there. Thalassophobia, though not without political implications, is a fear that strikes the very heart of what it means to be human. As the ocean drains color the deeper you go, all the soft xenophobia bleeds out of the film as Mexican and U.S. citizens unite against the true foreignness of the sea and its inhabitants.

When the locals are trying to convince the sisters to cage dive, one of them delivers another line that's key to our analysis here: "What are you gonna do, sit by the pool all day long?" The implication is that shark diving is a more authentic, and thus more meaningful, activity. It's a questionable proposition given the amount of gear involved—is a water experience mediated by chlorine and concrete that much less authentic than one mediated by a mechanical breathing apparatus and a steel cage? The fact that this assumption goes unquestioned, and is received as a teasing sort of challenge, is indicative of a usually unquestioned attitude about natural-water swimming.

Scholars Dagmar Dahl and Åsa I. Bäckström, who set out to discover "why wild swimming has become popular when there is no need for training and practicing swimming outdoors anymore," theorize that where pool swimming is seen as a mere activity, wild-water swimming is seen as an aesthetic experience. The Romantic (with a capital R) idea of communion with nature is "deeply intertwined with mastering other struggles in life."[24] Lisa is finally convinced to dive as a way to get over her breakup. An encounter with nature, however mediated, will help her master this life struggle, she thinks. But survival horror is not a Romantic genre, nature is not always spiritually uplifting. As viewers, we know that Lisa would have been better off staying in the pool.

We round off this chapter with Ken Wiederhorn's *Shock Waves* (1977), which is an outlier in two ways: It does not deal with wildlife, and it has a supernatural element. Nonetheless, it is spiritually similar to *Piranha* and features a memorable swimming pool death that encapsulates our themes.

Shock Waves begins on a tourist pleasure cruise around an island chain. After a glancing collision with a seeming ghost ship, a disappearing captain and a hole in the vessel, the crew and passengers evacuate in a lifeboat to the nearest island. The island is home to a formerly grand, now rundown hotel, which looks deserted until the newcomers discover a mysterious German resident. The old man is a former Nazi officer, creator and commander of a unit of undead soldiers that have apparently returned with the rising of their sunken ship. The group tries to escape the island as the Nazi zombies, who are weakened by daylight, pick them off one by one. A scene late in the film finds the last four survivors hiding in a walk-in refrigerator when one of them, Chuck, agitated by claustrophobia, fires a flare gun in the small space, injuring another survivor named Beverly. Chuck finds his way to the hotel's swimming pool, where the zombies drown him. The next morning, the last two survivors find Beverly dead in a fish tank.[25]

Like *Piranha*'s Dr. Hoak, *Shock Waves* features a morally ambiguous war criminal who created the monsters for use as a weapon and has been trying to contain them since the war's end. The two films play this containment differently. Much of *Piranha* is a race to intercept the fish and cut off their access to the rest of the world. The *Shock Waves* characters race to get off the island before they become the zombies' next victims. Here we encounter, once again, the pool as a symbol of both secrets and human attempts to control the uncontrollable.

The SS commander has tried, quite literally, to submerge his past. After the war's end, he took his "Death Corps" out to sea as far from human habitation as he could and then scuttled the ship, sending his misdeeds and their memory to the ocean floor. But as Dobbs, the pleasure boat's cook, says in the film's first reel, "The sea spits up what it can't keep down." The pool where Chuck is drowned to death represents this failed attempt to bury the past, which the film reminds us is never really past because it affects us today. At any moment, the ghosts of our misdeeds can rise from the murky depths.

The pool in *Shock Waves* also serves as a symbol of confinement. Every so often, the film cuts back to closeups of fish in a tank, a visual reminder of our characters' entrapment. There are other artificial habitats where the characters find themselves boxed in: refrigerator, furnace, and of course, swimming pool. After all, what is a pool but a scaled-up fish tank for humans? Just as the characters are besieged by Nazi-created zombies, they are also confined by the unnatural environments around them. In this respect, Chuck with his claustrophobia plays the part of audience avatar. The grisly shot of Beverly's dead body in the fish tank, one of the film's final images, drives the point home.

The commander describes his soldiers as "not dead, not alive, but somewhere in between." *Shock Waves* is a whole film of in-betweens: empty hotels with full fish tanks; glass-bottomed boats that show us the ocean while separating us from it; an island that sits between civilization and wilderness. At the center of it all is the swimming pool: an artificial body of water for a hotel that is itself surrounded by the sea.

We'll return to the ocean once or twice in later chapters, but this section is the last time the contrast between pool water and wild water will be a major theme. If, as it's speculated, human swimming began in prehistory as a way to escape predators,[26] it wouldn't be surprising if our ancestral memories linked being in the water with being hunted. As we head inland, let's keep in mind that every pool we encounter, no matter how domestic, has a bit of the untamed ocean in it.

Chapter 3

Synchronized Swimmers
Narcissus and the Mirror Self

> Words that tumble effortlessly from the lips of fools
> only cloud up what I see in my reflecting pool.
> —Bob Mould, "Reflecting Pool"
>
> Will you mistake it for somebody else, all enamored with you?
> Narcissus, Narcissus, which one of them are you?
> —Grant Hart, "Narcissus Narcissus"

I touched on the Narcissus myth briefly in reference to *Poltergeist III*, but for the next several films it bears a closer examination. In the most common version, Narcissus is a beautiful young man who spurns a certain water nymph. She curses him that someday he might know the feeling of unrequited love. One day, in a pristine natural fountain, Narcissus catches a glimpse of his lovely self reflected in the water. Thinking it the image of another, he falls in love. Since they reach for each other in tandem, he believes this reflected lover reciprocates his feelings, and is distraught that they can never seem to touch. Unable to consummate this love, he continues to stare into the pool. Depending on which version you read, Narcissus either withers away[1] or takes his own life.[2]

The story has multiple layers that are relevant to our purposes here. In addition to vanity, self-centeredness and misperception, it's also about identity contemplation. Characters in the Narcissus mold can either see themselves in others, see others in themselves, or both. Horror often portrays tension between exterior and interior, between how characters present themselves to the world and the reality of their internal lives. This tension can manifest as doppelgängers, secret identities or the psychological bifurcation of the self. The swimming pool is a handy symbol for this uncertainty, since it can both reflect and be seen through—but in both cases, the view it affords is a distorted one.

In the words of Seán J. Harrington, discussing Lacan, "We are not an image on a reflective surface; we are also the profound depth underneath."[3] Poolside identity contemplation can easily turn into identity slippage, a perspective shift resulting from a character's self-realization. Since we are talking about horror films here, we shouldn't be shocked when that realization comes with a side order of violence.

John Grissmer's *Blood Rage* (1987) exemplifies the identical-twin approach to the doppelgänger narrative. In the 1970s, a single mother named Maddy takes her twin boys, Todd and Terry, to the drive-in theater on a date with her boyfriend. Terry murders a young moviegoing couple with a hatchet and frames Todd, who is committed to a mental institution. Ten years later, the now-adult Todd has a breakthrough and begins to profess his innocence, but Maddy does not believe his claim that Terry really committed the murders. On Thanksgiving Day, Todd escapes from the hospital and returns to his family home in a suburban apartment complex called Shadow Woods. Despondent upon hearing of Todd's escape, Maddy starts drinking heavily and eating Thanksgiving leftovers. Terry, his psychosis revived, murders Maddy's new fiancé Brad, owner of the complex. Todd arrives at Shadow Woods and encounters Terry's girlfriend Karen, who flees once she realizes who he is. She later discovers that Terry is indeed the murderer. Several killings later, Terry chases Karen into the complex's indoor swimming pool, where the two brothers have a confrontation. Maddy arrives with a gun and shoots Terry, who is standing poolside with a bloody machete. Upon realizing that she has killed Terry and not Todd, and still thinking the latter is the murderer, Maddy takes her own life by shooting herself in the head.[4]

Shadow Woods is a suburban attempt at a planned community, complete with tennis courts, walking trails and swimming pool. Because it has not grown organically like a traditional neighborhood, nor is it zoned like one, there is an eerie sameness to the built environment. Similar trails lead to similar buildings made of similar apartments with similar layouts. There will be more discussion of suburban sameness in Part II, but for now let's focus on how *Blood Rage*'s identical twins embody this homogeneity.

Terry and Todd look the same, but they are not the same. As seen in the climax, even their mother has difficulty telling them apart. When Karen encounters Todd, she flees in fear, not just because she has been told that Todd is a murderer, but because of his eerie resemblance to her boyfriend. Todd's trauma has rendered him unable to protest his innocence, giving him the appearance of guilt. Terry, on the other hand, is charming and gregarious, hiding his psychopathy behind a socially acceptable presentation.

The bulk of the film takes place on Thanksgiving, a holiday that carries expectations of family togetherness and domestic normalcy. The plot struggles against this totalizing notion of the perfect American family, injecting it with barely concealed dysfunction and locating the family home in a place that is superficially tranquil but comes across cold and alienating. The family is already at a disadvantage where postcard perfection is concerned, since Maddy is a single mom, and has been since her boys were small. She has a lot riding on her engagement to Brad. "Looks like you're gonna get a chance to meet the rest of the family," Terry tells Brad at the

The murderous Terry (Mark Soper) is vanquished by a bullet from his mother Maddy (Louise Lasser) while Karen (Julie Gordon) leans over his injured twin Todd in *Blood Rage* (1987).

Thanksgiving table, ignoring his mother's plea to keep their business private. "My psychotic brother just escaped." The canned perfection breaks down further when Maddy turns to solo drinking in front of the refrigerator. In the climax, the twins symbolically return to the womb they once shared and wrestle in the complex swimming pool, a battle between two faces of middle-class America: one superficially strange but ultimately harmless, the other outwardly normal but secretly murderous. When they break the reflective surface of the water, they are breaking the illusion of sameness. Maddy, realizing she has shot the "wrong" twin, chooses to join him in death rather than let go of her attachment to a superficial ideal. Like the contradictions inherent in the Thanksgiving holiday—preaching community while celebrating dominion—she cannot accept that the way things appear is not always the way they are.

Horror films can also visualize the bifurcated self by depicting dissociation. When people dissociate, the normally integrated awareness of mind and body can uncouple, resulting in the feeling that they are watching, rather than experiencing, the things that happen to them. Dissociation is highly correlated[5] with the behavior known as non-suicidal self-injury (NSSI), which has been shown to be more common among women than men. One 2022 study found that female-identifying respondents were twice as likely to report NSSI than their male-identifying counterparts. The study noted, "Women's greater psychological distress contributed to their higher NSSI prevalence," and: "Empirically supported theory describes how … sociocultural factors (e.g., structural gender inequality, media exposure) contribute to higher levels of depressive symptoms and distress in women."[6] Negative body attitudes and self-objectification (including internalized objectification) have been identified as factors.[7] In other words, women may be more likely to self-harm because of a culture that imposes unyielding standards for how they are supposed to look and feel in their bodies. Marina de Van's *In My Skin* (2002) depicts self-harm behavior, with a pool scene as a symbol of that underlying alienation.

Before its narrative fractures in the final act, *In My Skin* presents an all-too-real portrait of the ravages visited on some women's bodies by the pressures of patriarchy in their personal and professional lives. The film's protagonist is Esther, who along with her colleague Sandrine is seeking a promotion at work. Sandrine finagles them an invitation to a company house party, where Esther falls and injures herself on some construction equipment. She does not notice how badly she is hurt until later, and her fascination with the wound precipitates a spiral of dissociation and self-harm behavior that eventually results in large-scale self-mutilation, auto-cannibalism and death.

At one point, Esther and Sandrine are at the health club where many of their colleagues hang out. Sandrine watches from the swimming pool as Esther talks to some of the higher-ups. Then Esther tells her that she has gotten the promotion they've both been eyeing. Even though Sandrine has been with the company longer (and got Esther into the health club in the first place), she suppresses her jealousy and responds supportively. Just then, three male colleagues emerge from the pool, pick up Esther, and try to throw her into the water. Esther reacts with horror, clutching the deck chair and begging Sandrine for help, but Sandrine does nothing. The men, finally recognizing Esther's terror, relent and release her. Sandrine apologizes, saying, "I panicked and froze." Looking down, Esther realizes that her leg wound opened during the struggle, and a streak of blood runs down the front of her trousers.[8]

Even absent the context of her self-harm, Esther's terror at the prospect of being thrown in the pool and the exposure that would result—"I don't have a swimsuit!" she pleads—is resonant. The blood on the front of her trousers suggests an exaggerated menstrual flow. There are lots of reasons why a woman might not want to be thrown into a swimming pool, and no good reason why she should be. During the struggle, Sandrine makes eye contact with the boss, who glances at the episode with a placid shrug. This is a boys-will-be-boys corporate culture, and Esther should expect no help from superiors when her dignity is on the line. Much later in the film, as Esther starts to cut pieces off herself, she also begins to miss days of work, and the narrative starts to fracture. Esther the professional, Esther the protagonist and Esther the body are all losing pieces. This sense of body-person unity is not one that Esther herself shares; her subjective point-of-view shots portray dissociation. She feels that her body parts don't truly belong to her. In a sense, she is right. At the health club swimming pool, women's bodies are public property.

The term "gaslighting" was popularized by a 1944 Hollywood film called *Gaslight* (a remake of a 1940 British film that was itself adapted from a 1938 stage play). *Gaslight* was about a husband who seeks to have his wife institutionalized, and

The distorted mirror: "Penny" (Susan Strasberg) carefully pilots her wheelchair around the swimming pool's edge in *Taste of Fear* (1961).

thereby inherit her wealth, by slowly making her doubt her own sanity.[9] Subsequent films riffed on the concept for decades. Seth Holt's *Taste of Fear* (1961) is one of a host of "let's drive the heiress mad" films to come out in this time period, but few are as thematically rich on the topic of mental and physical disability, and few portray identity slippage as a direct result of disregard for women's agency. In *Taste of Fear*, a young wheelchair user named Penny Appleby returns to the home of her wealthy father. Penny has not seen her father in the decade since her parents' divorce, and Penny has never met his new wife Jane. When Penny arrives, the household chauffeur Bob tells her that her dad had to leave urgently on business and it's not known when he will return. Getting to know Jane, Penny tells her that after her mother died, she lived with her best friend and former nursemaid Maggie, until Maggie's sudden drowning death three weeks prior. On her first night in the house, Penny follows a sound to one of the outbuildings, where she sees her father's corpse sitting in a chair. Terrified, she flees and falls, wheelchair and all, into the mansion's disused swimming pool. After she wakes, the group investigates the outbuilding but finds nothing out of the ordinary. Jane thinks the stress is causing Penny to hallucinate. As Penny and Bob develop romantic feelings, she is able to convince him she is telling the truth. Bob theorizes that Penny's father died before she arrived, and that Jane is using the corpse to try to frighten Penny into madness so that she can inherit the estate. Penny concludes that the body must be hidden in the murky pool. Late one night, Bob dives in and finds the corpse. On the way to notify the police, Bob stops and gets out of the car, leaving Penny inside with the brake off. The car begins to roll downhill and Penny sees her father's corpse in the front seat just before it crashes off a cliff into the sea. At this point it's revealed that Bob is Jane's lover and masterminded the plot to drive Penny mad—but dead is acceptable too. Mr. Appleby's lawyer comes to settle the estate and shocks Jane by telling her that Penny already died of suicide by drowning three weeks ago. "Penny" reappears at the house and reveals herself to be Maggie. Not really paralyzed, she was able to escape the car before it went off the cliff. Having surmised that Jane had murdered Penny's father (and wanting to see justice done on her behalf), Maggie traveled to the house posing as Penny. After explaining the ruse, Maggie walks away, leaving Jane sitting despondent in the wheelchair at the edge of the cliff. Bob then appears, having heard that "Penny" somehow survived the car crash, and kicks the wheelchair and its occupant off the cliff. He realizes too late that he has killed his lover Jane.[10]

Taste of Fear interrogates the concept of the "abnormal" female body and mind. Horror films have a sad history of equating or conflating physical disability with evil. Angela M. Smith's thesis in *Hideous Progeny: Disability, Eugenics, and Classic Horror Cinema* is that horror film audiences have a complex relationship with disability: a revulsion toward nonstandard bodies balanced by a fascination with "embodied vulnerability."[11] *Taste of Fear* leans away from the revulsion, with its wheelchair-using heroine whose disability is not the story's focal point. The other characters, though, are focused on Penny's physical and mental troubles to the exclusion of her other traits. Their inability to view Penny as anything but an invalid magnifies their moral corruption and hastens their undoing. The intersection of Penny's disability and her mental health struggles makes her a prime target for exploitation.

This is not the last time we'll cover a plot to drive an heiress mad, nor is it the last time we'll see a body hidden in a swimming pool, but it is the only time we'll see these themes through a disability lens. In several ways, the pool and the body in it represent Penny herself. To Jane's eyes, like the pool, Penny's body is ruined and her mind unclear. Jane wants her to be more social—partially so she won't become romantic with Bob—and suggests hosting a party for some of the other village men. "We might get the pool cleaned out," she says. To Jane, a restored pool is a restored Penny.

Early in *Taste of Fear*, Penny is said to have been a neurotic and fearful child, sometimes unable to distinguish fantasy from reality. Whether true or not, this characterization is used to justify disbelieving her over and over again, even going so far as to suggest that her physical disability is psychosomatic. Although the term "mental illness" is never spoken, different coded language is used in reference to Penny, like "over-imaginative" and "confused." The late-film revelation that the real Penny was a suicide confirms how troubled she was. But unlike many horror films, which use the confluence of physical disability and "madness" to convey evil, *Taste of Fear* makes Penny an object of sympathy, highlighting her vulnerability. Jane and Bob, believing Penny to be damaged goods, are surprised when she proves so resistant to their manipulation. Unlike the heroines of *Gaslight* and its progeny, Penny never once doubts the evidence of her senses—to the point where Bob has to

The young woman revealed to be Maggie (Susan Strasberg, right) cedes her cliffside wheelchair to the plotting Jane (Ann Todd) in the climax of *Taste of Fear* **(1961).**

switch tactics and pretend to believe her so he can kill her instead. She is self-assured enough to dress down the local doctor when he floats the idea that her paralysis might have a psychological component.

When we learn that the person we believe to be Penny is actually Maggie, the symmetry with the pool and the body it hides becomes even clearer. Two Applebys, both drowned before the movie even starts; both deaths concealed for the sake of a deception. Both are alive and dead simultaneously, the unseen corpse at the bottom of the pool all the action centers around, the pool that sits implacable in the background of many key shots. While Mr. Appleby's corpse is used as a prop, displayed in different places for the effect it will have on "Penny," Penny's body is absent from the main story. We see her dead in the opening moments of the film, but the ripple effects of her death propel everything that happens after.

Taste of Fear persistently links water to both femaleness and death. Penny, Mr. Appleby and Jane all die in water—plus Maggie, if the murder plot had worked. Images of dead women in water bookend the film. Water lubricates the shifting of identity—from Maggie to Penny and back again; from Penny the victim to Maggie the avenger; from Bob the manservant to Bob the love interest to Bob the murderous manipulator. All these changes happen, or are realized, when there is water in the frame. In *Taste of Fear*, the disabled female body and the troubled female mind pull double duty: as objects of manipulation, and as surfaces that conceal great strength. Like the murky swimming pool, which resilient nature has begun to reclaim, bystanders can only guess about what they encompass.

Before we exit the pool as a site of secrets and protean identities, I want to highlight a director who exemplifies those concepts across multiple movies. Although only three of M. Night Shyamalan's films have prominent swimming pools, each one is rich with symbolic importance. In Shyamalan's filmography, secret-keeping isn't just central to the stories, it's embedded in the storytelling itself. After *The Sixth Sense* and *Unbreakable*, he became known as "the twist guy," but that narrative was always unfair. John Kenneth Muir puts forward a compelling argument for Shyamalan not being a peddler of twist endings at all: "He cleverly and repeatedly plays on and subverts audience assumptions," Muir writes on his blog. "It's not the ending that twists, ... it's the audience's understanding of the imagery and symbols featured."[12]

There is a style of shot Shyamalan uses so often I've come to think of it as his signature: characters onscreen reacting to something offscreen. Usually the thing they are looking at is an object of fear, wonder or disgust, and it's usually situated behind or just below the camera. Shyamalan shows us the object of interest only after an uncomfortably long time, or sometimes not at all. Using this technique and others, he withholds visual information from the viewer the same way he withholds story information until just the right moment. To Muir's point, putting the audience in the position of trying to deduce what other people are seeing is a great way to interrogate misperception.

Lady in the Water (2006) opens with such a shot. It introduces us to Cleveland Heep, landlord and superintendent of a Philadelphia apartment complex, as he deals with a nasty unseen critter under a resident's sink. Cleveland, who we later learn lost his family in a home invasion murder spree, is a sad but gentle man who is devoted to his tenants. One night, a mysterious nude young woman emerges inexplicably from the swimming pool at the center of the complex. She tells Cleveland that her name is Story and that she is from "the Blue World." Cleveland gradually pieces together that she is a water nymph from a fairy tale reality who needs to fulfill an important mission, to which several of the residents, including Cleveland himself, are essential. One resident, Vick, is a writer who is working on a work of social critique that will spark the mind of a great leader one day. Story, who knows the future, needs to facilitate this by acting as a muse, inspiring him to finish the book. Hunted by a fearsome creature called a scrunt, she has just one more chance to be picked up by the giant eagle who will escort her home, and Cleveland must band together with his tenants to help her. According to the legend, several humans will play roles in getting her home, including a symbolist (interpreter), a guardian and a healer. Cleveland believes himself to be the guardian with the ability to keep Story safe from the scrunt. After he fails and she is almost killed, he realizes he is the healer, and manages to revive her in time for her rendezvous with the eagle. The awe-inspiring image of the eagle picking up Story and flying away is shot in dreamy distortion from beneath the water of the swimming pool.[13]

Like *Poltergeist III*, *Lady in the Water* relies on mirror imagery. Many shots of Story have her doubled by a reflection, and in the film's lore, the only way for an

Cleveland (Paul Giamatti) defends the titular character of *Lady in the Water* (2006), also known as Story (Bryce Dallas Howard), from an approaching scrunt.

earthbound person to detect the presence of a scrunt is in a mirror. You cannot see them by looking directly. Since Story is a water nymph, the Narcissus myth suggests itself. In Shyamalan's films, identity contemplation can lead to different outcomes depending on the character, and how rich they are in a trait that is key for the filmmaker: empathy.

When Cleveland looks into the pool, does he see what is there, or does he see what he wants to see? It's no surprise that he initially believes himself to be Story's guardian. Debilitated by guilt over not being able to protect his family, he wants to believe that he can make up for it by defending Story against danger. Like the audience in many Shyamalan films, Cleveland's expectations have made him overlook obvious signs pointing to the truth. He wants to be a protector, but his actions—fixing everything for his tenants, caring for Story—mark him as a skilled and empathetic caregiver. It's after he realizes his true role that the distorted reflections go away and the path forward is made clear.

Unbreakable (2000) tells the story of David Dunn, a security guard with a ten-year-old son named Joseph and a disintegrating marriage to Audrey, a physical therapist. David's train derails, killing everyone else on board but David, who is completely unharmed. An eccentric art gallery owner and comic book expert named Elijah Price, who suffers from brittle bone disease, begins trying to convince David that he has superpowers. Though David realizes he has never taken a sick day off work, can bench-press 350 pounds, and admits he has extraordinary intuition when it comes to identifying potentially dangerous people at his job, he maintains that these are unusual but mundane factors that do not add up to a superhero. He has two clear memories of being hurt: a childhood incident when he almost drowned in a swimming pool, resulting in pneumonia, and an injury from a car crash that ended his promising football career. Elijah theorizes, since both of those scenarios involved water, that water must be David's superhero weakness. Although Elijah turns out to be correct, we learn that only the pool incident was real; David was unharmed in the later auto accident but feigned injury in order to marry Audrey, who disliked football. He has kept this secret from her for their entire marriage. Eventually David embraces his superhero identity and sharpens his ability to see people's misdeeds upon physical contact. He follows an evildoer to the house where he is holding a family captive. During a fight, David is pushed off a balcony into a swimming pool, but he is rescued by the grateful family and ends up prevailing against the bad guy. David goes to thank Elijah for helping him discover his purpose, but when he shakes his hand, he learns that Elijah is a terrorist who orchestrated David's train derailment, among other massively fatal accidents, in search of the heroic counterpart to the supervillain he believes himself to be.[14]

Beat for beat, *Unbreakable* tells a straightforward superhero origin story. The only reason Elijah's villainy comes as a surprise is because the film was not marketed as a superhero movie, nor does it announce itself as such. If it had, we would know from the start that David is a superhero, and since every hero needs a villain, there is only one major character for whom that role makes sense. But since we were primed for a different genre—a supernatural mystery-thriller—we expected different storytelling conventions. (Shyamalan managed the exact same trick *again* 16 years later with *Split*, a stealth *Unbreakable* sequel which told a supervillain origin story presented as a psycho-thriller.)

Like *Lady in the Water*, *Unbreakable* is filled with mirror and glass imagery. The opening shot is a mirror reflection, in a flashback, showing a doctor arriving at the scene of Elijah's birth. The next flashback opens with another mirror shot, this time of the young Elijah reflected in a television, and the subsequent shot looks through a window. The first time we see David, he is leaning his head against a window. Like water, glass can both reflect and be seen through, albeit distortedly. In the same way, Mr. Glass himself has keen but skewed insight into matters that seem murky to other characters. He doesn't just break like glass; his gaze also embodies both properties of it. He sees things clearly, and yet everywhere he looks, he sees himself. His search for David, which cost so many lives, was motivated by self-interest. Looking for his mirror image—the person whose strength matches his weakness—is narcissistic in the classic sense. When Elijah sees his reflection in the metaphorical pool, the site of David's trauma and weakness, he becomes obsessed, despite being the only one in the film who truly understands what he is seeing.

Lady in the Water and *Unbreakable* both feature a general mood of melancholy and a protagonist in search of purpose. The precarious state of *Lady in the Water*'s world is underscored by background news reports about war. In *Unbreakable*, Elijah says they live in "mediocre times": "People are starting to lose hope. It's hard for many to believe there are extraordinary things inside themselves as well as others."

The protagonists of both films seem adrift. Cleveland Heep is devastated by the loss of his family; David Dunn grieves his decaying marriage and says he wakes up every morning feeling directionless. Both find purpose at the ends of their films, thanks to a swimming pool. David emerges from the pool near the end of *Unbreakable* accompanied by a triumphant flourish in the orchestral score. The last bit of doubt has been washed away. He now understands both his strengths and weaknesses, and steps into his role as a full-fledged superhero. Story emerges from the pool in *Lady in the Water* to awaken purpose in both Cleveland and Vick. She clears the cobwebs out of Vick's brain so he can begin to fix the broken world they live in, and reminds Cleveland of his true talents and rightful place in the world.

The aforementioned *Split* (2016) is pool-less, but it introduces Kevin Wendell Crumb, a serial killer with Dissociative Identity Disorder. One of Kevin's identities, known as "The Beast," gives him animal-like strength and speed and the ability to climb walls. He kidnaps Casey Cooke along with two other high school students, and Casey is the only one to escape alive.[15] *Split*'s sequel, *Glass* (2019), finds Kevin, Elijah and David in the same psychiatric facility, under the care of Dr. Ellie Staple, who we later learn is part of a secret organization committed to keeping the public ignorant of superhumans' existence.[16]

In *Unbreakable*, the childhood swimming pool accident that almost killed David and led to his aquaphobia is spoken of but not shown. *Glass* treats us to a flashback of the incident. Through a submerged camera, we watch in slow motion as two other boys hold David under the water. In *Unbreakable*, David describes the incident as mere roughhousing, saying the boys were doing nothing wrong, but in this reenactment it appears to be a clear-cut case of bullying. Whether David was lying to Elijah in the first film, or his memory of the incident changed in the two intervening decades, it makes sense for his superheroism to have its origins in victimhood. The Overseer, as he comes to be called, stands up for the little guy. Joseph

In *Glass* (2019), we see in a flashback the bullying incident that left young David Dunn (Colin Becker) with aquaphobia.

says as much in *Unbreakable*, when he gets in trouble at school for fighting in an attempt to stop another child from being harassed. Heroes, he tells his father, stick up for people who can't stick up for themselves.

Though Kevin does not interact with the pool directly, he does throw David into a water tank during their final fight as The Beast. Shyamalan plays fast and loose with the line between authentic D.I.D. and fantastical supervillainy, but one thing is clear: Kevin embodies the identity confusion element of the Narcissus myth. His self is as fluid as the water in which Narcissus mistakes himself for another. At the end of *Glass*, Joseph, Casey and Elijah's mother manage to circumvent Dr. Staple's efforts to keep the superhumans under wraps, and broadcast the footage of their fight to the world. If enough people can look into these waters and see themselves, perhaps the world can finally come to "believe that there are extraordinary things inside themselves as well as others."

David Dunn's superpowers aren't just strength and near-invulnerability; he also has super-empathy. He is able to see through the eyes of others simply by touching them. His ability to feel what others are feeling contrasts Elijah's callous disregard for all the lives he has taken. In *Lady in the Water*, a film without a real villain, nobody is motivated by self-interest. If they were, all would have been content to let Story die after she had accomplished what she came for. That everyone goes out of their way to help get her home proves them a true community, united not just by proximity but, more importantly, by mutual care. Shyamalan's films are arguments for empathy, for recognizing the limitations of any one perspective. The pools in these three films are layered symbols representing secrets (everyone in every film has them), rebirth and, via the Narcissus myth, both misperception and identity slippage. Whether the pools lead to disaster or greater self-knowledge depends on how much empathy we have. Who are we when we look into the pool? Like David Dunn and Cleveland Heep, can we learn to look through the water to the swimmer underneath? Or like Elijah Price and Kevin Wendell Crumb, are we unable to see past our own grotesque reflections?

Part II

Adult Swim
The Pool as a Site of Sexuality

Introduction

> He drifts off into the memory of the way she looked in school, with her body oiled and shining at the public swimming pool.
> —Joni Mitchell, "Harry's House"

Many of those who grew up going to the pool remember the transition point when they stopped seeing the people around them as just fellow swimmers, and started seeing bodies clad in practically nothing. People at swimming pools wear less than is acceptable anywhere else in public life. For this reason, the cultural consciousness has heavily sexualized the pool space. Of course, all sexual awakenings are not created equal. Some are sanctioned and taken for granted by our culture, and some are othered and made taboo. The blossoming of queer and other non-normative desires may well come later in life than adolescence, but it is just as likely to involve a swimming pool.

Although the pool can be a sexy place at any age, it has a special resonance for teenagers that deserves to be unpacked. The bare minimum of modesty afforded by a swimsuit mirrors the quasi-primal environment; at a pool, we are in something close to a state of nature, but not quite. Here we again encounter the pool as a liminal space, which coincides with the in-betweenness of adolescence—no longer a child but not yet an adult. The teenage pool party, as I touched on in reference to *Poltergeist III*, is coded as a slightly subversive activity, even if it is sanctioned by parents. Overtly, it's a chance to have fun in the water, but covertly it's a chance to see and be seen in swimsuits.

There is more to come on the public pool's social dimensions in Part III. Also in Part III, we'll drill down into adolescence, but right now it's important to address the plight of the teenage girl. While it is true that all adolescents live in a sort of twilight liminality, that state is even more acute for those who are female-presenting. This is a group of humans whom society incessantly sexualizes but condemns for owning their sexuality; society expects them to make adult decisions but also expects them to ask permission to go to the bathroom, and portrays them as vapid and immature but shows no mercy toward them when they make poor choices.

The pool too has its share of contradictions. It's water that you are supposed to bathe *before* getting into, and wash your hair again *after*. It's a place for kids, but also one imbued with lust, a public place of ritual undressing and attire more skimpy than most parents would let their kids look at under other circumstances. In some of the films we'll examine, the swimming pool is a symbol for teenage girlhood itself. Both are caught in the middle of a culture that shields children from the carnal on one hand but pornifies young women on the other.

Curiosity about bodies, of course, starts long before puberty, and it extends from the pool proper to the changing facilities. Poet Sharon Olds describes the forbidden allure of "the splintered pine wall, on the other side of which were boys, actually naked."[1] The summer I was six, my parents sent me to daycare at a neighborhood mom's house. Most afternoons, we would change in the house's bathroom and go to the pool. One day when I was getting my trunks on, I noticed someone watching through the crack in the door, and two girls ran away giggling. One of the curious girls squealed, "I saw it! I saw his penis!" It was the first time I'd heard the word *penis*, and I remember thinking it odd that the girl had mispronounced *peanut*, which was the cutesy word my mother used for it. The shame many people feel about being seen in a swimsuit stems from our acculturated understanding of the pool as a place for observing bodies, and that acculturation starts very early.

The pool in mass media is a site of the lustful gaze, particularly by men directed at women. Hence the long history of authorities policing women's swimming attire. Jeff Wiltse points out that at some point in the 20th century, the American notion of modesty changed from *keeping your body covered* to *keeping your body covered unless you have the right kind of body.*[2] But the association of water with femininity is much older; it was pervasive both in the classical world and in the *fin-de-siècle* weird and decadent fiction that laid much of the groundwork for modern horror.[3] In *The Interpretation of Dreams*, Sigmund Freud posited that immersion in water represented the womb, and the act of coming out of or going into water represented birth.[4] Freud's reading has proven durable as it pertains to horror films—nightmares written in light.

In the films of Part II, we will see these symbolic womanly water connections at work. We'll encounter women and girls as perpetrators of violence, victims of violence, and frequently both. I'll refer often to feminist theorist Barbara Creed's concept of the monstrous-feminine, described in her book of the same name. Creed draws heavily on Freud, including the abovementioned associations of water with femininity. "In the horror film," she writes, "the ancient connection drawn between woman, womb and the monstrous is frequently invoked."[5] The swimming pool as womb is a vital symbol for us going forward. We've already seen it in *House, Poltergeist III* and *The Pool*, as well as the Shyamalan films, where characters emerge from pools fundamentally changed—or reborn. More generally, the womb resonates in any film where the pool serves as a portal to another reality, e.g., the passage between the spirit world and our own, which is a common way to conceptualize the birth canal. For films that make use of Christian symbolism, a swimming pool also resembles a baptismal font, which itself is a surrogate womb.

If the pool can be read as a symbol for the womb, then the fear of it, and around it, would be coded fear of the reproductive body. Revisiting the crocodile terror of 2018's *The Pool*, we can see Day's anxiety about fatherhood manifest as a creature inside the pool (womb) that he is unprepared to handle. At the same time, the empty pool as an uncanny sight has implications for how the viewer is expected to receive the idea of an unproductive womb. To further complicate things, the monster herself is revealed to be a mother. When the crocodile lays eggs in the pool, Day and Koi boil one to keep from starving.[6] Amid this interspecies abortion, they discuss terminating Koi's pregnancy, but we never learn whether she ends up having the baby. For the film to resolve the abortion question would torpedo its own project: to cradle the womb, in all its complexities, as a place of the uncanny and the aspirational, of death and deliverance.

A twist on the empty swimming pool as barren womb can be found in Marc Carreté's *Asmodexia* (2014). During a bizarre December heat wave, exorcist Eloy and his teenage granddaughter Alba are preparing for a prophesied "resurrection" that is due in three days. They travel the countryside exorcising people possessed by entities that threaten the coming resurrection. One of the duo's visits is to an abandoned water park, where an exorcism is needed to undo the magic that imprisons a group of believers. Sitting by the empty, graffiti-covered swimming pool, Alba remarks that she can almost hear the laughter of children.

At the film's conclusion, we learn that Eloy is the leader of a Satanic cult, and the resurrection they are trying to bring about is a demonic, rather than a messianic one. Eloy is Alba's father as well as her grandfather. The violation of the incest taboo plus a little black magic resulted in Alba, who was born dead and then brought to life, giving her the ability to open the door to Hell. The exorcisms they have performed were to stop an angelic spirit called "The Nazarene"—possibly Jesus himself—from interfering with the plan by possessing cult members.[7] The rug-pull is reminiscent of Shyamalan: The film doesn't trick you so much as fail to dissuade you from assuming the main characters are the good guys. Also like Shyamalan, the film uses water and mirror imagery all the way through. Near the end, Eloy climbs a hill to a cathedral and gives a speech about everything having a "reverse" or negative image, as the camera slowly turns upside-down. Bound up in this theme is the notion of feminine power in opposition to Catholic patriarchy. Early in the film, Eloy tells a story about a woman who was posing as a man so that she could be a priest. In the end, we learn that, in opposition to the male Jesus, the apocalypse's chosen one is a teenage girl. Alba, a baby born dead, is the only one who can bring the Antichrist to life. Likewise, during a heat-wave winter, the graffitied swimming pool devoid of both water and children is a defaced symbol of fertility: an empty womb for a coffin birth; a hole in the ground that inverts the hilltop cathedral.

Through the lens of the pool as a site of sexuality, we'll see numerous examples of the horror film's obsessive tendency to equate, conflate and juxtapose sex and death. At this linkage, once again, horror and the swimming pool intersect. As Thomas A.P. van Leeuwen puts it, "The embrace of water is an erotic one, yet at the same time its cool fingers presage the immediacy of mortality. Eros and Thanatos occupy the two antithetical components of the complex sensation we call swimming...."[8] The only part of that quote swimming pool horror balks at is the word "antithetical." In these films, every drowning, every poolside murder, every stream of blood mingling with chlorinated water brings *la petite mort* face to face with *la grande mort*, reminding us how little distance really separates them. The pools in Part II, and the bodies that inhabit them, are sexualized and gendered. They are objects of desire, both accepted and taboo, both embraced and rejected, and their forms are as fluid as the water that fills them.

Chapter 4

The Changing Room

Atavism, Contagion and Transforming Women

> I just got a house here in L.A. with a pool. I pretend to be a mermaid in the middle of the night—it kind of de-stresses me.
> —Rebel Wilson[1]

Shapeshifting, both literal and metaphoric, is a perennial element in horror. This chapter focuses on pools that are connected to female shapeshifters specifically, and how the changes wrought by and on their bodies challenge the patriarchal fear of female power. Barbara Creed writes, "Feminist horror films imagine the non-human female protagonist through the aesthetics of the uncanny as she adopts a range of non-human and uncanny forms that appear human but are not."[2] She largely frames the feminist horror film drawing on non-human theory as a recent development, but as we'll see, these themes go back to some of the genre's foundational texts. Too often for it to be coincidental, these women do their transforming within spitting distance of a swimming pool.

Narratives about metamorphosis lend themselves to robust transgender readings, but I hesitate to provide many of them here. I leave it to critics who are trans themselves to put forward those interpretations. My queer readings of films encompassing non-normative sexuality and gender expression can be found in later chapters, but their absence from this one is not meant to foreclose on trans-affirming (or even transphobic) readings of these shapeshifting women's stories. Where my treatment of gender seems binary or bio-essentialist, it's because I think the film in question encourages that interpretation. The swimming pool is a flexible symbol for all kinds of fluid identities, so let this paragraph serve as my general acknowledgment that all the following films can, and should, be interpreted through a gender-critical lens.

Much of the horror of transformation in movies comes from the concept of *atavism*, which in biology means the reappearance of a genetic trait that has been lost in a population—like humans who are born with tails. In the 1800s, eugenicists used the atavism idea to suggest that certain types of people were inferior, and that their breeding could result in evolutionary regression. This idea has long been rejected as the racist pseudoscience it is, but since its prominence coincided with the birth of cinema, it had a lasting effect on how movies portray monstrosity.³ There will be more on eugenics and its lingering vestiges in Part III, but for now it's helpful to stay mindful of the atavistic monster trope's origins in bigotry.

Atavism and swimming are frequently linked, thanks to the understanding that all land creatures have waterborne ancestors somewhere in prehistory. Lidia Yuknavitch describes the experience of swimming with "the great intake of air, a breath that keeps a human able to move through water as if we were not gone from our breathable blue past."⁴

Filmic portrayals of atavistic women might be terrifying, but they are not always negative. In reference to the meme-fueled rise of "mermaiding" in popular culture, Maria Mellins writes that femininity, combined with strength, is "key to the mermaid identity."⁵ Buoying the classical link between water and femininity is the general attitude that women are closer to nature, which Creed both affirms and broadens: "The monstrous-feminine is represented in films as inter-species; she exists in a complex relationship with ... animals, machines, nature, matter, monsters, aliens, ghosts, the earth, forests, oceans and natural elements."⁶

Many of these new forms butt up against totalizing societal notions of femininity. In keeping with the image of the pool as womb, these films' transformations are often shorthand for the physical changes of puberty, menstruation and pregnancy. It's the push and pull of atavistic terror and feminine power that give the women in this chapter, and their swimming pools, such depth.

On the topic of transforming women, horror films and swimming pools, there's only one place we can start: 1942's *Cat People*, directed by Jacques Tourneur. Perhaps the most influential horror film of the 1940s, *Cat People* features the first important swimming pool scene in the genre's history. There is a reason for this. Although they existed in antiquity,⁷ swimming pools in cinema generally act as artifacts of modernity. Until *Cat People* came along, horror movies mostly clung to the vaguely medieval and/or remote European settings of the 1930s Universal monster movies. It wasn't until the 1940s that mainstream American horror films began situating their stories in the here and now. In *Cat People*'s case, the here is metropolitan New York City, and the now is in the midst of World War II. The film opens with a quote about atavism by a fictional doctor before introducing us to Oliver, an all–American engineer, and Irena, a commercial artist and immigrant from Serbia, who meet-cute at the zoo where she is sketching a panther. After a whirlwind but chaste courtship, Irena and Oliver marry, though she does not conceal her reservations. She fears she is descended from a race of werecats, per a superstition from her home village, who morph into panthers upon the incitement of intense emotion. When consummating a love affair, says the legend, these women transform and kill the men they partner with. Not appreciating that Irena's emotional distance and frigidity are for his own protection, Oliver grows closer to his colleague Alice, whose casual confidence Irena finds threatening. Alice, for her part, is not so secretly in love with Oliver. As their marriage erodes, Oliver refers Irena to a psychiatrist, but the doctor

The most imitated shot in swimming pool horror: Irena (Simone Simon) looms over Alice (Jane Randolph) in 1942's *Cat People*.

is more interested in putting the moves on her than helping her. The jealous Irena stalks Alice twice: once through Central Park, and again in her apartment building's swimming pool.[8]

Cat People has been written about hundreds of times, from as many critical perspectives. I cannot hope to do the film justice, but its status as the grandmother of swimming pool horror means I have to try. My reading focuses on the different femininities embodied by Irena and Alice, and how the swimming pool sequence contrasts them visually. The film takes pains to distinguish the two women from one another. Irena is dark-featured, Alice is blonde. Both are working women, but Irena's work seems solitary. Though we see her at work, we never see her colleagues. Alice, on the other hand, has an easy office rapport with Oliver and the others at her job, as well as the waitress at the corner cafe near their workplace. Alice works in engineering, a masculine-coded field, whereas Irena works in fashion, a feminine-coded one. Alice is pert and gregarious in a metropolitan 1940s way. In short, we get the impression that she is "one of the guys." The film compares the demure Irena unfavorably to Alice's male-approved cool. When Oliver thanks Alice for advice with a chummy "You're very swell," she replies, "That's what makes me dangerous. I'm the new type of other woman." The line doesn't just establish Alice as a threat to Irena's claim on Oliver, it also explicitly aligns her with the future.

Irena, by contrast, is associated with the past. In rejecting the "old country" settings of earlier horror films, *Cat People* leverages the World War II–era mistrust of European immigrants to craft a character who can't seem to let go of archaic ways of life.[9] In the film's lens, atavism, superstition and traditional femininity all go hand in hand, and Irena is an undesirable European representative of all three.

Despite Alice's American spunk, Irena still has the advantage when it comes to physical power. This brings us to the swimming pool scene, and a trope we'll see more of: role reversal at the pool. Pools, as we saw in the last chapter, are places that can mutate identity. When I was a child, my dad pointed out that the pool let me lift things too heavy to lift on land. I picked him up and cradled him in my arms while he babbled like a baby. Who is the parent and who is the child? The pool lets us blur the boundary. When Alice is in the swimming pool, being threatened by Irena, the latter has the upper hand in every way. In the words of scholar Alex Naylor, while Alice treads water with visible effort, "she becomes small, menaced and vulnerable, with the much physically smaller and usually less socially confident Irena towering over her from the pool's edge."[10] Alice may be able to take Irena's man, but Irena could tear her to ribbons without a second thought. This blocking has been repeated so many times I've come to call it the "*Cat People* shot." We'll see it throughout this book whenever a film wants to depict a power differential between two characters (usually women), especially one in which the tables have been turned.

The role reversal that finds Irena powerful and Alice powerless also finds Alice in a skintight swimsuit and Irena covered in a heavy black coat with shoulder pads that give her an imposing physical profile. In the world of *Cat People*, it seems, for a woman to embrace her sexuality is to surrender her strength. Irena is reluctant to be physical with her husband—not out of coldness or lack of love, but rather fear of her own destructive power. Keys are important symbols in the film: The key to the panther's cage is a plot McGuffin, a key looms large in Irena's nightmare sequence, and Alice needs a key to access the swimming pool. A key entering a lock is an obvious symbol for intercourse, but we should also pay attention to what the keys are opening. Irena's key opens the panther's cage—it lets loose the beast. When Alice asks for and receives the swimming pool key, the film is granting her symbolic access to a more wholesome form of sexuality, but the pool is also a place where she is vulnerable. Irena can only enter by invoking Alice's name, and as soon as she does, the pool loses its luster of health and vigor when the lights go out and the threat of death intrudes.

Paul Schrader's 1982 *Cat People* remake retains much of the original's subtext, though the remake expands the story considerably. This time Irena has a brother named Paul, whom she has not seen since they were orphaned in childhood and she went into foster care. Paul, we later learn, is aware of their werecat heritage, has spent much of his life in psychiatric institutions, and is now a religious zealot. Oliver and Alice are zookeepers instead of engineers. The lore of the cat people themselves is deepened: They transform when they mate with a human, and they remain trapped

The 1982 *Cat People* remake adds color, nudity and more overt menace to the iconic moment. Pictured: Nastassja Kinski, facing the camera, and Annette O'Toole.

in panther form until they take a human life. The only way to have sex without the metamorphosis is by mating with another werecat, and Paul informs Irena that their race has always been incestuous. Irena, a virgin, has never encountered this problem. In the interest of getting his rocks off, Paul has become a serial killer, having sex with women and then murdering them in cat form. Alice and Irena have a friendlier relationship in the remake, sharing drinks and intimate conversation, though this time it is Alice who feels threatened by Irena's allure. In the end, Irena has no good choices. She is in love with Oliver, but cannot have sex with him without turning into a cat. She must kill a human to resume her human form, which she is unwilling to do. Saying "I want to live with my own," she chooses to have sex with Oliver while safely tied to the bedpost, after which she lives out her life as a panther in the zoo.[11]

The original's swimming pool sequence is faithfully recreated, except this time Alice is topless, having been interrupted by her unseen stalker midway through undressing in the changing room. Irena still wears a heavy coat. Rather than being cautiously on guard, Alice screams about Irena trying to kill her, and Irena makes little effort to conceal her threatening attitude. This change in the scene's texture is part of the film's overall project to challenge the original's spirit of subtlety. Where 1942's *Cat People* is interested in drawing distinctions between different kinds of women, Schrader's film confronts the backwards reality that in American society, having a healthy relationship with one's sexuality requires a degree of rebellion and sometimes seems impossible—no matter what kind of woman you are. Religious zealot Paul's desire for his sister is repulsive to the viewer, but the cat people's culture normalizes incest. If acculturation can do that, what does it imply for our own society? When Alice expresses surprise that Irena is a virgin, Irena says, "Don't

Chapter 4. The Changing Room   53

make it sound so perverse." In the same conversation, Alice shares a tip for deflecting unwanted male attention: "I tell them I'm gay." Both of these moments point to a casual disregard for female sexual agency. A woman choosing to remain a virgin is as "incomprehensible" as a woman rejecting a man's advances without a "good reason," like being a lesbian, or even having a boyfriend. Just not wanting to, it seems, is insufficient. In this context, both Alice's nudity and her defensiveness in the swimming pool read less as vulnerability and more as defiance. In the bar scene when Irena says, "I was just being friendly, I was not trying to get laid," Alice responds, "Occasionally they're compatible." This attitude stands in contrast to Paul and Irena's world, where sexuality is irremediably entangled with violence. Some points demand to be made with a machete rather than a stiletto, and this is one that would be weakened by the original *Cat People*'s subtle approach.

Irena wants to live with her own kind, but they are extinct. Caught in a cycle of violence around her sexuality, she finds herself empowered but unable to use that power. So she chooses the closest thing: to live in passive proximity to the other big cats. Like Paul, who turned to religion with all its prohibitions out of guilt over his base impulses, she chooses bondage and calls it freedom. Alice, who is just as comfortable wielding a rifle as she is tits-out in the swimming pool, is the only one who seems to have it all.

Schrader's *Cat People* inspired a mini-wave of imitators in the 1980s. One of them, Pen Desham's *The Kiss* (1988), gives us another battle of female wills around the swimming pool, this time adding the element of adolescence to its psychosexual context, and crafting a much less subversive film in the process. *The Kiss* relocates the origin of its ancient curse from the original *Cat People*'s Eastern Europe to central Africa. In a prologue set in the Belgian Congo, a young girl named Felice is attacked by her aunt after her (Felice's) mother's death. The aunt passes something to her by means of a violent kiss. In the present day, Felice's sister Hilary, who has not seen her since the Congo, lives in the suburban U.S. with her husband Jack and their teenage daughter Amy. At a backyard pool party to celebrate Amy's Catholic confirmation, Hilary gets a phone call from Felice, who simply says, "It's time," before Hilary hangs up. Fearing danger, she goes shopping for a gun and is killed in a freak car crash. Months later, Felice shows up at Jack and Amy's house and begins to insert herself into their lives. As accidents continue to befall people around her, Amy becomes suspicious of Felice, who spends her time trying to seduce Jack. Eventually we learn that Felice is host to a wormlike parasite that gives her supernatural powers, including the ability to telepathically control a wild catlike creature. The parasite has been passed down through the female members of their bloodline for generations, and now it is Amy's turn. Jack and Amy engage Felice in a climactic fight in the swimming pool, which ends in an explosion that kills both Felice and the parasite.[12]

The Kiss' menstrual horror elements are hard to miss. Amy is a girl suddenly confronted with a hereditary "curse," one which only affects women, as she transitions into adulthood. The scene of Felice and Jack's first sexual encounter is cross-cut with Amy at school listening to a lecture about the human heart, as she hallucinates an anatomical dummy crying blood and is disturbed by her own menstrual flow. Amy's developing body and the sex act are connected, at least in her mind, with nothing but fear, pain and suffering.

The bringer of the curse, Felice, is a beautiful woman whose allure can easily tip into the sinister. She is a less ambiguous villain than Irena in either version of *Cat People*. She reminds us of Barbara Creed's words of caution against abuse of the "feminist horror" label: "I am not arguing that simply because the monstrous-feminine is constructed as an active rather than passive figure that this image is 'feminist' or 'liberated.'"[13] Although Felice is powerful, we are never invited to see her power as something desirable; although she is the victim of a curse-parasite, we are never encouraged to feel sorry for her. Her construction is that of a pure villain. Her body is dead, animated by the presence of the parasite, and it's possible that Felice isn't in there at all, having died back in the '60s when her own aunt did to her what she intends to do to Amy.

Even more regressively than *Cat People* from four decades earlier, *The Kiss* is interested in pitting women against each other. Felice is assertive, foreign, sexually predatory, and an evil witch—four traits that are combined often enough in popular culture that viewers begin to equate them. When casting her deadly spells, Felice suggestively strokes a carven phallic idol, resembling the creature that enters and exits her body through the mouth. Amy's struggle is to avoid becoming like her, *the wrong kind of woman*. To the extent that "the curse" represents puberty, though, it's womanhood itself, of any kind, that is the danger here. The film's antidote to the abject woman is the heroic man. Late in the film, the local priest grapples with Felice, buying Amy enough time to get away at the cost of his own life. Jack takes an active role in the climactic swimming pool fight, rescuing Amy multiple times from a watery demise. It is he who falls with Felice into the pool—returning the fight to the symbolic center of femaleness itself. Finally, it is Jack who throws in the propane tank that kills the monster. After Amy emerges from the pool, reborn and safe from scary womanhood, the final shot shows the pool water twinkling in the moonlight. Suburban bliss has been restored. Whenever the pool represents a border of propriety, there are films that counter the status quo, and films that uphold it. In what might be a first for this book, *The Kiss* is unquestionably one of the latter.

One of the quirkier takes on the monstrous-feminine can be found in 2016's *Colossal*, directed by Nacho Vigalondo. The film follows Gloria, an alcoholic writer who moves after a breakup from the big city to the small town where she grew up. She gets a job working at a bar owned by Oscar, an acquaintance from her youth. She accidentally discovers that when she sets foot on her childhood playground at a certain time of day, she manifests a giant kaiju-like monster on the other side of the world, menacing the city of Seoul, South Korea. The creature moves in tandem with her own movements—in essence, the creature *is* her—and because of its sheer

Oscar (Jason Sudeikis) completes his villain turn with a scummy pool dip in *Colossal* (2016).

size, she unwittingly destroys city blocks just by taking a few steps. It turns out that Oscar is capable of the same thing, although the creature he controls is a giant robot. Though they do not become romantically involved, Oscar grows increasingly possessive, manipulative and emotionally abusive toward Gloria. When Gloria's ex arrives in town to try to convince her to return, Oscar threatens to destroy Seoul if she leaves. Oscar's hostility unlocks a repressed memory for Gloria: When they were children, Gloria made a diorama model of Seoul for school. When the wind blew it away at the playground, young Oscar went after it, but instead of retrieving it, he destroyed it in a fit of frustration. At that moment, a bolt of lightning struck the playground, including the model, Gloria, Oscar and their toys, which were small-scale versions of the monsters they later manifested. In the present, upon remembering this, Gloria tells Oscar she now realizes how sad and jealous a man he is. Oscar races for the playground and Gloria tries to stop him, chasing him through her childhood home. The chase leads them upstairs, whence Oscar falls into the disused, leaf-covered backyard swimming pool. Wordless and stony-faced, Oscar stalks through the water while the monster's sinister orchestral theme plays on the soundtrack.[14]

Though brief, *Colossal*'s swimming pool scene does some heavy lifting by underscoring the conflict's primal nature. Prowling in the leafy pool, Oscar might as well be a predator in a jungle pond. The pool also acts as a symbolic womb. Like *Unbreakable*'s David Dunn, Oscar has fully accepted his part in this larger-than-life scenario. When he emerges from the swimming pool, a supervillain is born. On yet another level, the pool at Gloria's house is an extension of her person and, per the premise of this chapter, represents her gender. Oscar is driven mad by male fragility and entitlement. Seeing a woman living an exciting, successful life leads him to act vindictively, just as he did when he was a kid. (More on male possessiveness as a horror villain motive in a later chapter.) Oscar's tumble into Gloria's childhood swimming pool is a gendered gesture of dominance, and a disruption of her attempt to rebuild.

As I mentioned earlier, municipal pools in the U.S. had their origins in the 19th century as public baths. It was thought that pools slowed the spread of disease by encouraging the unwashed masses to rinse themselves in public tanks. In the 1890s after the germ theory of disease became widespread, the situation reversed. "Pools were especially hazardous because studies showed that germs could live longer in water," Jeff Wiltse writes. "[P]ools suddenly became obsolete and downright dangerous as public baths. Many cities consciously chose not to build municipal pools because officials now perceived them as threats to public health." Indeed, public pools would not have "survived the microbe," as Wiltse puts it, if not for their redefinition as facilities for fitness and recreation rather than hygiene.[15] A Brown University chemist pioneered the use of chlorine to sterilize pool water in 1910, and it soon became standard practice.[16] Still, concerns about swimming pools' disease transmission potential lingered in the public imagination, becoming part of the justification for excluding certain minorities from enjoying them.

In 1995, Greg Louganis, one of the greatest competitive divers in the sport's history and a recently out gay man, told ABC's Barbara Walters that he had been diagnosed with HIV six months before the 1988 Olympic Games. At those same Olympics, Louganis hit his head on the springboard during competition and fell bleeding into the pool. Without informing the doctor who stitched his wound about his HIV status, he returned to the competition and ended up winning gold medals in both the springboard and platform events.[17] The 1995 release of the ABC interview, and Louganis' autobiography, set off a media frenzy, with news stations replaying the slow-motion footage of Louganis' accident while pundits and the public debated the morality of his choice not to disclose his status. The mudslingers were ostensibly worried that Louganis had endangered others who used the pool, despite years of research confirming that the human immunodeficiency virus cannot survive the chlorine in pool water.[18] In fact, there had never been a known case of HIV transmission through sports of any kind.[19] Some speculated that the panic about the Louganis incident had more to do with homophobia than germophobia, noting that Louganis received harsher treatment than other high-profile HIV-positive athletes, like Magic Johnson and Arthur Ashe, who were heterosexual.[20]

The fear of contracting disease in a swimming pool is still a pervasive one, though weakly corroborated by data. As recently as May 2024, a false story circulated about a swimming pool in Texas that was supposedly linked to four cases of HIV.[21] In a 2009 survey, 47 percent of respondents admitted to "unhygienic behaviors in public pools," a category that included urinating (17 percent), swimming with a runny nose (11 percent) and forgoing a pre-swim shower (35 percent). When respondents were asked if they believed other swimmers were guilty of these behaviors, the numbers were much higher: 78 percent for urination and 38 percent for swimming with diarrhea (compared to the mere 1 percent who admitted to that particular gamble themselves).[22] These numbers indicate that most people believe the pool behavior of others to be far less hygienic than their own. In other words, widespread reckless

Chapter 4. The Changing Room 57

An infected Starliner Tower resident (actor unidentified) pushes Dr. St. Luc (Paul Hampton) into the waiting arms of sex zombies Betts (Barbara Steele, holding onto Hampton's leg) and Nurse Forsythe (Lynn Lowry) in 1975's *Shivers*.

swimmer behavior might well be a bugbear. While there certainly have been cases of illness from pathogens encountered in swimming pools, these have been rare (in the U.S., roughly 400 a year between 1971 and 2000, out of tens of millions of swimmers), especially when you consider a 2008 study that found 54 percent of pools had sanitation code violations.[23]

Given all this, it should be no surprise that fear of the swimming pool as a site of contagion, particularly of sexually transmitted disease, has made its way into horror cinema. Blood-borne disease is scary, and the image of blood in water is an irresistibly primal one. Women's status as an oppressed and sexualized group, and the archetypal womanliness of blood and water imagery, often put female characters at the centers of these narratives.

Women, contagions and swimming pools appear in two back-to-back films by David Cronenberg from the mid–1970s. *Shivers* (1975) and *Rabid* (1977) both depict the venereal spread of parasites with unwitting women as their origin points, but the two films handle their patient zeroes, and their swimming pools, differently. The outbreak in *Shivers* unfolds in Starliner Tower, a Montreal high-rise apartment complex. Mad scientist Dr. Hobbes, working with grant money earmarked for the creation of beneficent parasites to replace failing human organs, instead engineers one that makes its hosts sex-crazy and spreads like an STD. His goal is to "turn the world into one beautiful, mindless orgy." Hobbes uses his 19-year-old lover Annabelle as a guinea pig, murdering her and killing himself after the experiment goes wrong. Unbeknownst to him, Annabelle was also sleeping with at least three other men in the building, through whom the infection continues to spread. *Shivers* follows an ensemble of characters, but the most screen time goes to our *de facto* hero, Starliner's on-site doctor, Roger St. Luc. (Named, perhaps, after Saint Luke, patron saint of physicians, artists and butchers, and author of the line "This is my body, which is given for you; do this in remembrance of me.") Roger and Nurse Forsythe, his colleague and lover, spend the middle part of the movie searching the building for the parasites. As widespread acts of sexual assault accelerate the transmission, Roger and the nurse get separated, and Forsythe becomes infected offscreen. Roger, seemingly the only uninfected person left, makes it to the facility's swimming pool, where he is tempted by two women in the water. He attempts to flee the building, but the infected force him back inside and he ends up in the pool, swarmed by a mass of sex zombies. Later, Roger and Forsythe, both infected, lead a caravan into the city while a news report of the outbreak plays on the radio.[24]

Despite being killed in the film's opening scenes, Annabelle—specifically her body—looms large over everything that follows. For symbolic purposes, she is the parasite's mother, giving birth to it after being impregnated by Hobbes. We learn early on that Hobbes, her former teacher, sexually abused her at age 12. The parasite may have spread through Annabelle's body, but it was a direct result of sexual and medical abuse at the hands of an older man who took advantage of her trust. It's implied that her promiscuity, which hastened the parasite's takeover of the building, was also set in motion by that childhood abuse.

Shivers forefronts the conflict between science and savagery. It opens with an advertisement for Starliner Tower, showcasing its state-of-the-art amenities (including what is referred to as, but is obviously not, an "Olympic-sized" swimming pool), before cutting to Hobbes as he slaughters Annabelle. Hobbes reportedly believed that man is "an animal that thinks too much," and creating the parasite was an attempt to return man to "his primal self," albeit one mediated by the science of genetic engineering. Like the swimming pool, Hobbes' creation is an artificial attempt to return humanity to a state of nature.

Annabelle's dead body, absent from the proceedings, nonetheless lives on in the parasites that multiplied from it. Like Henrietta Lacks[25] and the enslaved test subjects of J. Marion Sims,[26] Annabelle is another in the long line of women's bodies sacrificed without consent on the altar of scientific progress. She is woman transformed into disease agent.

In another female metamorphosis, closer to the mermaiding I mentioned at the start of this chapter, two normal women become sirens in Starliner's pool. The pair of silent, floating temptresses reminds us of the aquatic women of ancient myth who lure seamen to their deaths.[27] Despite knowing them to be sex zombies who want to infect him, Roger is still susceptible to their allure, only just being able to wrench himself away and fling open the door, gulping the fresh air. Even the most level-headed among us, the film seems to be saying, are one little push away from giving in to our impulses. After Roger is submerged, the pool once again plays the role of womb, and he comes out of it reborn into Hobbes' "beautiful, mindless orgy."

Just before a parasite comes out of her mouth, revealing her as a zombie, Forsythe gives a speech about a dream she had where an old man told her, "Everything is erotic. ...Even old flesh is erotic flesh, that disease is the love of two alien kinds of creatures for each other." It is tempting to read this speech as the film blaming the free love movement for the spread of sexually transmitted infections, but that interpretation disregards the fact that the epidemic here is scientifically engineered. In fact, the film's lens seems to be sex-positive, especially in its frank portrayal of various kinds of queer love, which is unusual for the time period. At its heart, *Shivers*—like *Piranha*, *Alligator* and *Shock Waves*—is a mad scientist yarn, another entry in the proud horror tradition of cautionary tales against meddling with nature. In this case, that meddling targets the bodies of women. Mother Nature always finds a way to collect, and when the debt comes due, what better place to pay it than that sparkling, not-really-Olympic sized pool?

Cronenberg's follow-up *Rabid* (1977) is a thematic companion piece to *Shivers*. Another woman has a reckless scientific experiment performed on her without her consent. But this time, rather than an absent, passive agent, she is an active one, and the film centers her experience. In *Rabid*, main character Rose suffers a near-fatal motorcycle crash that coincidentally happens near a state-of-the-art plastic surgery clinic run by Dr. Keloid. Believing Rose to be too injured to survive the trip to a fully equipped hospital, Keloid attempts to save her life using what he has on hand. He applies a new skin graft technique, meant for cosmetic purposes, in an effort to repair her organ damage. Somehow, this results in Rose developing a vaginal orifice in the crook of her left arm, with a spiked appendage through which Rose feeds on human blood. She can no longer eat regular food and must sustain herself by attacking people, who subsequently turn into rageful zombie-like creatures. The infected's behavior resembles animals with rabies, although the virus, or whatever it is, does not affect Rose in this way. Seemingly unaware of what is going on, Rose makes her way to the city. After the outbreak grows to epidemic proportions, she is eventually killed by a man she infects deliberately as an experiment to see if she is really the cause of it all.[28]

In a news report, the film makes reference to "the infamous Typhoid Mary"—i.e., Mary Mallon, an early 20th-century domestic servant who was responsible for multiple typhoid outbreaks in New York. In 1907, when an early form of contact tracing led to her arrest and forcible quarantine, the germ theory of disease was not widely accepted, and most laypeople had no idea what an asymptomatic carrier was.[29] Like Mallon's, Rose's complaint is simple: How can she be sick if she doesn't feel or look sick? The ethics of how Mallon was treated—quarantined in a hospital until her death 23 years later—are still being debated.[30] A similar question arises about Rose. How much responsibility does she have to the people around her, especially if she doesn't understand what's happening? Must she, like the rabid animal the film's title invokes, be put down for the good of all, despite none of it being her fault? Does her gender make that question easier for society at large to answer?

Mallon herself cast her plight in gendered terms, writing in a letter that she has been "a peep show for everyone." She concluded the letter with, "I wonder how ... Dr. William H. Park would like to be insulted and put in the Journal and call him ... Typhoid William Park."[31]

It is worth noting that almost all of Rose's victims are male. Though the film allows us little access to Rose's interiority, leaving us to guess about what's happening in her head, we can infer that Rose's attacks are crimes of opportunity. She assaults whoever happens to be nearby when the urge to feed becomes too great to suppress. This is usually a man, because men won't leave her alone—from a patient at the clinic to a farmer in his barn to an adult movie theater patron to a random apartment building tenant, a parade of men lines up to hit on Rose and they pay with their blood. Of all the people we see Rose feed on, only two of them are women. The second victim is her friend Mindy. Rose seemingly tries to protect Mindy by leaving before the hunger overtakes her, but when Mindy catches her sneaking out, Rose cannot resist the urge to feed on her.

Rose's first female victim is a Keloid clinic patient named Judy, a wealthy young woman whose father has paid for multiple nose jobs. Judy is relaxing in the facility's hot tub when Rose approaches her, acting strangely. Judy is visibly unsettled, but Rose strikes before she can get away. Judy, however, is spared the indignity of becoming a rabid creature: When the police investigate the outbreak at the clinic, they find her body in the walk-in freezer, frozen solid. Neither of the two women we see Rose infect comes back as a zombie. Although there are two other infected women who do commit violence onscreen, on the whole the viral rage reads as masculine.

Like *Shivers*, Judy's hot tub scene plays on the presumed seductiveness of a woman in water. Rose's attraction to her, though impelled by hunger, has a sexual quality to the way it's performed, and the attack, like most of the attacks in the film, plays out like a rape. Judy is not trying to be alluring. Rose sees her minding her own business in a vulnerable, feminine space, and victimizes her. In short, Rose treats Judy the way men treat Rose. After all, Judy is there in the first place because her father—a male figure with power over her—has paid for surgery to make her appearance more attractive. Rose's erotic gaze is intertwined with violent assault, and culture teaches us that a woman in a hot tub is fair game for both.

I set a rule that, for the purposes of this book, hot tubs do not count as pools. I am bending it for *Rabid*, because in the film's 2019 remake, directed by Jen and Sylvia Soska, the hot tub is transformed into the plastic surgery clinic's swimming pool, and the victim is gender-swapped—factors that reflect a change in the remake's sexual politics. The 2019 version gives us more insight into Rose as a person. At the start, she is an aspiring designer working in an entry-level position at a fashion house. She bears facial scars from a car crash that killed the rest of her family. Chelsea, her foster sister from the family that cared for her after the accident, is a model at the same fashion house. Chelsea convinces a photographer (whom Rose has a crush on) to ask her out; Rose finds out about the subterfuge, leaves in a huff on her motorbike and

Chapter 4. The Changing Room 61

Pretty but not nice: Rose (Laura Vandervoort) approaches her quarry Dominic (Stephen Huszar) in the 2019 *Rabid* remake.

winds up in a near-fatal accident. This time her face is majorly disfigured, in addition to the internal injuries. After experimental cosmetic surgery, which also eliminates her need for eyeglasses, the new Rose is a stunner. The day the bandages come off, the first thing she does is visit the facility's swimming pool where she meets a fellow patient named Dominic, a TV actor who is at the clinic for "routine maintenance." After some aggressive flirting, Rose starts to kiss Dominic before biting him hard enough to draw blood. She then runs away, ashamed.³²

By spending so much time with Rose's professional life in the cutthroat fashion business, the film reminds us of that world's superficiality and naked ambition. We find ourselves back in 1942 with *Cat People*'s Irena, the mild-mannered fashion illustrator who transforms into a powerful poolside predator. Simply put, Rose's world encourages ruthless competition among women. Later, though sick and rapidly getting worse, Chelsea insists on pushing through rather than let another model close the fashion show in her place. This results in a zombified Chelsea wreaking havoc in her feathered designer dress and war paint–like makeup, "pretty and not nice" personified.

Both versions of *Rabid* stage assault scenes in the clinic's aquatic therapy facilities. Since healing and nurturing are coded as feminine, this adds another dimension to the pool's associations with wellness and the "water cure" discussed in Part I. Both *Rabid*s' pervert expectations with the passing of infection in a medical place of healing. The idea of woman as a passive sexual partner is upended too. Far from the coy smiles of the '70s Rose, the 2019 version clamps her legs around Dominic in the pool and later flings a male partner against the wall of a nightclub hallway, both to her subsequent chagrin. Like Irena, Rose is afraid of the aggression her own sexuality unlocks. She enters the pool and finds it more natural to murder than to demur. Disturbingly, the more she does it, the more people seem to like her.

From the absent body of the woman-cum-disease vector in *Shivers*, to the active but guiltless lead in *Rabid* 1977, to the woman whose viciousness is rewarded and encouraged in *Rabid* 2019; from the shapeshifting predators of *Cat People* to the woman's unwitting destructive power in *Colossal*—these films showcase the swimming pool's complicated relationship with the female body.

Over the next few chapters, we will meet more transforming women. While the changes they undergo will not always be physical, the body consciousness we've laid bare in this chapter will never be far from the surface.

CHAPTER 5

The Back Stroke
Aquatic Female Vengeance

> The town pool is an inverted block of flats, something gathered and gently milling. Container for a small revolution.
> —Katherine Pierpoint, "Going Swimmingly"

Like the pools themselves, each of the previous chapter's monstrous women are "manmade" in the strictest sense. The inciting incidents are symbolic rapes: for selfish reasons, men put things into women's bodies that turn them into monsters. We can find this same setup in a film that emerged in the waning days of the 2000s and laid the groundwork for much of the following decade's feminist horror. Karyn Kusama's *Jennifer's Body* (2009) follows the friendship between high schoolers Anita and Jennifer. Anita, nicknamed "Needy," is insecure and still finding her way in high school, while Jennifer is popular and hot. Jennifer is kidnapped by a rock band, who sacrifice her in an occult ritual intended to bring them fame. But the ceremony called for a virgin, which Jennifer was not. The ritual works, but rather than killing her, a demon permanently possesses Jennifer's body. Needing to eat humans to survive, she starts seducing and consuming high school boys. After determining that Jennifer has been transformed into a succubus, Needy breaks up with her boyfriend Chip, fearing for his safety. On the night of a school dance, Jennifer intercepts Chip as he walks through a park and seduces him. Leading him to a disused public swimming pool, she pulls him into the water and begins to feed on him. Following his cries for help, Needy arrives to find Chip bitten but still alive, and jumps into the pool to rescue him. Jennifer demonstrates her power, first by shrugging off the effects of pepper spray and then by levitating above the pool, her long white dress dripping in a parody of an angelic pose. Needy confronts Jennifer verbally, accusing her of being insecure. Just as Jennifer begins to attack, Chip stabs her with a broken pool skimmer and dies.[1]

Comparisons to *Rabid* are irresistible. There is even a scene that also occurs in both versions of *Rabid*, where Jennifer attempts to eat a chicken and vomits it up, learning that she can no longer digest anything but human flesh. But unlike *Rabid*'s surgery scene, the *Jennifer's Body* ritual plays out overtly like a sexual assault. The band members pick Jennifer out of the crowd and usher her into their touring van

"She's just hovering, it's not that impressive": a *Cat People*–style shot with a plus-one as Chip (Johnny Simmons) and Needy (Amanda Seyfried) cower before the levitating Jennifer (Megan Fox) in *Jennifer's Body* (2009).

in a vulnerable state—in this case, in shock from a fire that broke out at the venue. She asks, "Are you guys rapists?" The band physically restrains Jennifer, surrounds her and taunts her as they perform the act. The staging in the woods is reminiscent of Wes Craven's *The Last House on the Left* (1972), a foundational film of the rape-revenge format.[2]

The pool, representing the female body, is the film's symbolic as well as literal battleground. Like other seductresses we have seen, Jennifer plays the siren, using her beauty to lure men to their deaths. The water symbolizes both her sexuality and her seeming atavism. After eating her second victim, Jennifer swims naked in a lake, looking like an aquatic predator, and emerges feeling deliciously empowered. "I am a god," she tells Needy over the phone. Meanwhile, the community pool has undergone its own kind of atavism. Nature has retaken the abandoned premises, with vegetation growing through the windows and across the water's surface. Jennifer's semi-bestial self is at home here, and by bringing Chip here she has brought him completely into her power.

The film borrows its title from a 1994 song written by Courtney Love, whose lyrics reference an abusive relationship.[3] Although Jennifer is victimized by men, the abusive relationship at the film's center is her friendship with Needy. Jennifer, the more assertive personality, acts condescendingly toward Needy, ordering her around and dismissing her opinions. They are still best friends thanks to their childhood bond, despite no longer having anything in common. Minus the shark-toothed demon element, many viewers will relate to the pain of trying to sustain a friendship past its expiration date. This dynamic drives the swimming pool confrontation.

Chip has little power in this female space, but Needy can, and does, challenge Jennifer's dominance. Jennifer's levitation recalls *Cat People*, with the animalistic woman in the superior position, looming over the more vulnerable woman in the pool. *Jennifer's Body* also echoes *Cat People* in its illustration of a disintegrating relationship hastened by a woman's monstrous metamorphosis. When Needy emerges from the pool, she undergoes her own rebirth: She now has the confidence to stand up to Jennifer, saying, "You were never a good friend." Jennifer may be taking symbolic revenge against the men who wronged her, but it takes another wronged woman—a victim of Jennifer herself—to defeat her.

Despite its clear sexual assault resonances, the sacrifice of *Jennifer's Body* is still only a metaphorical rape. We'll turn now to some films where the assault is literal. The rape-revenge movie, which dates back to Ingmar Bergman's *The Virgin Spring* (1960), became a recognized subgenre of exploitation film in the 1970s.[4] With a few exceptions (Roberta Findlay's *A Woman's Torment* [1977], Janet Greek's *The Ladies Club* [1986]), rape-revenge films were almost exclusively made by male filmmakers until the 21st century. Even the best of them had a hard time escaping the male gaze. As public dialogue about sexual assault and harassment became mainstreamed in the 2010s, a new wave of female-directed rape-revenge films challenged the conventions of the form—and a few of them gave us memorable swimming pools. As mentioned above, *Jennifer's Body* was influential to this wave, which likely crested in 2020 with Emerald Fennell's Oscar-winning *Promising Young Woman*. But the best year for feminist rape-revenge movies was 2017, which saw the release of Coralie Fargeat's *Revenge* and Natalia Leite's *M.F.A.* (as well as the pool-less Indonesian film *Marlina the Murderer in Four Acts* by Mouly Surya).

In *Revenge*, our heroine Jen is the mistress of rich businessman Richard, who flies her out to his remote vacation home in the desert, accessible only by chartered helicopter, in advance of the arrival of his friends for their hunting trip. The friends, Stan and Dimitri, arrive early, intruding on what was supposed to be Jen and Richard's private time. At first everything seems okay—the quartet spends an evening drinking and dancing by the pool. The next morning, Stan—frustrated with Jen for rejecting him—rapes her. When Dimitri wanders in, Stan invites him to join. Dimitri chooses instead to ignore what is happening, first turning up the volume on the television and then diving into the pool so he doesn't have to hear Jen's cries. When Richard appears, he sides with his friends and tries to buy Jen's silence. She insists on leaving immediately, and when he refuses, she threatens to tell his wife about his infidelity. Richard slaps her and Jen flees into the desert with the three friends in pursuit. Jen stops short at the edge of a cliff, and Richard pushes her off it. Thinking her dead, impaled on a tree at the cliff's base, the men come back the next day to clean up the body and find her gone. Having managed to free herself, Jen takes gruesome revenge on the three men one by one as they hunt her across the desert.[5]

The first-act poolside party montage finds us in familiar territory with the pool as a sexy place of indulgence. Shot from beneath, Jen is a sleek naiad, her body

Another *Cat People*–style shot, *minus* one: Having dispatched her attackers, the victorious Jen (Matilda Lutz) takes a poolside moment to reflect at the end of *Revenge* (2017).

slicing through the water. Richard drinks liquor straight from the bottle while fully submerged. A drunken Jen does a sexy dance with Stan, which he misinterprets as a come-on. As with *Rabid*'s Judy, *Revenge* problematizes the way culture equates women in water with objects of desire. Using familiar cinematic language, Fargeat encourages the viewer to see Jen like Stan does: as a temptress. The male gaze does not recognize her personhood. Since she is Richard's mistress and is at the vacation home to have sex with him, all three male characters view her as a slut. When he learns about the rape, Richard defends his friend by telling Jen, "You're so damn beautiful, it's hard to resist you." Stan thinks Jen had it coming for being a poolside tease.

In the context of *Revenge*'s topography, its location in the middle of the forbidding desert, the pool takes on another quality: that of oasis. A perfect rectangle of pristine blue in the midst of the untamed land, it becomes an escape from the world's harshness. Dimitri dives under to avoid hearing Jen's cries as she is assaulted. After realizing both his friends have been killed, Richard rides his motorcycle back to the house and immediately plunges his head into the pool, to wash off the dust of the desert and the violence of the day. Jen is no stranger to harsh realities, but she does not have the luxury of ignoring them—she needs to face them. Her transformation is from sex object to angel of vengeance. She recovers from two kinds of penetration: the sexual violation and her impalement on the tree. The latter leaves her with a gaping abdominal wound, a symbol of her abused womanhood. She cauterizes it by heating a beer can and pressing it against the wound, which leaves her branded with the image on the can: a bird of prey, evocative of both the reborn phoenix and her new role as huntress. The impression left by the can is backwards, legible only in a mirror, recalling Stan's gaze at Jen in the pool, which saw only a distorted reflection.

In fact, *Revenge* is bookended by mirror imagery. Its opening image is a wide establishing shot of the desert, with a black speck growing in size that turns out to be the helicopter. The following shot is of the same desert, this time as a convex reflection in Richard's sunglasses. The film's closing image is a low-angle wide shot of Jen standing at the far end of the pool, her reflection in the gently lapping water and the vast desert beyond. In skimpy underwear for most of the film, she stands in her feminine strength above the pool—a *Cat People* shot with just one subject, empowered reality elevated over the objectified fantasy.

Another rape-revenge movie from 2017 by a female director, *M.F.A.*, takes a different approach to both its metamorphosis and its swimming pool. Noelle, the protagonist, is pursuing a graduate art degree as a painter. She attends a party at the home of classmate Luke, who rapes her. Back at home, the traumatized Noelle tells her roommate Skye what happened. Skye advises her to keep quiet, saying she is unlikely to get justice by telling the authorities, and the process will only hurt her further. Noelle reports the incident anyway, and Skye's warning proves to have been apt. The next day, Noelle confronts Luke. Angry and defensive, Luke seems to be about to hurt Noelle again when she accidentally pushes him off a second floor landing and he falls to his death. Soon afterward, she learns about a recent gang rape on the same campus; the perpetrators went unpunished. Newly empowered, she murders the three rapists one by one. Meanwhile, Noelle's art has taken a new, darker direction to the delight of her professor and classmates, and her campus women's group debates the morality of a vigilante rumored to be targeting rapists.[6]

Two important scenes feature the swimming pool at Noelle and Skye's apartment complex, and in both scenes the pool accompanies Noelle's transformations—first into a trauma survivor, and later into a vigilante. After she is assaulted, Noelle goes home and collapses by the pool. She tips forward into the water, and there is an underwater shot of her floating, blank-eyed and possibly dissociating. The shot

The traumatized Noelle (Francesca Eastwood) tries to wash off her violation in *M.F.A.* (2017).

captures the surreal, out-of-body nature of the experience. Noelle's subaquatic sojourn underscores that she has entered another world. This incident is now part of her life.

After she commits her first deliberate killing—seducing one of the gang rapists and drugging him so that he chokes to death on his vomit—Noelle takes another dip. This time, she is serene and confident. She treads water, head above the surface, like a satisfied predator with a belly full of prey, as Skye says, "Seems like you're in a good mood. Meet a boy?" Where *Revenge*'s Jen transforms into an angel of retribution, Noelle becomes a different archetype: the vigilante. Her mission is to hunt down evildoers who have escaped justice and balance the scales.

M.F.A. bears some similarities to *Unbreakable* in the way it plays with the visual language of the superhero. Noelle wears a wig, mask and heavy makeup to a party where she makes one of her kills. When police question witnesses, they can only describe the wig and the mask, not the woman underneath. Like David Dunn's green raincoat, her getup works as a superhero disguise while remaining realistic in context. Also like David Dunn, she stands up for those who cannot stand up for themselves—and like David Dunn, she completes her heroic transformation in a swimming pool.

Noelle's change is not lost on those around her. They don't know she is the masked vigilante, but they know something about her is different. It manifests in her new artistic direction, which reflects both the despondency and the risk-taking that have recently entered her life. Her professor makes direct reference to the theme of metamorphosis: "Who are you and what have you done with Noelle?" Like Rose in 2019's *Rabid*, the more ruthless she becomes, the more approval she gets. This dynamic suggests that women's suffering is acceptable—even desirable—if it makes for good art.

M.F.A. teems with water imagery. In an early scene, the art professor, admonishing his students against playing it safe, says, "Let's jump in the deep end this year." In the scene where Luke invites Noelle to the party, she first sees him standing in front of a fountain. When the police detective questions Skye, she too is sitting by a fountain. Noelle tells Skye she is nervous about how to present herself to Luke, whom she has a crush on, and Skye suggests inviting him "for a midnight swim." Twice during scene transitions, the film cuts briefly to B-roll of a swimming pool for no plot-relevant reason. If Noelle's two transformative swims represent her changing relationship with her own body, the fountain scenes interrogate patriarchy's presumed entitlement to women's bodies in general. While Noelle's apartment pool is a private one, the fountains are part of the commons. (More on public vs. private water in Part III.) Skye alludes to one reason many women choose not to report sexual assaults: because of the exposure involved. Private matters are forced into public; effectively, the victims' bodies become part of the commons. The scene with the rapist near the beginning of the film and the scene with the detective near the end, both addressing women next to public fountains, underscore that the men are on two

Reborn as a huntress: Noelle (Francesca Eastwood) takes a satisfying swim after claiming her first victim in *M.F.A.* (2017).

ends of the same violation. When a member of her women's group, arguing against the vigilante, invokes the phrase, "An eye for an eye leaves the whole world blind," Noelle responds, "The world's already blind." Blinded, perhaps, by the sheet of falling water at the public fountain that obscures the person behind it, while Noelle's two dips in the clear pool have taught her how to keep her eyes open underwater.

Not many rape-revenge films have been made by men since female directors reclaimed the form. One that straddles the gap is Lucky McKee's *The Woman* (2011), and like *M.F.A.*'s Noelle, the titular character avenges not just her own assault, but those of other women as well. Like *The Kiss*, *The Woman* opens its main narrative with a poolside scene. At a neighborhood party, Peggy, teenage daughter of the Cleek family, sits in a deck chair while a boy in the pool tries to get her attention, muttering "strumpet" when she blows him off. Peggy looks back and sees her father Chris staring at her from the back porch of a house. His insistent gaze evidently makes her uncomfortable. A few scenes later, Chris encounters a feral woman in the woods while hunting. He watches her bathe in a creek, a natural parallel to the concrete pool where he gazed at his daughter. Chris kidnaps the Woman, who does not speak English, and imprisons her in a shed where he says he will "civilize her." In reality, she soon becomes a plaything for him and his middle-school–aged son Brian. Chris is an abusive, tyrannical patriarch who beats his wife Belle, has raped and impregnated Peggy, and keeps another daughter with birth defects in the barn like a dog. But he lavishes Brian with all the love and respect he denies the women in his life. He takes a "boys will be boys" attitude when Brian mutilates the Woman's nipple with a pair of pliers while masturbating. In the climax when the Woman gets free and wreaks bloody revenge, her first victim is Belle—who stood by and allowed Chris to

Imprisoned by the male gaze: Peggy (Lauren Ashley Carter) is unnerved by her father's penetrating stare in *The Woman* (2011).

terrorize while instilling his values in Brian. The film ends with the Woman leading all the Cleek daughters by the hand into the forest, perhaps to start a new utopian community of wild women.[7] This is the final metamorphosis in a film that observes the degradation of one daughter to beast and the parallel changes wrought on Peggy's body by incestuous pregnancy, but there is no room for enablers like Belle in the future that the Woman leads them toward.

Chris is obsessed with appearances: He needs his family to look picture-perfect. He puts on a genial public persona for the same reason he hides his deformed daughter from the world. He keeps the Woman on display like a hunting trophy in the shed, a cruel manifestation of the idea that women should be seen and not heard. Chris' gaze, and the gazes of the men around him, are all that matters to him. The POV shot when Chris sees the Woman for the first time through the scope of his rifle is a blunt literalization of the threat of violence that accompanies the male gaze, but this threat was established even earlier, in the quietly possessive glare he directed at Peggy while she sat poolside.

Jayro Bustamante's *La Llorona* (2019) depicts another avenging woman whose grievance is both personal and political. But this time it's not just on behalf of her gender, but of her ethnic group as well. The film focuses on former Guatemalan general Enrique Monteverde, an elderly man who is on trial for war crimes (he ordered the massacre of native Mayan people 40 years before). The court convicts him of genocide, but the conviction is overturned on a technicality. This sparks a protest of hundreds who gather outside Monteverde's house. Inside with the old man, who requires oxygen from a tank, are his wife Carmen, their daughter Natalia and Natalia's daughter Sara. Sara's father, who is implied to have been of indigenous heritage, disappeared years before. Every member of the house staff quits except for housekeeper Valeriana, who we later learn is Monteverde's illegitimate daughter, fathered with an indigenous woman. Seeking more help, Valeriana hires young Alma, who is supposedly from her village, although it's later revealed that nobody in the village seems to know her. Alma strikes up a relationship with young Sara, telling her about her two dead children and training her to hold her breath underwater. Alma also has a habit of wading in the house's swimming pool late at night.

Meanwhile, Carmen, who has thus far stood by her husband and dismissed his accusers as liars, begins having nightmares about being an indigenous woman fleeing the general's forces with two children. Natalia notices that the protesters' faces match the photos of long-disappeared civilians on flyers that litter the grounds. Sara takes her grandfather's oxygen tank and jumps into the pool to practice her underwater breathing. Monteverde, thinking she is Alma, shoots into the pool and wounds Sara's arm. During a ritual Valeriana performs to dispel the spirits, Carmen returns to her hallucination and realizes she is reliving Alma's final moments from decades before, when Monteverde forced Alma to watch her two children drowned in the river and then shot her dead. Carmen, realizing the truth, strangles her husband to death.[8]

La Llorona belongs to a long history of ghost stories about abusive men who escape worldly justice but are punished for their crimes by supernatural means. The film uses water imagery from the beginning: one of the first ghostly manifestations is faucets turning on by themselves. This represents not only the river where Alma's children were drowned, but also the tears of the titular figure—La Llorona, the crying woman, a well-known legend in Latin American folklore.[9] The two bodies of water—the river where Alma's children died and the pool that echoes it—also evoke the movie's various mother-child relationships. Mothers' love for and desire to protect their children is what drives events. Perhaps because of Sara's indigenous heritage, Alma symbolically adopts her and tries to teach her a lesson that might have saved her own children. When asked what Alma said to her, Sara replies, "She asked me not to drown." Sara takes this lesson to heart when she plunges into the pool with Monteverde's oxygen tank, rewriting the fate of Alma's children. Monteverde's pool symbolizes both his ill-gotten affluence and the dominion that he exercised over the indigenous people, attempting to bend nature to his will. When Carmen in her trance sees the reality of what happened, it is her outrage as a mother that finally overcomes her loyalty as a wife, causing her to turn against her husband.

The identities of *La Llorona*'s female characters are fluid, slipping and blending into one another. Carmen takes the place of Alma in the flashback scenes. In the same way that Monteverde sees Alma in the pool instead of Sara, he also mistakes Carmen for an enemy at the start of the film, when he accidentally shoots her in the darkened house. All these women are united in the struggle against masculine domination. In a shot near the end of the film, Carmen, Claudia, Sara and Valeriana stand together at the window, looking out at the vengeful spirits surrounding

Alma (María Mercedes Coroy), servant of justice, plucks the damning missing-persons posters out of the Monteverde family pool in *La Llorona* (2019).

the house. These four women, three generations of the same family, confront the consequences of the patriarch's misdeeds while that same patriarch lies unconscious on the floor. He has created a mess and left the women to clean it up. But the spirits are not insensitive to this dynamic. "You know it's not fair for innocents to pay for the consequences," Valeriana pleads during her ritual, and indeed, as soon as Monteverde is dead, the supernatural threat appears to be over. The spirits thus prove themselves more humane than Monteverde, indiscriminate killer of women and children.

When Alma asks Sara not to drown, she's talking about more than the fate of her own children. In Sara's generation there is the opportunity to create a more just future, but only if they open their eyes to the inhumanity and oppression that surround them and if they avoid taking part—avoid drowning in their privilege. Where Monteverde sees a woman in the pool as a predator, a dangerous guerrilla in hiding, Sara and Alma see salvation.

The theme of mothers avenging their murdered children brings us to 2010's *Confessions*, directed by Tetsuya Nakashima. It leverages the fear of HIV and swimming pools discussed in the last chapter to tell a morality tale of social exclusion and expiation. After serving cartons of milk to each member of her class, middle school teacher Yuko announces that she will resign at the end of the term. She proceeds to tell the story of her four-year-old daughter Manami, who was found dead in a swimming pool, and how she discovered that two of her students had murdered her. Yuko then announces that she injected the HIV-positive blood of Manami's estranged father into the milk of the two guilty boys, Naoki and Shuya. We later learn that after his scientist mother abandoned him in early childhood, Shuya became an electronics prodigy in an attempt to win back her love. He won a regional science fair, but a high-profile case of patricide by a young girl overshadowed his achievement in the press. Shuya then enlisted Naoki, a lonely boy in search of friends, to help him accost

Manami. Naoki, mistaking Manami for dead after an electric shock rendered her unconscious, threw her into the swimming pool, where she drowned. In the aftermath of the milk incident, Naoki becomes a shut-in, until he kills his mother when she attempts to put him and herself out of their misery. Another classmate, Mizuki, starts dating Shuya and reveals herself as the killer whose crimes stole the spotlight from Shuya's science fair victory. After learning that his mother has remarried, Shuya plants a bomb in his school. Yuko secretly relocates the bomb to Shuya's mother's office, leading him to accidentally kill her when he triggers it.[10]

Confessions' female characters embody dynamic, constantly shifting identities, while the male characters, though their actions drive the plot, are static by comparison. Yuko starts the film as an exhausted educator, morphs into a bereaved, avenging mother, and then reveals herself to be a calculating manipulator. Shuya's mom abandons her child to become a career scientist, and later starts a new family. Mizuki, an apparently normal teen, hides a patricidal past. Even Manami, a symbol of hope in her parents' otherwise tragic lives, transforms via the swimming pool into a symbol of death. Naoki and Shuya, by contrast, end the film as they started it: lonely, disturbed boys whose yearning for belonging drives them to murder.

Christopher Brown and Pam Hirsch mention *Confessions* in their introduction to *The Cinema of the Swimming Pool*, pointing out: "The pool with its intruding body is likened to a milk carton with intruding blood; both bespeak deliberate, immoral acts of pollution."[11] The imagery becomes more potent when we consider the centrality of motherhood to the narrative. The three adolescents the film focuses on—Shuya, Naoki, and Mizuki—all kill their mothers. Yuko is a mother who kills on behalf of her murdered child. In the world of *Confessions*, motherhood is a position of both power and peril. Like the swimming pool, it can lead to destruction as easily as joy. Shuya and Naoki's mothers both turn against their sons, actions which lead to their deaths. The narrative is full of absent, cold or dangerous mothers, and the death-corrupted pool represents the womb gone wrong. The infected milk is an image of polluted nurturing, as all the film's characters grapple with the contagious disease of loneliness and the epidemic of social disconnection.

Maybe the ultimate aquatic avenging woman movie is 1984's *Mermaid Legend*, directed by Toshiharu Ikeda. The protagonist, Migiwa, lives a humble and peaceful life with her husband Keisuke, fishing for abalone in a coastal village. A local developer is in the process of buying land to build an amusement park, but the park is a smokescreen for the real goal: the construction of a nuclear power plant. One landowner refuses to sell, so Miyamoto, the wicked industrialist behind the scheme, hires thugs to murder him by blowing up his boat. Keisuke witnesses the crime and reports it, so the mob murders him too. In a dreamlike sequence, Migiwa is diving for abalone when Keisuke's lifeless body falls into the water from the boat above. As they speed away, the killers fire a harpoon into the water, wounding Migiwa. When she washes ashore, she tells a policeman about the murder, but the cop believes she is confessing to having killed him. In a struggle, she ends up pushing him off a wall

Naoki (Kaoru Fujiwara) tosses the young Manami (Mana Ashida) into the pool to make it look like she drowned in 2010's *Confessions*.

onto the rocks below. Now a fugitive, she reaches out to Keisuke's friend Shohei, who helps her escape to Watakano Island, where "only women live," and there are no police. While Migiwa hides out in a bordello on the island, she and Shohei grow close and sleep together. In a moment of remorse, Shohei confesses that Miyamoto is his father, and tries to convince her to flee to the city. Instead, Migiwa volunteers to work in the bordello for a gathering of Miyamoto's men the next night. She takes one of Keisuke's assassins to bed and gets him to tell her the story. The goon then informs her that he knows who she is, and that Shohei instructed him to kill her. He tries to rape her, but Migiwa chokes him with a towel, gets ahold of his knife and stabs him to death. When the deed is discovered, she swims away from the island. Back on the mainland, she drowns Miyamoto in his backyard swimming pool. Shohei, who has inherited the position of company president and *de facto* mob boss, tracks down Migiwa. His men throw her off a cliff wrapped in a fishing net, once again leaving her for dead in the ocean. She washes ashore near the power plant construction site, where she finds Keisuke's body and the Buddha statue Migiwa prayed to, half-buried in the sand. The next day, she asks the Buddha to make it storm that night, and goes to the plant's groundbreaking gala. She confronts Shohei and kills him with a fishing trident, and then proceeds to stab about a dozen others, screaming, "I'm insane!" The police show up to stop the rampage but are thwarted by the arrival of a raging storm. Migiwa stands unaffected by it, though it scatters the cops like leaves. The film ends with Migiwa leaping into the ocean and emerging in a fantasy where Keisuke is still alive.[12]

Mermaid Legend, though not a pure rape-revenge movie, is a spiritual sister to films like *M.F.A.* As in that film, Migiwa's violence begins accidentally, when she pushes a man during a confrontation, causing him to fall. As in *M.F.A.* (and many other films in the subgenre), Migiwa uses sex appeal to lure male victims and relies on them underestimating her. Finally, as in *M.F.A.*, a series of swims underlines Migiwa's multiple transformations. Each time she comes out of the water is a symbolic rebirth. Like *M.F.A.*'s Noelle, she emerges as a survivor after being wounded at the scene of her husband's murder. Migiwa swims away from Watakano Island as a two-time fugitive, but surfaces as a confident avenger able to walk straight up to the big boss and announce her purpose. The third time she rises from the sea, she is an elemental creature with a mythic weapon and the power to call down storms.

When people analyze films with female killers, they often assume that violence is inherently masculine—or at least that when a woman does violence, she is enacting maleness. Many horror theorists, chief among them Carol Clover in her groundbreaking 1987 paper "Her Body, Himself: Gender in the Slasher Film," have pointed out the preponderance of phallic weaponry in slashers and other horror films. Clover, who coined the term "Final Girl," writes, "The killer's phallic purpose, as he thrusts his drill or knife into the trembling bodies of young women, is unmistakable." She then points out the "qualified" masculinity of many slasher killers, that murder is often an outlet for their sexual frustration, and the Final Girl's "phallicization" as she picks up the killer's weapon and turns the tables at the film's end.[13] Building on Clover, Barbara Creed takes the Freudian view that female killers represent men's castration anxieties.[14] This framework ignores the fact that not all killing in horror movies is penetrative. If death by stabbing, slicing or impaling can be construed as phallic, then deaths by smothering, strangling, devouring or otherwise engulfing a victim—especially when the assailant is female—are what we'll call "vulvic murders." We've already seen one in *M.F.A.*, where Noelle kills her first victim by making him asphyxiate, but the form of vulvic murder that resonates most with this book's theme is drowning. We saw Ben Rolf in *Burnt Offerings* almost drown his son in the pool under the influence of the female-coded house; likewise, we saw *Night Swim*'s Ray attempt to drown a neighborhood boy under the influence of the vulvic pool itself. Amy survives a drowning attempt by her witchy aunt in *The Kiss*. *Mermaid Legend*, though, is the first time we've seen a drowning carried out by an avenging woman. It will not be the last.

Mermaid Legend's swimming pool scene operates on many of the levels we've already discussed. Like Migiwa's titular, symbolic mermaidness, it is a border between the human and natural worlds. Like the feared nuclear plant, it draws a line between the privileged and unprivileged, and represents a human attempt to harness dangerous natural forces. When she drowns Miyamoto in his own pool, plunging him into the wrath of a woman scorned, Migiwa sends the same message as the tempest at the film's end: Humans, don't forget how frail you are in the face of Mother Nature.

If not for the sex scenes—including the rape—being shot in a titillating softcore-porn style in keeping with the Japanese *pinku* films of the time, *Mermaid Legend* could pass for a thoroughly modern, sex-worker-positive feminist revenge movie. But its ambiguous ending, with Migiwa appearing to manifest supernatural powers, flirts with another feminine horror trope. We'll turn our attention to it now.

CHAPTER 6

The Sunken Sorceress

Pools, Witchcraft and Youth

> I want to be the color of the pool.
> I want to hold the fire part of fuel.
> —Lala Lala, "Color of the Pool"

One of Barbara Creed's monstrous-feminine archetypes, the figure of the witch,[1] has a special connection to swimming. Bonnie Tsui points out one of the things that made swimming lessons for girls a hard sell in Victorian England: the practice of "swimming a witch," i.e., throwing a suspected witch into water to see if she floated, and judging her guilty if she did.[2] The swimming of witches was still done occasionally in the 19th century,[3] the act of swimming thus being directly linked to the "wrong" kind of female power. As a woman, in society's eyes, maybe you were better off not knowing how to swim.

European witch folklore is full of shapeshifting, with witches transforming both themselves and their victims into animals. One witch-hunt victim confessed to "gather[ing] around a basin of water in which a lance had been placed upright" in order to summon the Devil.[4] If you've been paying attention so far, I won't insult your intelligence by unpacking that image's implications. Although most were female, witches of European folklore got their power from a male-coded Devil through fornication and blasphemous marriage. There is not much of the Devil himself in the films we're about to look at, but they do support Creed's suggestion that man's fear of the witch is grounded entirely in her body's reproductive capabilities.[5]

Creed declares the witch to be the only "incontestably monstrous role in the horror film that belongs to woman." *The Monstrous-Feminine* includes a lengthy analysis of Brian de Palma's 1976 film *Carrie*, focusing on how blood imagery connects the aspects of what she calls "abject femininity"—that is, elements of the feminine that patriarchy has labeled negative. She points out that superstitions about menstrual blood have historically been similar to notions of witchcraft.[6] Given all this, it's too bad that *Carrie* doesn't have a pool scene. But lucky for us, Kimberly Peirce rectified that in her 2013 remake. While both versions open with a volleyball game, *Carrie* 2013 relocates it from the gym floor to the pool. In an underwater shot, the camera pushes through an aquatic forest of girls' legs to a shy pair of legs in the corner of the pool, separated from the group. In the female space of the pool—where we only see bodies from the waist down—the other girls seem to be performing femininity with ease, but Carrie is awkward and unsure how. When she accidentally beans Sue with the volleyball while trying to serve, it isn't just a sports mishap; it's a failure to be the right kind of girl.[7]

In a sentence that should remind us of *Mermaid Legend*, Creed writes that the witch "is closer to nature than man and can control forces in nature such as ... storms."[8] The real terror of the witch is not in her specific actions—traditionally, witches were healers and prognosticators, not necessarily evildoers[9]—but in her inability to be controlled. Though it is not commonly thought of as a witch movie, *Carrie* is the preeminent exemplar of menstrual horror—and Creed contends that the two are synonymous: "The young female witch (*Carrie*) evokes both sympathy and horror because her evil deeds are associated with puberty and menarche."[10] Keeping this characteristic of the adolescent witch in mind, let's leave behind *Carrie* 2013's brief but significant pool scene and look at a *Carrie* movie that stages major parts of its climax in and around a swimming pool.

At the start of director Katt Shea's *The Rage: Carrie 2* (1999), high schooler Rachel Lang's only friend, Lisa, tells her that she has lost her virginity. Later that day, Lisa takes her own life by jumping off the school's roof. It turns out that the high school football team has been playing a "game," complete with elaborate rules and a scorebook, competing to see who can bed the most girls, with point values assigned to each conquest. Eric, the jock Lisa slept with, told her that he only had sex with her to pad his score, and this led to her suicide. With Rachel's help, the authorities learn about the game and seek to charge Eric with statutory rape. To get back at Rachel, football player Mark leads the team and their friends in a campaign of intimidation and harassment. Rachel manifests telekinetic powers that only seem to emerge when she is overwhelmed by emotion. Sue Snell, Carrie White's reluctant tormentor

The 2014 *Carrie* remake gives us a brief swimming pool scene to establish the social isolation of the title character (Chloë Grace Moretz, center).

from the original film, now works as a high school guidance counselor. Recognizing Rachel's power, Sue visits her mother in the psychiatric institution and learns that Rachel and Carrie have the same father. One football player, Jesse, takes a romantic interest in Rachel. This creates friction between Jesse and Mark, until Mark offers an olive branch: the use of his family's vacation house for a romantic night with Rachel. Jesse accepts, and he and Rachel have sex at the house. After the season-opening football game, everyone gathers for a party at Mark's big fancy home. Surrounding Rachel on the dance floor, the team taunts her. They play a secretly filmed video of her sexual encounter with Jesse on huge screens for everybody at the party to see. Rachel lashes out telekinetically, murdering several people at the party and starting a fire that destroys most of the house. Mark and his friends attack Rachel with harpoon and flare guns. Both wounded, Rachel and Mark grapple and fall together into the house's swimming pool. As the water turns red with blood, Rachel telekinetically closes the pool cover, trapping Mark inside so that he drowns. When Jesse arrives, Rachel accuses him of being in on the plot. She doesn't believe his denial until she hears his voice on the video saying "I love you" to her when she was asleep at the vacation home. It's too late to live happily ever after, because Rachel has already loosened the bolts of a walkway above their heads, which falls on her and traps her in the burning building. Rachel stops Jesse from trying to free her by using her power to fling him to safety; he lands atop the covered swimming pool.[11]

While it replays most of the original *Carrie*'s plot points, *The Rage*'s details alter the subtext. Most obviously, it does away with the menarche angle. There is no direct reference to menstruation in the movie, and instead of tying the emergence of Rachel's powers to her first period, it seems to associate them with her burgeoning sexuality instead. Unlike Carrie, Rachel is not a sheltered innocent who needs to be told what a period is. Instead, she is a different kind of outsider: what was known in the '90s as an "alternative kid," toughened by the foster system until she has enough moxie to brush off Mark's offer of a date with, "I'm a dyke." Moreover, the film narrows *Carrie*'s exploration of high school cruelty to focus specifically on high school boys' gendered cruelty toward high school girls. In the blunt words of horror theorist Alexandra West, "*The Rage: Carrie 2* is about misogyny."[12] In this, the film seems to anticipate many of the #MeToo movement's concerns, high-profile sexual assault cases involving sports teams and the rise of "revenge porn."

Cultural critic Anita Sarkeesian popularized the expression, "In the game of patriarchy women are not the opposing team, they are the ball."[13] The football team in *The Rage: Carrie 2* compete with each other using every girl at their school as an up-for-grabs game piece, public property worth points to be claimed by the first guy to bed her. Mark, by broadcasting Rachel's sex tape, is forcing her body into public. Rachel punishes him for this transgression by drowning him—killing him with the feared power of her reproductive womanhood. She closes the pool cover over him, symbolically declaring that her body is her own business, not for public entertainment.

The pool drowning sends another message: that Mark's wealth and privilege will not save him. When a young female assistant D.A. (played by director Shea) tries to bring charges against Eric for statutory rape, the older male D.A., entreated by the boy's well-connected family, says, "Do you want to be responsible for ruining these boys' lives?" The scene feels even more familiar after the intervening years. Mark and Eric's family money have gotten them out of every scrape so far, but no longer. The pool water, fast turned red by bloodshed, serves the same womblike function as the bloody bath Carrie took after the prom massacre—but instead of washing herself clean of menstrual shame, she is cleansing herself of Mark and other men's power over her.

Another significant symbol in the film's climactic sequence appears when Mark goes looking for weapons. He smashes open what we assume is a rifle case, but to Eric's surprise, it contains harpoon guns. Mark also arms himself with a flare gun. Like the fishing net with which Shohei's minions snare *Mermaid Legend*'s Migiwa, these maritime weapons suggest that Rachel is being hunted like a sea creature. They remind us of Rachel's dehumanization at their hands, her outsider status, and the mermaid's dilemma: being part of two worlds but not truly belonging in either. The room with the harpoon guns also contains a fish tank, which Rachel's power causes to explode. Like the folkloric witch raising storms at sea, Rachel is impossible to control.

The film uses visual language to set up Jesse as a foil for Mark. He is an outsider like Rachel, just not as visibly. He plays the sex game only reluctantly, disliking its casual exploitation. Near the end of the film when the rest of the team members shave their heads, giving them the appearance of neo–Nazis, Jesse is the only one who rejects the pack mentality and keeps his hair. When Rachel saves Jesse's life by throwing him onto the covered pool, the message is twofold: Her love is saving him from the fire, but her body will be forever closed to him.

At the vacation home, a background swimming pool illuminates Jesse and Rachel's sex scene with its waving light. Here the pool retains some of its wholesomely erotic connotations: This is not the pool of death that Mark will later encounter. As West notes, "While the film attempts to show the romantic, consensual part of sex that is part of a healthy relationship, it also shows how that experience can be coopted and turned against the participants."[14] The film's two pools symbolize this dichotomy: the passive pond whose lapping casts sensual reflections on the lovers, and the fearsome weapon Rachel uses against Mark. The friendly pool remains part of the background, never interacted with, while the angry pool is a main character in the climax, revealing the power gap between these emotions in the film's point of view.

By dropping the menstruation angle, *The Rage: Carrie 2* loses some of the original film's subtext—but it gains just as much of its own. Creed takes pains to note that menstrual horror is a patriarchal construct. "Woman is not, by her very nature, an abject being."[15] I differ with Creed in that I do not believe that portraying the

Chapter 6. The Sunken Sorceress

Power reversal in a *Cat People*-style shot as Rochelle (Rachel True) lets racist bully Laura (Christine Taylor, right, with towel) break her concentration on the high dive in *The Craft* (1996).

reproductive body as monstrous is part of "the ideological project of the horror film,"[16] and this movie proves it. By rejecting its predecessor's insistence on linking menstruation with monstrosity, *The Rage: Carrie 2* announces itself as a major work of 1990s feminist horror.

You can't talk about the 1990s, high school and witches without talking about director Andrew Fleming's *The Craft* (1996). A quartet of high school girls forms a coven to practice witchcraft. Each is an outcast in her own way: Sarah, the new girl in town, is lonely and has a history of self-harm. Soon after she arrives at her new school, a jock named Chris humiliates her by spreading a false sexual rumor. Bonnie bears scars on her shoulders and back from an automobile fire, and has also struggled with suicidal ideation. Nancy's family is poor and she lives with an abusive creeper of a stepfather. Rochelle, apparently the only Black student at the school, suffers racist bullying led by classmate Laura. The girls' earliest spells are attempts to overcome these social and emotional problems: Sarah casts a love spell on Chris which makes him grovel at her feet; Bonnie makes her scars go away; Nancy causes her stepfather to die of a heart attack, after which she and her mother become rich from the life insurance; Rochelle casts a spell which causes Laura to lose her hair.

Our first glimpse of Laura's bullying occurs during diving practice. Laura shouts "Shark!" when Rochelle is in mid-dive, startling her and causing her to land gracelessly in the water. Back in the changing room, Laura makes a crude joke about "one of Rochelle's little nappy hairs." Later in the film, Rochelle is back on the diving platform, watching with satisfaction as her spell takes effect and Laura's hair begins to fall out. Rochelle then executes a perfect, graceful dive.[17]

It shouldn't surprise us that this racist harassment occurs around a swimming pool. As we'll discuss more in Part III, swimming pools have historically been a major site of racial conflict in the U.S. Poolside acts of racist terror and resulting court cases have led directly to major legislation and legal precedent around discrimination. As Jeff Wiltse points out, as soon as public pools became gender-integrated, they started to be segregated racially. The white public apparently had no problem with Black men swimming with white men and Black women swimming with white women, but as soon as the genders were mixed, they had a change of heart.[18] The intersection of Blackness, gender and swimming is a fraught one, and Rochelle's poolside trauma is part of a very old story.

Appropriately, hair is central to Rochelle's conflict with Laura. Laura taunts Rochelle by likening her hair to pubic hair, in contrast to Laura's long blonde locks. Rochelle calls Laura a "racist [piece] of bleach-blonde shit." When Rochelle makes Laura's hair fall out, she is directly repudiating the Eurocentric beauty standard that elevates Laura above her socially. The intersection of hair, Black womanhood and swimming pools adds another layer of symbolism. The "black people can't swim" stereotype is partly rooted in many Black women's reluctance to get their hair wet.[19] On some level, Laura is offended by Rochelle's diving skill because she does not conform to her preconceptions. In their own ways, all four of *The Craft*'s witches fail to perform the kind of femininity that is expected of them. Chris wants Sarah to put out; when she does not, he tells everyone that she did. Because of her burn scars, Bonnie is self-conscious about her appearance and hides her body beneath layers of baggy clothing. Nancy wears her hair short, dresses in goth style, talks openly about her menstrual cycle, and otherwise presents herself as decidedly un-dainty. When a bus driver warns, "You girls watch out for those weirdos," and Nancy famously responds, "We are the weirdos, mister," she's not just announcing the coven's outsider status. She is also answering his implied warning about sexual harassment by assuring him that potential harassers should watch out for them instead.

Like European folklore witches, *The Craft*'s coven derives their female power from a source—in this case the supernatural entity known as Manon—that is designated as male. *The Rage: Carrie 2* also goes this route by making the telekinesis gene patrilineal. But where *The Rage* directs its, well, rage at sexually exploitative men and their enablers, *The Craft*—like *Cat People* and *The Kiss*—is more interested in pitting women against one another. The film's main conflict is the coven's fracturing, as Nancy becomes power-mad and turns the other two against Sarah. We get another *Cat People* shot when Rochelle stands on the high dive, looming over the less powerful woman below. Creed's analysis of the adolescent witch holds true here: the viewer's main response to these girls is sympathy, since they use their power mostly to right wrongs in their world. The edge of their threat to patriarchy, though, is blunted when they turn against one another.

We meet another sympathetic teenage witch in *Hellbender* (2021), directed by the mother, father and daughter team of Toby Poser, John Adams and Zelda Adams.

Chapter 6. The Sunken Sorceress

Two of the directors play a mother and daughter living in an isolated mountain home with very little contact with the outside world. Mother, who remains unnamed in the film, has kept Izzy isolated her whole life, claiming that she has a rare immune disorder. Izzy is not allowed to accompany her mother on supply runs to town. One day, Izzy leaves her family's property while hiking and comes across a house with a backyard pool where Amber, a girl her age, is swimming. Izzy befriends Amber, who tells her that the house is a vacation home belonging to someone who only uses it on the weekends. Later, Izzy returns to the pool and meets two of Amber's friends. They play a drinking game that requires Izzy to eat a live earthworm. She has never eaten meat before—another one of her mom's rules—but she ends up caving to peer pressure. Just then, the house's owner shows up unexpectedly and the kids scatter. The owner catches Izzy, who is behaving strangely after consuming the worm. The film implies that Izzy kills the owner and eats him. Back at home, Izzy's mother finally tells her the truth: They are part of an ancient hereditary line of witches called Hellbenders. Eating the flesh of any animal awakens and fuels their power. Mother has invented the story of Izzy's illness to keep her isolated until she learns to control her abilities. Izzy now must navigate her relationships with her mother and her new friend Amber, both of which are complicated by her new self-knowledge.[20]

While menarche is not directly mentioned, *Hellbender* fits into the menstrual horror canon. The plot is driven by Izzy's discovery of new things about her body and its capabilities. Furthermore, the Hellbenders' magic is explicitly linked to blood. Each spell we see them cast has a blood component, culminating in the scene where the mother and daughter eat maggots—their version of getting high—and vomit blood onto each other's faces while they roll around laughing in the snow. The film also features a straightforward example of the pool party as a site of adolescent self-discovery. Izzy first sees Amber through the trees from afar, like a glimpse of a woodland nymph or a rare species—but a role reversal, since Izzy is the exotic forest creature. Indeed, we earlier saw her swimming in natural water, clearly in her element, in a sister scene to *Jennifer's Body*'s primal lake swim. Amber senses that she is being observed and thinks she is being leered at. She yells the name of one of her male friends, calling him a pervert. The scene establishes the power of the gaze to both captivate and violate. Izzy's first swim in the pool is a small rebirth: She enters friendless and emerges with a friend. The illicit nature of the abovementioned pool party is on display here too. The kids are trespassing, a fairly benign crime, but the transgression of being where they aren't supposed to adds to the subversive thrill of the affair. Izzy's first physical transformation comes in the form of a wardrobe change when Amber loans her a swimsuit. Izzy, who normally favors loose-fitting clothes, wears a bikini for what is probably the first time. She gains confidence, shows off her drumming skills, and enjoys the approving gaze of her friends. This blossoming foreshadows the final metamorphosis into her primal, animalistic form. This, by Hellbender standards, is adulthood.

To our familiar adolescent witch coming-of-age story, *Hellbender* introduces a

An isolated teen catches a glimpse of a social life: Izzy (Zelda Adams) gazes through the trees at Amber (Lulu Adams) in *Hellbender* (2021).

new figure: the witch mother. In the Hellbenders' lives, the mother-daughter relationship is all-encompassing. Hellbenders, the film strongly implies, do not have fathers. How exactly Izzy was made is left to the imagination, but we get a hint when Mother shows Izzy a fern and says, "Self-reproducing, like us." This makes the maternal Hellbender what Creed, building on Kristeva, calls the archaic mother: "She is the mother who conceives all by herself, the original parent, the godhead of all fertility and the origin of procreation. She is outside morality and the law."[21] In *Hellbender*, morality and the law are represented by men. There is the lost hiker—Amber's uncle—the serpent in the Hellbenders' Eden, who tempts Izzy with knowledge of the outside world. Mother kills and consumes him. There is the owner of the pool, who castigates Izzy for trespassing, and meets the same end as the hiker. There is AJ, Amber's friend, who sets and enforces the rules of the drinking game. There is a cop who shows up briefly to discuss the hiker's disappearance and the owner's death, and has a granular conversation with Mother about the details of property lines and public land. Each of these men is preoccupied with normalcy, boundaries and order. Mother, though, imposes her own kind of order, which Izzy later suggests is a result of the world of men having tamed her nature.

There is tension between the witches' opposition to maleness and its laws, and the women's conflicts with each other. After a pre-credits sequence, the film opens with an original song by the Hellbender duo, whose refrain is "Women cut women." With this song, the film sets itself up as a critique of the intra-gender competition we've seen in *Cat People* and *The Craft*, but also acknowledges that Izzy's conflicts with her mother and Amber are what move the plot along. Izzy is frustrated with her mother for not wanting her to grow up. Amber rejects Izzy when, in her bloodlust after eating the worm, Izzy tries to choke her. She forgives Izzy later, only to become wary again after Izzy reveals that she kept Amber's hair clips, and that Izzy somehow knows where Amber works. Mother and Izzy perform mutual surveillance, entering each other's dreams. It's a classic complaint for rebelling teenagers: "Mom, stay out of my business!" Every transgression in the film is a violation of privacy, the same kind of boundary-crossing that Amber accuses Izzy of, mistaking her for a peeping Tom when she first glimpses her at the swimming pool.

If Mother had told Izzy the truth earlier, and given her a fuller understanding of her power, would things have turned out differently? The film doesn't seem to think so. There is an inevitability to events as they unfold, indicating that Mother's mistake was thinking she could control Izzy in the first place—as, in turn, her mother once controlled her. The film's totemic words are, "Winter eats fall, fall eats summer," etc. This hints at the only way a Hellbender can die: consumed by her daughter. The witches' life-and-death cycle is a closed, asexual system. Late in the film, in what may or may not be a dream, Mother crawls into a fleshy hole in the ground and emerges in Izzy's secret realm. Comparisons to the birth canal are irresistible. Thus we have Izzy and Mother undergoing parallel rebirths. Izzy comes out of the surrogate womb of the swimming pool with a new experience of power, and Mother carries out a backwards birth, emerging into Izzy's reality in a mother-daughter role reversal. Izzy's journey of self-knowledge prepares her to usurp her mother. Like Carrie White's mom, in the logic of the film, the elder Hellbender's attempt to impose rules and standards on Izzy puts her in both a maternal and paternal role. Nevertheless, as soon as Izzy spies that pool, we know the battle against adulthood has been lost.

Adolescent witches evoke sympathy. The same cannot be said for older female witches. For every film like *Hellbender*, with its friendly witch mother, there is one like Dario Argento's *Suspiria* (1977), which provokes nothing but loathing of its maternal sorceress through a witch archetype we haven't encountered yet: the crone. In *Suspiria*, American Suzy Bannion travels to Germany to study at a prestigious dance academy. Upon arrival, she sees a student named Pat rushing away during a violent rainstorm. Later that night, Pat is murdered by an unseen assailant. Strange things continue to happen: maggots rain from the ceiling, the school's blind piano player is killed by his own service dog. Suzy keeps hearing about the school's mysterious directress, who is never seen.

Suzy befriends classmate Sara, who opens up about her friend Pat. While swimming in the academy's pool, Sara tells Suzy that Pat had learned something troubling about the school and its faculty, and had left notes behind. That night, after finding that the notes have vanished, Sara is chased through the school and murdered. Suzy learns that the academy was founded by a witch named Helena Markos, who supposedly died in a fire in 1905. Alone in the school that night, Suzy follows the sound of footsteps and discovers the entrance to a secret passage. Pursued by faculty members, who belong to a witch coven that plans to sacrifice her, she ends up in the headmistress' bedroom. Revealing herself to be Helena Markos, now well over 100 years old, the headmistress turns invisible and taunts Suzy while Sara's zombified corpse attacks her. Suzy is able to discern the outline of Markos' hidden form and stabs her with a shard from a broken ornament. Markos' grotesque figure becomes visible as she dies, and the death of the coven's leader causes the other members to perish.[22]

Like many of Argento's films, *Suspiria*'s storytelling hinges on the subjective gaze. We see Pat leave the school from Suzy's point of view, and she spends much of the film trying to remember and understand exactly what she saw. In the world of dance, bodies and appearances are paramount. Key to *Suspiria*'s portrayal of witchcraft is the contrast between the students' young, healthy bodies and the decrepit bodies of the witches. The Tanz Academy, in the classic gothic mode, is more than meets the eye both architecturally—with its hidden passages and chambers—and spiritually, with its secret purpose. In the pool scene, Sara shares knowledge with Suzy that endangers them both. The pool here is literally a site of secrets, where Sara feels comfortable telling what she knows. But they are not alone. A point-of-view shot shows the girls being observed from a balcony overhead. In this vulnerable position, partially unclothed, Suzy and Sara's youthful bodies are subjected to the coven's deadly gaze.

The gaze is further weaponized in the climax when Markos turns invisible. She can see Suzy, but Suzy cannot see her. Barbara Creed mentions the figure of Helena Markos—retroactively dubbed *Mater Suspiriorum*, or the Mother of Sighs in a later film—as an example of the maternal abject.[23] Of equal symbolic importance in this scene is the mutilated, reanimated body of Sara. Markos bringing her back to life is a gesture toward motherhood, a variety of asexual reproduction like that referenced in *Hellbender*. The contrast between Sara's "clean and proper body"[24] when alive and her abject grotesqueness when dead visualizes the corruption witchcraft has wrought upon her. Hers is the most literal transformation in the film. By the time we finally see Markos' withered form in the moment of her death, the point has already been made. *Suspiria* still makes a monster out of the female body, but in a different way from the aforementioned adolescent witch movies. Instead of coding menstruation and fertility as horrible, the film portrays the youthful female body as wholesome, and saves the horror for the crone figure—the aged female body and, implicitly, menopause. This preternaturally old woman cannot give birth by normal means, so she creates zombies as a perversion of lifegiving. Only by turning the power of the subjective look to her own advantage, by seeing what she is not meant to, does Suzy escape the violence of the unwanted gaze—violence that started in the swimming pool.

Another variation on the witch as abject mother can be found in Fruit Chan's *Dumplings* (2004). Mrs. Li, a former television star, visits an enigmatic woman known as Aunt Mei, who lives in a Hong Kong tenement and makes dumplings that reputedly restore youth and beauty. Aunt Mei, it turns out, is a former doctor whose

Suzy (Jessica Harper, top) and Sara (Stefania Casini) don't know they're being watched in the Tanz Academy pool in *Suspiria* (1977).

secret ingredient is aborted fetuses. Mrs. Li and her husband have been living in a hotel for months while their house is being renovated; when we first see Mr. Li, he is swimming in the hotel pool and flirting with his young masseuse, whom we later learn he is having an affair with. Mrs. Li, disappointed with the slow progress of the dumplings, pesters Aunt Mei for something more potent. After visiting Mrs. Li's house, still under renovation, and swimming in her pool, Mei agrees to perform a black-market abortion on 15-year-old Kate, who has been impregnated by her father. She serves the fetus to Mrs. Li, whose appearance becomes dramatically more youthful. After Mei begins an affair with Mr. Li, she cuts off the supply of fetuses to his wife and eventually disappears. Mrs. Li takes matters into her own hands, paying her husband's mistress to abort their baby and preparing the fetus herself.[25]

World folklore is full of cannibalistic witches, from the Native American Ho'ok to the Russian Baba Yaga to the Japanese Yamamba.[26] Also relevant is the figure of Elizabeth Báthory, the 16th-century Hungarian noblewoman who allegedly bathed in the blood of over 600 young girls believing that it would preserve her youth.[27] *Dumplings* puts a modern spin on the child-eating witch, interrogating youth-obsessed beauty standards that apply unequally to men and women. Mr. Li is visibly older than both his wife and his mistress, but that does not make him sexually undesirable. Like *Suspiria*, *Dumplings* countenances the fear of the aging female body, but unlike *Suspiria*, its lens is a critical one. The film's two swimming pools represent two different views of feminine beauty. The pristine hotel pool where Mr. Li woos his mistress represents that woman's idealized youth. The under-construction pool at the Li house represents a deteriorating body in need of repair. Aunt Mei plays in this pool, partially covered with a tarp, while singing an old song from her childhood. Mei, a literal witch doctor, specializes in the renewal of youthful beauty through the application of folk magic, like the construction workers who go about their jobs silently in the background. In the half-renovated house, Mrs. Li tells Mei how she met her husband: She was a 20-something TV star and he was a producer on her show. "It's the law of nature," she says of men, "they just can't resist the body of a 20-year-old." Mei, who calls herself her "own best advertisement," appears to be in her 20s but is in fact 64 years old, having maintained her youthful appearance with abortion dumplings. Later in the film, when Mei seduces Mr. Li, he is initially repulsed by her true age, but she retorts, "It's my body that counts. ...Is my body young enough?" By continuing the affair, Mr. Li proves his wife's words literally correct: Men like him do not care about the actual ages of their partners, they just want "the body of a 20-year-old."

The same fetish for young female bodies that results in the masseuse being impregnated by Mr. Li also results in Kate being impregnated by her father. Both pregnancies, which end up being terminated, are linked to swimming pools in the narrative. Mei decides to perform Kate's abortion after swimming in Li's home pool, and the masseuse's first appearance is poolside at the hotel. The former fetus results in Mrs. Li's first transformation, granting her the youth and desirability that she craves. The latter one prompts her second transformation: After the vacuum left by Mei's disappearance, Mrs. Li becomes the witch herself. In doing so, she shapeshifts into the abject mother, taking her husband's illegitimate offspring not to nurture, but to use for herself. The two wombs, at the end of the film, become one: Resources are taken from the new pool to revitalize the old, and the cycle continues.

In the saga of demon-haunted families that unfolds over the course of seven films in the *Paranormal Activity* franchise, only one features a swimming pool. *Paranormal Activity 2* (2010), directed by Tod Williams, takes place both before and after the events of the first film, and depicts *two* possessed mothers. Kristi and Daniel Rey live in the suburbs with their baby son Hunter, and Daniel's teenage daughter from a previous marriage, named Ali. After an apparent burglary in which nothing is stolen, the family sets up security cameras around the house. The cameras begin to capture odd occurrences, beginning with an automatic pool cleaner that somehow makes its way out of the pool overnight. Kristi and her sister Katie, the protagonist of the first *Paranormal Activity* film, make oblique references to similar things happening to them as children, but Katie is reluctant to discuss the subject. Ali begins to suspect that someone in Kristi's family has bargained with a demon in exchange for the soul of their first-born son, noting that Hunter is the first male to have been born in the family for decades. The supernatural happenings, which started as nuisances, increase in severity, culminating in an attack on the family dog that causes her to have a seizure. While Daniel and Ali are at the vet, Kristi is dragged by an invisible force into the basement, where the demon possesses her. Daniel enacts a plan to pass the possession to Katie. Weeks later, the possessed Katie enters the house, murders Daniel and Krisi, and kidnaps Hunter.[28]

Most of the footage in the *Paranormal Activity* franchise is from static, diegetic security cameras. The visual rhythm of these films gives us repeated views of the same environment from the same angles, often shown in long takes where nothing

Chapter 6. The Sunken Sorceress

We don't talk about that here: Sisters Katie (Katie Featherston, in the water) and Kristi (Sprague Grayden) want to keep the pool a place for family fun, free of the ghosts of the past, in *Paranormal Activity 2* (2010).

happens. As a result, the viewer is trained to look for small differences, and over the film's runtime becomes familiar with a handful of locations to the point that the mere absence or presence of something mundane can be unnerving—or to use Mark Fisher's terminology, eerie.[29]

The series, with its reliance on static wide shots, challenges the found-footage format's supposed immersiveness. Because we know that the footage exists in the universe of the film, there is an extra level of abstraction. The images we see are mediated by two screens: the one we are watching and the one the characters are watching. This puts the viewer in the role of an analyst rather than a participant. Because the security camera will not cut to a closeup to draw our attention to important details, we learn to scan the frame; and because we are merely observers, we are powerless to do anything about the horrors unfolding on the multiple layers of screens before us.

One of the Rey family's cameras affords a view of the pool. This allows us to see it in different contexts: populated by day, a center of recreation, leisure and family life; empty at night, with subaquatic lighting and the pool cleaner going about its dispassionate business. Multiple scenes find the family relaxing at the pool, including one where Kristi and Katie discuss the strange incidents of their childhood. At one point, Daniel catches Ali and her boyfriend at the pool after hours, when they are not supposed to be there. Like other films in the series, *Paranormal Activity 2* leverages the most basic application of Fisher's theory of the eerie: places look different at night, and places where we expect to see people look wrong when they are empty. The logic of the film is binary: light and dark, order and disorder. This extends to a rather simplistic view of the woman's conventional role in the family: as mother and housekeeper. The first sign that something is wrong is when the pool cleaner, like a derelict homemaker, stops doing its job. The fabric of the household is unraveling; chores are not getting done.

The two views of the pool—the happy domestic and the eerie abandoned—mirror the two versions of motherhood the film portrays. The Kristi we meet at the start is a devoted mother to Hunter and a willing, nurturing stepmom to Ali. After being possessed by the demon, she transforms into a passive, neglectful mother, who sits in bed and stares into space before suddenly attacking Daniel when he approaches her with a cross. Immediately after, the film cuts to a surveillance shot of the lights going out at the pool, signaling the extinguishing of care in the domestic scenario. Once Daniel and Ali get their bearings, they find that the possessed Kristi has taken Hunter into the darkened basement. After Daniel succeeds in subduing the demon and passing it to Katie, we next see Katie sitting poolside, domestic tranquility seemingly restored, with Hunter on her lap. But she mentions that disturbances have begun at her house, which leads into the events of the first *Paranormal Activity*. When she returns to the Rey household, Katie has transformed into the abject mother, achieving a version of asexual reproduction by killing Hunter's parents and taking him as her own. At each juncture, the pool serves as a visual shorthand for domestic order, or lack thereof.

The monstrous-feminine is more likely than male-coded monsters to be sighted in or around water. Putting her in a pool juxtaposes her non-human qualities with a fabricated version of a natural setting. The pool's birth and rebirth symbolism facilitates the shifting of identity. Despite its ostensible purpose for recreation and wellness, the pool in these films is a place to see and be seen. Most of the poolside gazes we've seen have been harmful, or at least menacingly objectifying. Next we will look at an often more wholesome variety of gazes that, in true horror film style, affirm the humanity of those with outsider status.

CHAPTER 7

Matching Two-Piece
Queer Femme Awakenings Poolside

> I AM 15.
> In the women's locker room after swim practice and skin and wet. Little girls holding in youth in V-shaped torsos. Almost women shaving their legs. The bodies of women and girls safe in a room with heat and steam and let loose hair. My head swimming, swimming. I want to stay.
> —Lidia Yuknavitch, *The Chronology of Water*

While many of the films in this book—especially in Part II—support queer interpretations, I am limiting the next few chapters to films where queerness is explicit in the text, or where a swimming pool is key to my queer reading. Regardless of orientation, most of us can relate to the experience of the pool as a sexy place, but it is especially significant for the stirring and indulging of same-sex desire. After all, it's the only public place where men can frolic nearly nude with other men, no questions asked. In fact, in the early days of municipal pools, same-sex gatherings weren't just sanctioned, they were mandatory![1] Gay culture has often gravitated to watery spaces: Bathhouses, docks, lakes, restrooms and public pools have been popular cruising spots.[2] Implicitly repudiating conventional masculinity by embracing—and being embraced by—a feminine space, the plunge into a pool can be deeply symbolic for both men who love men and women who love women. In the latter case, immersing oneself in a surrogate female body is a subversive act that can be safely done out in the open.

On the other hand, for those experiencing gender dysphoria or, more broadly, those insecure about their bodies, the pool can provoke anxiety. Between 2017 and 2020, a study in the United Kingdom interviewed trans and non-binary people before and after private, safe-space swimming sessions at an indoor pool. A typical story from a participant discussed how they had felt unwelcome at a public pool because of the binding attire they wore to feel comfortable. However, after the sessions, many participants reported feeling "pleasure and freedom," and a few produced drawings of mermaids to describe their experiences.[3] The mermaid is not just a symbol of feminine power; it has also come to represent the trans and non-binary imagination of water metamorphosis. For queer people, the poolside experience of being free to gaze is balanced, or challenged, by vulnerability to the gazes of others. This push and pull of freedom vs. repression in the queer experience of swimming pools makes them fertile ground for representation in the horror genre.

In his survey of queer themes in classic horror, *Monsters in the Closet*, Harry Benshoff analyzes the 1950s cycle of teen monster movies by American International Pictures. He points out that these films often feature an older character of the same sex—usually a queer-coded authority figure—who seduces the young protagonist into monstrosity. To Benshoff, who coined the term "monster queer," these films in context of the '50s "can be understood as metaphoric reworkings of the increasingly common idea that older homosexuals were out to recruit young people into their ranks."[4] This evolved into a substrate that underlies queer horror films to this day—minus, for the most part, the implications of pederasty the gay-panic '50s movies worked in. Horror cinema has long been sympathetic to outsider figures, and queer horror theory has embraced the monster as an emblem of the ostracized. While the queerness in these films can be presented in a crass or exploitative way, seldom is it depicted as bad or perverse. Gay characters in these films might be monsters, but usually the source of the horror is not their queerness but rather the forces that oppose it. It's not uncommon for the monsters and wrongdoers to be the heroes of these texts.

Benshoff notes that villains in the '50s AIP cycle often use mesmerism or other coercive methods that the author calls "exploitative seduction."[5] Most of the films in the following chapters are missing that element: characters seduced into queerness go of their own free will, and when there is an element of coercion, other factors in the story tend to complicate it.

The figure of the older seducer has likewise been reclaimed. Since being queer is not hereditary, many gay people with straight parents have to find more experienced surrogates to teach them the cultures of their non-mainstream lifestyles. Another common element in the queer horror film is what I'll call the "threesome murder." This is when a novice murderer makes their first kill while their mentor shows them the ropes, either by assisting or by standing by and observing. In horror films, especially of the queer variety, murder is never just murder. It represents taboo transgression, the rejection of repressive notions of propriety. In movies where the queer couple do not actually have sex, the *meurtre à trois* can be a stand-in for the act. A same-sex couple committing murder together has served as an analogue for queer consummation in films at least since Alfred Hitchcock's *Rope* in 1948.[6] Even in films where the queerness is more explicit, it marks the moment the young killer, usually the protagonist, plants their flag outside the mainstream.

Sadly, the 1950s moral panic that Benshoff describes—the fear of queer adults turning our children gay—has made a comeback in recent years. In the 2020s, framing adult affirmation of children's queer identities as a form of "grooming" became a talking point for the American far right.[7] Thus, it is important to put forward alternative readings of films like these that do not conflate the queer seducer with the

Swimming pool horror's original star-crossed lovers, Nicole (Simone Signoret, left) and Christina (Véra Clouzot), prepare to dispose of the body of the man who wronged them in *Les Diaboliques* (1955).

corruptor of youth. While implying that gay people are violent is a classic smear tactic, and heteronormativity is often reasserted by the ends of these films, we should not limit our readings by assuming that any story where a queer person commits murder is homophobic.

Another character type, almost as common as the gay seducer himself, is the heterosexual love interest who tries to rescue the main character from their clutches. Sometimes the love interest is also the victim of the threesome murder. This can represent the protagonist killing the the old version of herself and emerging as a new, more authentic version. Given what we know about the swimming pool's functions of identity negotiation and rebirth, it's no surprise when we see this transformation happen around a pool.

The threesome murder trope probably owes its popularity to Henri-Georges Clouzot's *Les Diaboliques* from 1955. The film follows two boarding school teachers, Christina and Nicole. Christina, who owns the school with her family wealth, is married to Michel, the tyrannical headmaster. Nicole is Michel's mistress, a fact known to pretty much everyone, including Christina. The two women have an unlikely friendship, and the vulnerable, sickly Christina depends on the confident Nicole for emotional support. Fed up with Michel's abuse, the pair decides to murder him over a holiday break. Christina calls Michel from Nicole's house and threatens divorce, prompting him to travel there to talk her out of it. Christina gives him drugged liquor, and they drown him in the bathtub after he passes out. They smuggle his body back to the school and dump it in the disused swimming pool. They hope that when the body is discovered, the authorities will conclude that Michel drowned by accident over the holiday. When the body fails to surface after several days, Nicole has the pool drained but the corpse is nowhere to be found. Amid a series of happenings that suggest Michel is still alive, the increasingly anxious Christina falls ill from her heart condition. Although the doctor orders bed rest, she wanders the school one night investigating a noise. Upon returning to her room, she finds what appears to be Michel's corpse in her bathtub. He rises from the tub, seemingly undead, and Christina suffers a fatal heart attack. It turns out that Michel's death was staged, and he and Nicole collaborated on a plan to scare Christina to death so he could inherit her money. But Christina had confided in a private detective, and he was on hand to witness the reveal. The detective declares that they will go to prison.[8]

Though queer themes are not explicit in the text of *Les Diaboliques*, the film allows for a robust queer reading, with the pool—feminine symbol and site of hidden truths—at its center. In the opening scene, a student comments that Nicole and Christina are "always together." At Nicole's house, Michel reacts with surprise when Christina tells him that they are sharing a bed. Back at the school, they seem one morning to have woken up together. Later, when they discuss going their separate ways, Christina calls it "separating." But the symbolic queerness of their actions speaks louder than their physical closeness, and the other indications that they might be more than friends.

Nicole fits the monster queer seducer role in all its particulars. The short-haired, broad-shouldered Nicole is the dominant partner both physically and psychically. She seems to be older than Christina and is certainly more experienced. Although it's not specified whose idea the murder plot was, Christina tries to back out several times and Nicole exhorts her to follow through. During the murder itself, it is Nicole who physically holds Michel's head under the water. As it turns out, this is convenient and perhaps necessary for her part in the deception, but the fact that Nicole double-crosses Christina does not negate her part in the sapphic relationship. What makes Nicole a villain is not her lesbianism, but rather her mirroring of the husband's possessiveness and greed.

The importance of swimming pool symbolism is apparent from the film's opening credits, which play over a closeup of the pool's surface. The water's twinkling reflections contrast the scum that covers it, pointing to Christina's characterization. Christina is the pool, beautiful but neglected. The first time the women discuss their plot, they are standing next to the disused pool, symbolizing their mistreatment at Michel's hands. When they drown Michel in the bathtub, they are committing vulvic murder while washing themselves clean of his influence. By dumping his body in the pool, they are submerging masculine violence by way of their own femininity, a literal rejection of the male body and their peonage to it. The last seven decades of swimming pool horror are fed by the twin wellsprings of *Cat People* and *Les Diaboliques*, both of which depict a battle of wills between a pair of powerful women to decide who sinks and who floats.

The 1996 remake *Diabolique*, directed by Jeremiah S. Chechik, follows much the same plot until the point where the seemingly undead headmaster (now named Guy) frightens his wife (now named Mia) into a heart attack. In this version, the heart attack is not fatal. Nicole, meanwhile, has had a change of heart about the plot against Mia. Guy chases Mia outside in a murderous rage and almost drowns her in the refilled pool. Nicole rescues her, Guy pulls Nicole into the water, and the three of them end up in the pool, where Nicole and Mia work together to drown Guy for real this time. The detective, who is a woman in this version and aware of Guy's cruelty, offers to help them cover up the crime.[9]

The remake is more explicit about the women's queer coding. Before the murder, Nicole kisses Mia sensually on the hand and forearm. They then exchange a gentle cheek kiss before Nicole goes to distract the neighbors. After the murder, they lie in bed together; Nicole, shirtless, lights a metaphoric post-coital cigarette and Mia embraces her. The first morning back at the school, Mia and Nicole are first seen in the same bedroom and Nicole appears once again in lingerie. Mia gives dictation to her French class on the verb "desire," ending with, as she stares at the pool, "They desire, feminine."

When things start to unravel, Mia threatens to go to the police and says that, when asked about Nicole's motive, "I'll say we were lovers." Nicole does not challenge the assertion. Instead, she strokes Mia's hair and agrees that they had the same reason for committing the murder, then gives her another cheek kiss. Later, one of the videographers hired to shoot a promo for the school calls the women a homophobic slur while declaring his belief that they murdered Guy. Guy, taunting Mia near the end while choking her, asks suggestively, "Was it a lonely week? Or did you two keep each other company?" Finally, when it looks like Guy has drowned Mia in the pool, Nicole gives her mouth-to-mouth resuscitation, effectively kissing her back to life.

Most of the changes *Diabolique* makes to the original seem designed to turn the film into more of a feminist text. Nicole is a reluctant, rather than enthusiastic, partner in the plot against Mia, and ends up turning against Guy at last. Guy's physical violence, hinted at in the original, is shown explicitly in this version. The name change from Michel to Guy could also be taken to suggest that the cruel husband's disagreeable qualities are generalizable to all men. But the biggest change in the film's gender politics is the private detective. Shirley Vogel is a tough-talking cancer survivor who refuses to disguise the results of a mastectomy, wears her hair short and dresses in pantsuits. Though she mentions an ex-husband and talks about dating men, she seems to have no particular love for the male of the species. "Testosterone," she remarks in her first major scene, "they should put it in bombs." When she interviews the videographers about Guy, one of them says, "This guy gives 'prick'

In the 1996 *Diabolique* remake, Nicole (Sharon Stone, left) and Mia (Isabelle Adjani) stay close together to protect their secrets.

a bad name," to which Shirley responds, "What doesn't?" Her final act in the movie, declaring her willingness to cover for Nicole and Mia, suggests solidarity with wronged women, and the film closes on the image of her lighting a cigarette while she watches Guy's body sink into the pool. This noir-esque touch might indicate that we are to consider Shirley as the viewer's conscience, and approve of how things ended up. It also mirrors the cigarette Nicole smoked after they "killed" Guy the first time. Shirley may be joining the other women in a symbolic consummation—the threesome murder adding another partner.

Diabolique's water imagery matches that of the original. The credits again play over closeups of water, but instead of the dancing light on the pool's surface, it is the falling and cascading of raindrops. Instead of a heavy statue, the women use the large bottle from the water cooler to weigh Guy down in the tub. Later, as the pool is being drained, the boys in Mia's class recite a rote list of the world's oceans and seas. Most importantly, the remake spends more time with the theme of religion, which the original touched on lightly. It adds a scene where Mia—who in both versions is a former nun—donates a chunk of Guy's embezzled money to the church in an effort to assuage her guilt. When Nicole confronts her about it as Mia sits poolside, Mia dips her hand in the pool and says, "It's holy water."

That isn't the only time the image of consecrated water shows up in the remake. When Shirley enters Nicole's house to snoop around, she touches the water cooler as if genuflecting at a church font. When he attempts to kill Mia in the climax, Guy performs a mock baptism, dunking her head in the pool repeatedly while asking if she wants to confess her sins. There is also an abortion subplot where one of Guy's other girlfriends shows up to demand payment to terminate her pregnancy.

"Abortion is a sin," says Mia, but she does not object to the check being written. All of these threads intersect in the image of the pool as baptismal font—which is just one layer of abstraction away from the pool as womb. Guy's offscreen emergence from the pool, when Mia believes him dead, is a symbolic rebirth. Nicole's resuscitation of Mia literally brings her back to life, and after drowning Guy—Nicole having redeemed herself and Mia having found her strength—they both emerge wholly changed.

As we'll see later, nineteen seventy-two was a good year for poolside queer desire in Spanish horror films. *Tombs of the Blind Dead*, directed by Amando de Ossorio, opens at a seaside swimming pool where Betty runs into her old school friend Virginia, who is accompanied by her friend Roger. Roger invites Betty to come on vacation with them, and Betty agrees. Though she says she will bring a boyfriend, she shows up for the train ride alone. On the train, Virginia is so upset by Roger and Betty's flirtatiousness that she jumps off and walks alone into the countryside. In flashbacks, we learn that Virginia and Betty had a romantic relationship while in school together. Virginia is jealous not because she wants Roger, but because she wants Betty. Virginia stumbles upon the ruins of a medieval town, spends the night there, and is murdered by the zombies of Templars who haunt the town.[10]

Roger repeatedly insists that he and Virginia are not together. While the viewer is led to believe that he is lying to woo Betty, it turns out that he is probably telling the truth. Later in the film, he insists the same thing about Betty. Betty, for her part, seems to have no relationship of any kind with a man. The boyfriend she mentions in the beginning never materializes. When a character named Pedro comes on to Betty, she rebuffs him, saying that she has trouble getting close to men: "It's a fear that was instilled in me as a child." Pedro proceeds to re-traumatize her—since the childhood experience she alluded to was probably sexual assault—by raping her in the haunted graveyard. It's after this act that the dead rise from their tombs, symbolic of the terrifying ghosts the assault has raised from Betty's past.

All the evidence indicates that Virginia and Betty are both living as closeted lesbians. Their affection when they meet at the pool, verbal flattery about each other's beauty and bodies, and the intense way they look at one another drive the point home. It's surprising to me how many critics, John Kenneth Muir[11] and Jamie Russell[12] among them, seem to think that Virginia gets upset on the train because of Roger's flirtatiousness with Betty, when to me it seems clear that she is bothered instead by Betty's apparent receptiveness to it. *Tombs of the Blind Dead* doesn't often get talked about as a queer film, but it's a great example of the way a public pool can provide cover for the queer gaze. Like another pair of Spaniards we'll meet later, Betty and Virginia take advantage of a zone where they can be nearly nude together in public, right under the noses of Franco's fascist watchdogs.

Again depicting the closet's disastrous consequences, Joachim Trier's *Thelma* (2017) finds us back in the familiar territory of adolescent witchcraft. The title character is a college student who finds herself attracted to a classmate named Anja—an

In *Tombs of the Blind Dead* (1972), Betty (Lone Fleming, left) and Virginia (María Elena Arpón) only have eyes for each other. Roger (César Burner) doesn't seem to notice.

attraction she feels shame about due to her conservative Christian upbringing. After Thelma notices Anja for the first time, sitting next to her in the library, she (Thelma) has a seizure. A short time later, Thelma is swimming laps in the pool when Anja approaches and introduces herself. Thelma is reluctant to pursue a relationship, but she ends up joining Anja and friends at a bar. That night, Anja appears outside Thelma's dorm, seemingly having sleepwalked there. Upon seeing her, Thelma suffers another seizure, after which they spend a chaste night in the same bed. Anja invites Thelma to accompany her and her mother to a ballet performance, where Thelma becomes overwhelmed by physical contact before they share their first kiss. During an epilepsy test, a clinician tries various verbal prompts to trigger a seizure in Thelma. It finally happens when she begins to think about Anja. In the midst of Thelma's seizure, back at home, Anja inexplicably vanishes. Having looked into her medical history, the specialist informs Thelma about her institutionalized grandmother, who her father claimed was dead. Visiting the institution, Thelma finds her grandmother drugged into insensibility. A staff member tells her that the old lady was wracked with guilt about her husband's disappearance many years ago. She believed that she could make things happen by thinking about them. Back in the pool, Thelma has another seizure and imagines being pulled into a dark abyss. When she tries to swim back to the surface, she finds a tiled barrier trapping her in the water. She wheels around and manages to get out, but collapses on the pool deck. Believing that she caused Anja's disappearance, Thelma returns home and tells her parents everything. Her father reveals that Thelma inherited her grandmother's

Chapter 7. Matching Two-Piece

power to manifest her desires, and unwittingly killed her baby brother years ago by teleporting him beneath the ice of a frozen lake. Thelma's mother attempted suicide after the incident and ended up paralyzed. Hoping to "fix" Thelma, the family made a hard turn into conservative Christianity, which seemed to be working. The incidents stopped until she went away to college.

Upset about her parents' manipulation, and realizing that they plan to neuter her with heavy drugs like her grandmother, Thelma causes her father to combust and burn to death in the same lake where her brother died. She then enters the water herself and, amidst a seizure, envisions diving deep in the lake, through the abyss, and emerging back in the school's swimming pool where she finds and kisses Anja. Thelma returns to the house, uses her power to heal her mother's paralysis, and leaves. The end of the film finds Thelma back at college with Anja, returned from wherever she banished her to, as her girlfriend.[13]

The swimming pool, the place where Thelma and Anja officially meet, comes to symbolize both the relationship and Anja herself in Thelma's mind. The pool evokes feminine sexuality, and the thrill and vulnerability of young love. But for the closeted Thelma, it is also a prison, as seen in her vision of being trapped in the pool. As in many of the films from Part I, the pool is conceptualized as a human-made container for something natural and only tenuously tamable. Thelma's magic seems to be strongest around bodies of water, particularly the lake near her house. When she fatally teleports her brother, she sends him from his bath—a miniature swimming pool—to the lake. The lake is also where she kills her father. Though we don't get details, we know that Thelma's grandfather vanished on the water as well: "They never found his body, just the boat." This recalls Creed's portrait of the witch as being specially attuned to the elements,[14] as well as the larger symbolic womanliness of water.

The link to water is not the only way Thelma's power parallels her queerness. She is full of guilt and confusion about both, thanks to her family's tactic of using religion to suppress them. Instead of acknowledging and accepting her powers and her queerness, learning how to embody them in a healthy way, the religious suppression taught her to deny, to be ashamed and fearful. What is not acknowledged cannot be integrated. The self-loathing is so intense that her wish for the "problem" of her queerness to go away manifests in Anja, the object of her desire, being literally zapped out of existence. In the end, Thelma learns to embrace both her queerness and her magic in defiance of mom and dad—never with their support. The father's encouragement of prayer and piousness to tamp down her psychokinetic abilities has real-world resonances with religious "gay conversion therapy."

Thelma's three visits to the swimming pool represent three different stages in her journey out of the closet. Her first poolside encounter with Anja has the bashfulness of a blossoming schoolgirl crush. She is intrigued, but still uncertain. This recalls one of the opening images of the film, in a pre-credits flashback when a young Thelma looks down at the frozen lake to see a fish swimming under the sheet of ice.

The title character (Eili Harboe) in *Thelma* (2017) experiences one of the seizures that seem to accompany the blossoming of her reality-warping powers—and her queer sexuality.

Like the fish, she is swimming around in a cage, but does not know it yet. She realizes her entrapment in the second pool scene, pushing against the tiled barrier in a visual echo of her dead baby brother trapped beneath the ice. In the last pool fantasy, she has embraced both her power and her sexuality. In a recurrence of the pool as portal between realities, she swims from the lake into the pool, creating a magical bridge from the natural and reclaiming the pool as a space of liberation. One possible reading of Thelma's choice to kill her father but heal her mother (though it relies on the ableist notion of wheelchair users as "broken") is that she needs to make the maternal figure whole in order to facilitate her own symbolic rebirth when she emerges from the pool waters to embrace her lover Anja.

There is a disturbing dimension to Thelma's power that complicates a reading of the ending. Thelma's father pushes back on the idea that Anja loved her by saying, "Do you think she had a choice? With what's within you?" Maddeningly, Thelma can never know the answer. She finds herself on the other side of Benshoff's "exploitative seduction" trope, uncertain of the extent to which Anja's affection is genuine rather than unknowingly coerced. Her father, on the other hand, may be invoking the queer manipulator trope, ironically playing mind games of his own. This is Thelma's cross to bear. We are left with an invitation to ponder exactly how happy an ending we've been given. As the camera slowly pulls out on the scene of dozens of people walking around the campus, we wonder just how much of it Thelma is controlling. Are these people going freely about their lives, or are they all being subtly manipulated?

As Barbara Creed observed, like other young female witches, the character of Thelma provokes sympathy.[15] For most of the film she is bewildered by the emergence of a power she does not yet know how to wield. The influence of *Carrie* is clear, both in the way Thelma's abilities manifest and the way her family seizes on religious fervor to try to contain them. But the addition of queer themes changes the dynamic, particularly as it pertains to Thelma's social life. Unlike Carrie White, Thelma is not a social outcast. In fact, Anja and her friend group seem to accept her readily, subconsciously influenced or not. The challenge to Thelma's social flowering comes from within, from the insecurity of the closet. Thelma is not excluded from the swimming pool, she is trapped inside it.

Any teen horror movie made since the mid-2010s has to reckon with how the Internet and social media have changed what it means to be an adolescent. In 2012, Pew Research found that 23 percent of Americans aged 12 to 17 owned a smartphone.[16] By 2015, that number was 73 percent, and in 2024 it had risen to 95 percent. In the same 2015 survey, 24 percent of teens reported being online "almost constantly"; by 2024, that percentage had almost doubled.[17] Today's discourse is rife with speculation about the effects of this technology, and its attendant erosion of privacy, on teen mental health. Cyberbullying can lead to body image issues, disordered eating and self-harm.[18] Like other forms of bullying, the consequences can be devastating for queer and gender-nonconforming teens.[19] Because it is mediated by a screen, this kind of bullying can feel less real and serious for those who perpetrate it. Some films feature the swimming pool as a reminder of the real-world sites of teen socialization the online world is increasingly displacing. In others it suggests an experimental environment we have thrown our children into without considering the consequences—one that just might be full of predators.

One movie that does both is Sam Levinson's *Assassination Nation* (2018). The film focuses on four high school girls—Lily, Bex, Sarah and Em—in a town called Salem. An anonymous hacker steals the mayor's phone data and uploads it publicly. Photos of the conservative mayor cross-dressing and engaging male sex workers cause an uproar and accusations of hypocrisy, leading him to publicly take his own life. The next hack targets the high school principal, whose porn search results and bath-time photos of his young daughter lead to mob demands for his resignation

Bex (Hari Nef) is surprised by a masked attacker in the house-storming centerpiece of *Assassination Nation* (2018).

and imprisonment. Before the dust from these incidents settles, the hacker uploads leaks of literally half the town. Lily's sexting history with Nick, a married man, is made public, and her bitter boyfriend identifies her as the high school "slut" in the leaked selfies, making her the target of a harassment campaign. Evidence of a sexual encounter between Bex, who is transgender, and football player Diamond is also leaked. The football team vows vengeance on Bex for seducing Diamond into acts they perceive as homosexual. Meanwhile, a local hacker falsely claims, under duress from a masked mob demanding justice, that Lily admitted to being the uploader. The mob, which includes one of the town's police officers, descends on Em and Sarah's house in search of the four friends. One of them attacks Bex near the pool with a nail gun. They fall together into the pool, where she manages to wrest the nail gun from her assailant and kill him with it underwater. Lily flees to Nick's house, where he reveals himself as the leader of the mob. She kills him to escape, frees Em and Sarah, and arms them with guns from Nick's house. Together they rescue Bex from being lynched by the football team. In response to Lily's vlogs explaining her victimization by the town, a growing crowd of women and other victims joins the four girls in self-defense against the frenzied townspeople. In an epilogue, it's revealed that Lily's younger brother Donny is the hacker responsible for the leaks, and he cites his motive as "for the lulz."[20]

Central to *Assassination Nation* are the impossible standards our culture holds teenage girls to. As Lily puts it in her closing monologue: "Smile. Open up. Cross your legs. Spread your pussy. Speak softer, scream louder. Be quiet, be confident. Be interesting. Don't be so difficult. Be strong. Don't fight back. Be an angel, be a whore." In the film, when the pressure of trying to hold all those contradictions finally causes society to snap, it's the youngest and most vulnerable who bear the brunt of the damage. "You can't live by the rules you set, yet you still pretend," Lily concludes. "This is your world. You built this. ...Don't take your hate out on me, I just got here."

At one point, a high schooler named Reagan says everyone needs to "come to terms with [the fact that] privacy is just dead." Later it's revealed that Reagan had previously published her friend Grace's private nudes to the whole school. Grace retaliates by beating Reagan to death. A callous act that Reagan committed on the other side of a screen suddenly feels a lot more real when she pays for it on the business end of Grace's baseball bat.

In *Assassination Nation*'s first pool scene, the girls hang out in Em and Sarah's backyard pool discussing the mayor's hack and subsequent suicide. Lily argues for compassion, saying it's sad the mayor felt the need to live a double life. Bex retorts, "People like me kill themselves every fucking day, and bigots like him aren't shedding tears." Observing this conversation, the camera is positioned half-in, half-out of the water, two perspectives that mirror the two girls' points of view. The cisgender Lily argues from a position of privilege: Although Bex is her friend, the reality of rampant transphobia is still somewhat abstract because she herself does not

Chapter 7. Matching Two-Piece

In *Assassination Nation* (2018), Lily (Odessa Young, foreground) thinks she sees both sides of the issue where compassion for bigots is concerned, while Bex (Hari Nef) knows better.

experience it. She can argue the moral high ground (above water), while Bex is immersed in the issue and cannot be objective. Later, when Bex struggles with her attacker in the pool, the camera plunges fully underwater. All ambiguity is gone. As in *The Pool* (2018), the swimming pool has changed from a place of friendly leisure to a primal battleground. The issue of clemency for bigots is no longer academic for anyone: It's kill or be killed.

Assassination Nation is about abstraction. Our actions' impacts feel farther away when they are mediated by screens. By hacking the town, Donny caused a landslide of death and destruction, not to mention allowing his own sister to become a target for violence. His reason? He was bored. Internet alienation collides with suburban alienation to create a superstorm that washes away the commons, leaving people atomized in the glow of their screens, each a microcosmos of one, sending signals into the void whose real-world consequences usually, but not always, remain theoretical. Floating in her water wings under a sunny sky, Lily bumps up against the limits of allyship; after night falls, Bex is the one who must fight tooth and nail against her oppressors.

CHAPTER 8

Fish Out of Water
Challenging Masculinity

> Every time you dived in—the classic spear entry came naturally to you—there was the vestigial hope that you might just hover, then ascend....
> —Bill Broady, *Swimmer*

For the most interesting riff on Benshoff's 1950s tropes, we'll return to the *Nightmare on Elm Street* franchise. *A Nightmare on Elm Street Part 2: Freddy's Revenge* (1985) is one of the most infamously queer-coded horror movies ever.

The protagonist of Jack Sholder's *Freddy's Revenge*, a teenage boy named Jesse, has just moved with his family into the Elm Street house occupied by Final Girl Nancy in the first film. Jesse's nominal love interest is classmate Lisa, but he also has a rather fraught friendship with Grady, a boy in his gym class. Jesse and Grady keep getting in trouble with the gym coach Mr. Schneider, who is rumored to "[hang] around queer S&M joints downtown."

As Jesse's family settles into their new home, strange things happen. The house is hot, with indoor temperatures approaching 100 degrees despite an air conditioner. Jesse has recurring nightmares about a grotesque, scarred older man, who says they have "work to do" together. After Jesse finds Nancy's old diary and learns about Freddy Krueger, the dreams start to bleed into reality, and he realizes that Freddy wants to possess his body so he can be reborn into the waking world. One night, unable to sleep, Jesse wanders downtown and ends up in a leather bar. He encounters Schneider, who takes him back to the school gym, presumably for punishment. An invisible Freddy attacks Schneider with sporting equipment, ties him up in the shower, strips him naked, and whips his backside with a towel. In the steamy shower, Jesse appears to transform into Freddy and slices Schneider's back open, killing him. That weekend, Lisa hosts a pool party for a large friend group at her house. Jesse, fearful for the other teens' safety, is nervous about attending and tries to leave. Lisa stops him and they begin to make out. Before they can get past first base, Freddy again tries to take over Jesse's body and starts to emerge through his mouth. Jesse flees to Grady's house and begs to spend the night there. Grady agrees but ends up going to sleep despite Jesse's admonition. Freddy uses Jesse's body to murder Grady and then returns to the pool party. Teens panic as the water begins to boil and

Chapter 8. Fish Out of Water   105

The return of the repressed: Freddy Krueger (Robert Englund) devastates a teenage pool party in *A Nightmare on Elm Street 2: Freddy's Revenge* (1985).

Freddy rampages poolside, killing multiple partygoers. Lisa's father appears with a rifle and Freddy vanishes. Lisa goes to the defunct industrial area where Freddy used to work, seeking to rescue Jesse. When Freddy corners Lisa, she tells Jesse that she loves him. Freddy's reincarnated body catches fire and he apparently burns to death. The charred remains fall away, revealing Jesse alive and unharmed underneath. An epilogue shows Lisa and Jesse riding the school bus together, normalcy apparently restored, until Freddy bursts through the chest of Lisa's friend Kerry and the bus careens out of control.[1]

Freddy's Revenge's queer coding has been examined extensively[2] elsewhere,[3] so I won't belabor the details. Suffice to say that all the tropes we're interested in are present here: Freddy is the elder monster queer who supernaturally seduces Jesse into his world of wrongdoing. Lisa is the hetero love interest who rescues Jesse from Freddy's corruption—but only temporarily. Schneider's death is a notable example of the threesome murder because of how subordinate Jesse is: Freddy doesn't just take control, he subsumes Jesse's identity inside his own body.

In the pool party set piece, adolescent poolside thrills and anxieties are on full display. Though the party is overseen by Lisa's parents, the kids see it as a subversive space. Everybody tolerates her dad spinning big band records and commandeering the grill while they wait for the parents to go to bed so the party can really start. Once the parents retire, the music and the mood both change, from a wholesome kid's gathering to a sexy rager. In terms of teen pool party politics, Jesse is an evident outsider. His swimming attire is a matching two-piece set of powder blue shorts and tank top, modest by male standards. In familiar adolescent style, Jesse is self-conscious about the changes happening to his body and uncomfortable around his more confident peers. He enters the pool house to change back into street clothes: long pants and the same button-up shirt he wears in the leather bar scene. In the pool house, he tries to conform to heteronormative expectations and make love to Lisa, but he cannot resist the influence of the man who is inside him trying to get out. After he flees to Grady's house, Grady says the quiet part aloud: "She's female and she's waiting for you in the cabana, and you want to sleep with me."

Back at the pool, the film's theme of building heat and pressure—the growing temperature in the house, the increasing strain of two personalities trying to fit into one body—culminates in an explosion of adolescent id. The pool water boils (echoing *Burnt Offerings*). Freddy knocks the top off the barbecue and a pillar of flame shoots out, backlighting Freddy as he delivers the iconic line, "You are all my children now"—a clear expression of the simmering social fear, noted by Benshoff, of queer elders trying to turn our children gay *en masse*.[4] In a poolside transformation, Freddy overtakes Jesse's body, it seems, for good this time.

More heat, fire and steam accompany Lisa's last desperate bid to save Jesse from Freddy's queer talons. In an apparent heteronormative victory, it turns out that all Jesse needed was the love of a good woman to straighten him out. But the bus epilogue makes it clear that you can't fight nature, only beat it off for a while.

It took another iconic slasher franchise, *Halloween*, four more decades to get its "gay chapter." It finally arrived in 2022 with David Gordon Green's *Halloween Ends*—and it came complete with a poolside threesome murder. *Halloween Ends* is the first film in the series to feature a serial killer other than Michael Myers. In a prologue, it introduces us to Corey Cunningham, a young man who accidentally kills Jeremy, a boy he is babysitting, on Halloween night. Corey is charged with aggravated manslaughter but ends up going free. Four years later, Haddonfield is a depressed community where suicide, aggression and callousness are rampant. Most believe Corey killed Jeremy deliberately and he has become a social outcast, more ridiculed than feared, working as a salvage yard mechanic. Meanwhile, series heroine Laurie Strode has bought a house with her nurse granddaughter Allyson, whose mother—Laurie's daughter—was murdered in the last movie. Laurie takes Corey to Allyson for treatment of a wound on his hand, inflicted during in an encounter with some bullies. Corey and Allyson start dating, but after a Halloween party where he is confronted by Jeremy's mother, he gives up on trying to re-socialize himself. On his way home from the party, another bullying episode leaves him unconscious beneath a bridge among Haddonfield's homeless. Michael Myers drags Corey into the sewer tunnel where he lives, but does not kill him. Instead, Corey appears to undergo a personality shift when he looks into Michael's eyes. Immediately upon leaving the tunnel, he kills a homeless man in what may or may not be self-defense.

The newly confident Corey takes Allyson to a diner where they encounter Doug, Allyson's policeman ex-boyfriend. The two have a tense exchange, and that night Corey lures Doug to Michael's tunnel and helps Michael kill him. Later, the pair murders Allyson's boss Dr. Mathis and his nurse mistress Deb at the doctor's home, next to the swimming pool. On Halloween night, Corey attacks Laurie, who has caught on to what he is doing, at her home. She defeats him, and he stabs himself in the neck just before Allyson walks in. Allyson leaves in horror, believing her grandmother murdered Corey, but returns in time to help her defeat Michael in a final, bloody battle. In full view of the town, Laurie pulverizes Michael's body in the shredder at the salvage yard. With this impromptu ceremony, it's suggested, perhaps the town can start to heal.[5]

Arriving as it did amidst the "queer adults turning our children gay" panic's latest revival, *Halloween Ends* is careful about depicting Corey's murderous transformation. The differences between Corey and his spiritual predecessor, *Freddy's Revenge*'s Jesse, are significant. We first meet Corey in the feminine-coded role of babysitter. In a series with a lot of babysitters, he is the first male one, giving the character a gender-nonconforming touch similar to Jesse's unisex name. Like Jesse, Corey is groomed as a successor or surrogate by the franchise's boogeyman. Corey's relationship with Allyson echoes Jesse's with Lisa: Both are drawn to their hetero love interests but seem reluctant about physical intimacy. But unlike Jesse, a victim of Freddy's supernatural coercion, Corey embarks on his queer-coded murder spree wholly of his own will. Furthermore, it's Corey's ostracizing by the community that sets him on his antisocial path.

I will emphasize again that the queer coding of murder in horror films does not always equate queerness with violence. To the extent that murder in these films is symbolic, it represents transgression of social norms. Returning to Kristeva via Creed, the abject can be anything that challenges the symbolic order,[6] and in slasher films it's represented by one of humanity's major taboos: senseless killing.

The first threesome murder between Corey and Michael happens under the bridge among the unhoused, a subterranean autonomous zone set apart from mainline Haddonfield. Corey lures Doug the cop, a representative of authority and cishet male ego, into this lawless space. Corey begs Michael, "Show me how to do it," and holds Doug from behind as Michael stabs him, bucking Doug's body upward to meet Michael's thrusts, eyes locked on the knife and gasping with each penetration. Corey later goes to Allyson's house and greets her with the line, "I don't know what's happening to me," a sentence that recalls Jesse in *Freddy's Revenge* and a familiar refrain for adolescents struggling with confusion or guilt over the blooming of non-normative desire.

The next threesome kill is the reason we're here: the poolside murders of Dr. Mathis and Deb. Deb walks onto the pool deck to investigate a noise. The viewer sees a murder happening behind her, but in the dim firelight we cannot make out details. When Deb turns on the patio and pool lights, she sees Corey seated on the ground, stabbing the doctor in the neck with a corkscrew as twinkling blue pool light plays over the scene. This is Corey's first fully premeditated solo murder, and the illuminating pool light suggests something "turning on" within him, making clear what was obscure. Deb flees into the bedroom and locks Corey outside the glass door, but

The first half of a foursome murder? Corey (Rohan Campbell) skewers Dr. Mathis (Michael O'Leary) in his first masked kill—but there will be more before *Halloween Ends* (2022).

Michael emerges from within and stabs her. As Corey watches, still backlit by the pool, he compulsively unbandages his wounded hand, revealing the vaginal gash in his palm and pressing it against the glass as he leers at the murder.

Corey and Allyson's relationship is built on wounding. Psychologically, she is drawn to him in part because of the trauma he's endured. He thinks she is trying to fix him, while she seems to merely relate to his ordeal because of her own Halloween night of death. She tells him, "I know what it's like to have everybody looking at you, thinking that they know you, thinking they know what you've been through, but they don't." On a literal, physical level, it is Corey's wounded hand that brings them together, when Allyson treats him at her work. His physical wounding, then, is linked to his psychic wounding, and when he unbandages it at the scene of the second threesome murder, it's a signal that he does not want either to heal.

Slasher theorists talk a lot about the obvious "phallic purpose" of slasher killers stabbing young women,[7] but in *Halloween Ends*, Deb is the only woman we see stabbed. Every other time a knife plunges onscreen into flesh, it's the flesh of a man. One of those men is Corey himself, and in his case the wound is self-inflicted. According to a 2023 survey by a suicide prevention group, The Trevor Project, 41 percent of young LGBTQ+ people reported seriously contemplating suicide in the last year. These suicidal thoughts often stem from bullying and feelings of being disrespected and outcast by the community.[8] Many a teen and young adult, after being told enough times by their tormentors to "kill yourself,"[9] has done just that.[10] *Halloween Ends*' Corey has heard so many taunts accusing him of being a murderous "psycho" that he eventually decides he might as well *be* one. That's what he's really deciding, with finality, in that moment when he unwraps his hand as he stands by the pool and embraces its gender-queering power.

Of course, the tropes we're zeroing in on do not appear in every queer horror movie. Whether or not they know it, the films that play with Benshoff's monster queer seducer tropes are in conversation with a short-lived wave of 1950s drive-in fare. There are many ways to queer the horror genre. A film like Jim Sharman's *The Rocky Horror Picture Show* (1975) is in dialogue with even older movie traditions—in this case the 1930s' "old dark house" pictures, mad scientist films and Busby Berkeley musicals. *Rocky Horror* follows an engaged couple, Brad and Janet, who find themselves stranded on the road and seek refuge at a mysterious castle inhabited by a gender-nonconforming mad scientist, Dr. Frank-N-Furter. Frank and his butler Riff Raff artificially animate a muscular man named Rocky, whom Frank takes to bed. Later that night, Frank visits Janet and Brad in their separate bedrooms and seduces both of them. After learning about Brad's fling with Frank, Janet ends up seducing Rocky. Eddie's uncle, a professor who once taught Brad and Janet, arrives in search of his nephew; Frank serves him a meal made from Eddie's remains. Frank turns Brad, Janet, the professor, Rocky and a hanger-on named Columbia into stone statues, dresses them in cabaret attire and then reanimates them for an elaborate musical number with a swimming pool and a replica of the radio tower in the RKO Pictures logo. It turns out that Frank, as well as Riff Raff and another servant named Magenta, are aliens from a planet called Transsexual, Transylvania. Apparently the aliens are just as intolerant of Frank's flamboyance as Earthlings are, because Riff Raff and Magenta declare mutiny and shoot Frank with an energy weapon. The last time we see Frank, he is dead and face down in the pool.[11]

The film emphasizes the homoeroticism implicit in the mad scientist's desire to create the perfect man, or more generally to create life without hetero intercourse, but with the aid of a same-sex partner, like Henry Frankenstein and Dr. Pretorius' efforts in gay director James Whale's *Bride of Frankenstein* (1935).[12] It also uses the template of the "old dark house" movie—named after another Whale film, 1932's *The Old Dark House*. Isolated from the normal world both physically and psychically, the old dark house is an autonomous zone where anything can happen. It is full of quirky characters and, in the gothic tradition, every secret seems to hide another secret. With both of these traditions in mind, Benshoff wrote that *Rocky Horror* "laid bare the queerer implications of the genre for all to see."[13]

In addition to the mad scientist, Frank embodies another queer horror archetype: the seducer. He makes love to Janet and Brad in separate scenes that play out with almost identical dialogue, blocking and composition. The only significant difference is a cheeky bit of color-coding: Janet's scene is backlit in pink, Brad's in blue. In both scenes, Frank pretends to be his target's partner and begins the lovemaking before he is unmasked by the removal of a wig. This begs for a conversation about consent. On one hand, Frank enters Brad and Janet's beds under false pretenses. On the other, both of them accede to Frank's lovemaking after making him promise not to tell the other partner. In Brad's case, it comes uncomfortably close to the myth of sexual deception—that trans people are out to "trick" others into having sex with them, believing that they are cisgender.[14] In the context of the queer horror film, Frank is embodying the "exploitative seduction" tactics of Benshoff's monster queer

Banished from their fantasy pool, Rocky (Peter Hinwood) prepares to carry the unconscious Frank-N-Furter (Tim Curry) to higher ground at the climax of *The Rocky Horror Picture Show* (1975).

archetype. Sexual coercion, murder and cannibalism are clearly on the other side of the morality divide from victimless transgressions like pansexuality and crossdressing, but Frank is a character designed to revel in the confusion of such boundaries.

As in other films we've seen, the pool in *Rocky Horror* represents sexual freedom, but the reference point is a new one for us: classic Hollywood musicals. The swimming pool musical number echoes Busby Berkeley's *Footlight Parade* (1933),[15] as Frank is lifted from the pool on a rising piece of scenery like Berkeley's famous "human waterfall." But instead of carefully choreographed geometric movements, the activity in the pool among Frank, Brad, Janet, Columbia and Rocky is a five-way tangle of lust that recalls the gender-expansive swimming pool orgy at the end of Cronenberg's *Shivers* from the same year. "Swim the warm waters of sins of the flesh," Frank encourages his listeners. In *Something for the Boys: Musical Theater and Gay Culture*, John M. Clum writes that musicals' "heightened theatricality, their exaggerated, almost parodic presentation of gender codes, and their lyrical romantic fantasies" meant "an escape from the masculine rites that disinterested and threatened" young queer men.[16]

Frank-N-Furter's love of classic Hollywood glamor takes the notion of fantastical escape one step further, reveling in cinema's ability to construct entire worlds free from the constraints of physical space. The title of Frank's song, "Don't Dream It, Be It," evokes Berkeley's feat of capturing his abstract, surreal imagination on the screen.

The other reference set Frank draws from, the 1930s horror film, is equally untethered from mundane modern reality. His character is Benshoff's monster queer writ large, embodying the queer viewer's tendency to identify with movie monsters and interpret their monstrosity as coded queerness.[17] The titular beast of 1933's *King Kong*, an RKO picture, is portrayed as a tragic hero in a doomed, forbidden romance with the film's leading lady Fay Wray. Frank sings about Wray directly, saying that he "wanted to be dressed just the same." Moments later, Rocky plays the Kong figure and carries Frank's body in a climb up the RKO tower before being shot down by Riff Raff, playing the part of *King Kong*'s fighter planes, enforcing institutional normalcy. Unwelcome on Earth and outcast from Frank's home planet, nothing is left for Rocky and Frank but the refuge of "rose-tinted" fantasy, so they tumble back into the pool.

Another 1970s horror film interested in flouting taboos is *The Cannibal Man* (1972), by queer director Eloy de la Iglesia. In Spain during the fascist Franco regime, a young man named Marcos works at a slaughterhouse and lives in a neighborhood where expensive high-rise apartments have started to displace humble old houses like his. On a date with his girlfriend Paula, Marcos quarrels with a taxi driver who asks the couple to stop making out in the back of his car. Marcos strikes the driver down, and the next day he learns from the newspaper that the man died. Paula insists on going to the police but Marcos, fearful that his life will be ruined, strangles her to death. Marcos' brother comes home early from a trip and Marcos ends up murdering him as well, followed in turn by the brother's fiancée and her father. As the corpses accumulate in his small house, he figures out a way to dispose of them: He chops them up and takes the pieces to his job, where he adds the human flesh to the industrial meat grinder, turning the customers who buy his company's meat into unwitting cannibals. The plan has a flaw: He can only safely transport as much meat as can fit in his gym bag. Unable to control the smell in his house, he buys gallons of air freshener and perfume, but that doesn't stop the neighborhood dogs from gathering around his door.

Nestor, a wealthy young man who lives in the neighboring high-rise, has been trying to strike up a friendship. At first Marcos rebuffs him, but the two slowly grow closer, culminating in a nighttime swim together at Nestor's health club. After Marcos murders a waitress who has a crush on him, Nestor invites him up to his apartment. He shows Marcos that with binoculars he can see clearly from his balcony into Marcos' house. Knowing he is caught, Marcos almost cuts Nestor's neck with a broken wine glass, but he cannot go through with it. Nestor encourages him to do the right thing. Marcos goes home, calls the police, and turns himself in.[18]

The Cannibal Man is a film about repression, an observation of the obstacles imposed by fascist rule to people living as their authentic selves, and more specifically a film about the closet. Marcos is lonely and aimless, as Nestor observes, even before he starts killing those around him. He enjoys spending time with Paula, but he is ambivalent about marriage. His overreaction to the taxi driver suggests that he is performing machismo. At one point he taunts the driver with, "What are you, some kind of homosexual?"

Criminalizing homosexuality is not the only way the totalitarian state keeps Marcos in thrall. The threat of the police hangs over the whole film. It is Paula's insistence on going to the cops that leads Marcos to kill her. Though he has a fair claim to self-defense, Marcos is convinced the police will not believe him. The cops hassle Nestor and Marcos when they are sitting at a cafe together, for no reason other than, implicitly, they look gay. Nestor is not carrying his ID, even though he is required to by law, but he faces no consequences. That scene is one of several where the pair discusses the economic disparity between them. Nestor makes little attempt to hide that his interest in Marcos is romantic; he goes out without an ID card, he names his dog Trotsky in a fiercely anti–Communist state, and he knows he can get away with it all because he is insulated by his class privilege. Marcos has no such luxury. There is no escape from his station in life, and he muses that it's only a matter of time before his house gets bulldozed to make way for another bourgeois high-rise. The system is making Marcos sick, and he is literally feeding that sickness back into the system, in the form of decaying human meat. Even the glimmer of upward mobility he manages, the promotion he receives midway through the film, is soured by the behavior of his colleagues. His former peers at the plant mock him ("You aren't one of the gang anymore") and play keep-away with his gym bag, which unbeknownst to them contains human remains. In this episode, the casual violence of heteronormative society toward queer people intersects with capital's interest in turning workers against one another using petty differences.

Roughly midway through the movie, Nestor invites Marcos to a night swim at his health club, where the pool is open late. What follows is an idyllic scene of queer delight, complete with gentle music on the soundtrack and underwater shots of the men's bodies snaking around each other. Like Betty and Virginia in the same year's *Tombs of the Blind Dead*, they are taking advantage of the one space where same-sex couples can frolic together nearly nude in a way that is socially condoned. At one point, they toss a beach ball in the form of a globe: In this moment, they have the world in their hands. The scene ends with the two men gasping side by side beneath an artificial waterfall. It is a brief sojourn in a utopian spot where they can be themselves and enjoy each other's company, a space that exists outside brutal reality, but a space they can only access thanks to Nestor's class privilege.

Marcos later sits alone in his chair, flashes of the pool scene playing in his memory as he grimaces with internalized homophobia. The film cuts from Marcos rocking back and forth in the grip of the memories to an extreme closeup of a pinball machine that reads "Top Secret." I do not think the word "top" has the significance we English speakers might think, but there is certainly a meaning to "secret": In his shame, Marcos is deflecting, denying, sublimating—doing everything he can to protect his secret.

As in the other queer horror films we've looked at, murder is symbolic in *The Cannibal Man*. The stress of the closet, like the other forms of fascist repression, causes Marcos to do extreme, irrational things. For both his queerness and

Chapter 8. Fish Out of Water

Nestor (Eusebio Poncela, left) and Marcos (Vicente Parra) finally get to spend some time together away from prying eyes in *The Cannibal Man* (1972).

his murdering, fear of being caught only makes him dig his hole deeper. The bourgeois Nestor may have the luxury to be his authentic self, but for Marcos there is no escape, as the final scene makes clear. The world's brutality and coldness are maddening, and the only relief for Marcos, like Frank-N-Furter, is the fantasy dreamscape of the swimming pool.

Chapter 9

Night Swimming Prohibited
Queer Vampires at the Pool

> Like a vampire at the swimming pool trying to hide,
> I don't know why I even came, I just feel so out of place.
> —Skylar Grey, "Vampire at the Swimming Pool"

Barbara Creed's most vivid description of the archaic mother reads like this: "As the oral sadistic mother, she keeps her lover/child by her side in a relationship which symbolically collapses the boundaries between milk and blood as well as violating the taboo on incest."[1] If you squint, she could be writing about *Hellbender*'s matriarch or a similar witch mother. But she's actually analyzing Tony Scott's 1983 vampire movie *The Hunger*. The film focuses on the relationship between Miriam Blaylock, an ages-old vampire, and Dr. Sarah Roberts, a specialist in research on aging. At the start of the film, Miriam's lover John realizes that the supernatural longevity she bestows has an expiration date. After 200 years of looking the same, he is suddenly aging at a frightful rate. He seeks out Sarah's help, but she dismisses him as a crank before realizing too late that he is telling the truth. By the time Sarah finds his house, he is a shriveled husk. The next time Sarah visits, Miriam seduces her. During their sexual episode, Miriam mixes their blood together, thereby vampirizing Sarah with the intent of taking her as her new lover.

Sarah goes to a fancy restaurant with her boyfriend Tom. They sit next to a window that overlooks a swimming pool. The suspicious Tom wants Sarah to account for the three and a half hours she spent at Miriam's house. He becomes increasingly aggravated as she gives evasive answers. Meanwhile, Sarah's attention is continually drawn to the swimmers outside the window. In a series of point-of-view and reaction shots, we see Sarah distracted by the bodies of women entering and exiting the pool. She seems uninterested in Tom, who is also irritated when she refuses food. The implication is clear: Along with turning Sarah into a vampire, Miriam has turned her into a lesbian. Sarah returns to Miriam's house and, after swooning from lack of sustenance, ends up in Miriam's bed again. When Tom arrives looking for her, Miriam shows him upstairs, then retreats behind a curtain to watch what happens. Sarah, unable to suppress her hunger, kills Tom and drinks his blood, completing her transition into full-fledged vampire. She joins Miriam in the next

Chapter 9. Night Swimming Prohibited

Hunger of a different kind: The newly vampirized Sarah (Susan Sarandon) can't focus on her dinner, or her boyfriend Tom (Cliff DeYoung), with all those swimmers frolicking next door in *The Hunger* (1983).

room and indicates her willingness to be Miriam's new lover, but then attempts suicide.[2]

The story doesn't reveal whether Sarah has had, or desired, queer experiences before. The way she flirts with Miriam ("Are you making a pass at me, Mrs. Blaylock?") suggests it's not wholly unfamiliar territory for her. Tom's distrust upon learning she spent a whole afternoon with the glamorous blonde indicates that Sarah might have a history of cheating on him with women. The film is also unclear as to what extent Sarah is in control of her actions. This is a common ambiguity in vampire films with sexual overtones. When vampires are portrayed as having hypnotic powers, to what degree they are using Benshoff's "exploitative seduction," and to what degree they are just that sexy, is frequently left up to the audience. If we read Sarah's queerness as being innate and uncoerced (my preferred interpretation), then Sarah is merely a non-heterosexual woman conflicted about her dalliance with Miriam. We can read a homophobic element into that version of the story—the male fear of losing a woman to a lesbian—but Benshoff's monster queer seducer trope is moot. In this case, the queer lust does not add an extra element of terror to the vampire scenario as Creed seems to suggest by writing, "It is the sexual desires of the lesbian vampire that render her the most abject of all vampire monsters."[3]

While Tom's offscreen death isn't a pure example of the threesome murder, it clearly marks a transition. Sarah, Miriam and the viewer all know there is no going back. But we also know the moment was inevitable, and it was telegraphed when Tom lost Sarah's attention to the wet bodies of bathing beauties, slipping in and out of the pool.

Another poolside lesbian vampire seduction can be found in *The Velvet Vampire* (1971), directed by Stephanie Rothman. A married couple, Susan and Lee, meet a mysterious woman named Diane at a Los Angeles art gallery. Diane invites them to spend a few days at her house in the desert. Their car breaks down on the way, but

Diane comes to their aid in a dune buggy and has their car towed to a service station. When they arrive at Diane's house—a sumptuous mansion, with no sign of human habitation for miles around—she begins to flirt aggressively with Lee. Susan knows Lee is going to sleep with Diane, and seems peevish but wearily resigned. On the first night, with the help of her manservant Juan, Diane attacks the auto mechanic and drinks his blood, revealing herself to be a vampire. The next day, Susan is bitten on the leg by a rattlesnake, but Diane springs into action, cutting the wound open and sucking out the venom. Each night, Susan and Lee share the same dream: They are making love in a bed in the middle of the desert, and Diane arrives to pull Lee away. The night after the snakebite, Susan wakes up alone, wanders into the living room, and sees Diane and Lee having sex. The next day, chiding Susan for being upset about his cheating, Lee playfully picks her up and throws her in the swimming pool. After this, Diane seems to turn her attention to Susan. The shared dream changes: Now Diane is romancing Susan while Lee runs toward them but can't seem to reach them. Diane flirts with Susan while she is sunning herself by the pool, delivering a speech about female pleasure. Susan refuses to leave, even after Lee reveals that Diane has trapped them. Angered, Lee goes in search of Diane and finds her in a bedroom, where she seduces him again. But instead of making love, she bites his neck and kills him. Exploring the house, Susan finds a secret room from which Diane has watched them in their guest bedroom through a two-way mirror. Upon finding Lee's body, she flees, but Diane pursues her back to the city. In a street market, Susan realizes that Diane is afraid of the Christian cross symbol, so she enlists a mob of people to wield crosses and subdue her. When Susan tears off Diane's cape and exposes her to the sun, Diane rapidly ages and dies.[4]

In *The Velvet Vampire*, we again encounter the intertwining of queerness, monstrosity and outsider status. Diane lives apart from civilization, deep in the unforgiving desert. Susan and Lee are established as members of the early 1970s counterculture, attending an alternative art gallery and having, at least in Lee's case, a carefree attitude toward sex with multiple partners. But Lee holds himself and his wife to different standards: While he acts entitled to bed Diane, he is angered by the prospect of Susan doing the same. Susan spends the second half of the film needling him on this point, exposing his fragility. The morning after Lee and Diane have sex, Susan's sarcastic attitude prompts him to admit to the infidelity. Susan claims she is not upset, saying, "Why should I put you down for something I could do myself?" When they awaken from a shared dream of Diane romancing Susan, Susan says pointedly, "This one was *my* dream."

Diane fills the role of Benshoff's elder queer monster seducer, but like *Les Diaboliques*' Nicole, what makes her evil is not her queerness, but rather the way she mirrors Lee's masculine possessiveness. While the scene where Diane rescues Susan from the snakebite is sexually charged, showing Diane applying her mouth to Susan's inner thigh, it's not the rejection of patriarchy that a surface reading may suggest. Diane does not cast away the phallic snake and perform an intimate act of rescue in gender solidarity. Really, Diane is just getting rid of the competition. She is the gender-swapped tempter in the garden, the one with the deadly fangs, and she vanquishes her competitor for Susan just as she does later when Lee tries to take her away.

Diane's possessiveness extends to her feeling of entitlement to the land and to the indigenous figure of her manservant Juan, the only character who is not sexualized. Although he lives with Diane, their relationship to all appearances is chaste. Perhaps Diane saves her seduction for people she wants to victimize. Or, more likely, Diane considers Juan somewhat less than a person because he is an indigenous American. Juan's family, the ancestral stewards of the land, "died on the reservation," according to Diane. There are several coded dehumanizing references to Juan in the dialogue, including Susan calling him a "watchdog" and Lee saying, "I don't get the feeling that Juan is someone to trust." Diane blames Juan's death on "his own tribe," saying, "They can be very brutal. Juan became an outcast when he left them to live here." In fact, it is Juan who sacrifices himself to Diane for the sake of her nourishment. This relationship, a microcosm of the colonial exploitation of Native Americans by Europeans, drives home Diane's avaricious essence. As in *Poltergeist*, the unnatural spectacle of Diane's artificial oasis, the swimming pool in the deep desert, is built atop bones.

The Velvet Vampire is a rich text that resists easy reading as either an empowered queer feminist film, or one of Benshoff's monster queer scare vehicles. One thing is clear: the fragility of modern heteromonogamy in the face of older forces. But in sidelining Juan, the film complicates the in-group/out-group dynamics that culminate in the cross-wielding mob subduing the vampiric transgressor in an extravagant reassertion of the symbolic order. Everyone is othered in some way, but which is the "abject other" seems to be in constant flux.

Speaking of dominance, this is the second time (after *In My Skin*) we have encountered a man throwing a woman in the pool. Though seemingly playful, the act of getting a woman wet without her consent has an edge of sexual aggression. Tellingly, before tossing her in, Lee asks Susan, "Do you want to see what Diane showed me last night?" Lee may think he is asserting his control over Susan, but Diane has been in charge the whole time, even if he doesn't realize it. When he tosses her in the pool, he may as well be tossing her into Diane's bed.

During Diane's poolside come-on to Susan, she asks, "Have you ever noticed how men envy us? The pleasure … that only we can have?" The pool is now fully a place of feminine power, and Diane is inviting Susan to embrace it. "In their secret hearts they hate us for it," she says, invoking Lee's discomfort with the prospect of Susan making love to Diane. Susan takes pleasure in watching Lee squirm as she turns the tables on his casual philandering. During their poolside confrontation, when Susan tells Lee that she wants to stay at Diane's, he replies, "I think you want *her*." Susan fires back: "Maybe I do. How does it feel?" In classic fragile male fashion, Lee responds with a gendered slur: "Where is that bitch?"

Andreas (Johan Sömnes, right) is the lone survivor of Eli's rampage at the end of *Let the Right One In* (2008).

Like *The Hunger*'s Tom, Lee plays the role of the hetero love interest in the queer horror film. This character type is defined by stiff principles but ultimate frailty. Even when the character succeeds in restoring heteronormativity, like Lisa in *Freddy's Revenge*, it's often a symbolic failure. But Lee doesn't even get the cold comfort of a pyrrhic victory. He stands as little chance of getting his woman back from the vampire as Tom does, and they're both at the pool when that fact becomes clear.

We'll round out our survey of queer poolside vampires with 2008's *Let the Right One In* and its 2010 remake. The original film, directed by Tomas Alfredson, is set in the early 1980s and tells the story of an ostracized 12-year-old named Oskar. The friendless boy lives in a suburban apartment complex with a single mom. He is bullied daily by a group of classmates and though he seems resigned to it, he harbors revenge fantasies. Around the same time that a series of nearby murders sets the community on edge, two new arrivals move into the apartment next door to Oskar: a 12-year-old girl named Eli and an older man, Håkan, who everyone assumes is her father. Oskar and Eli meet on the playground and though she is reluctant at first—flatly declaring that they cannot be friends—a bond develops. The viewer learns before Oskar does that Eli is a vampire, much older than she appears, and that Håkan is her human assistant. He is responsible for obtaining blood for Eli, but he manages to botch the job twice, forcing Eli to do the killing herself. She attacks and feeds on a neighborhood man. Håkan's second failed attempt to harvest blood ends with him disfiguring his face so he cannot be traced back to Eli. Eli visits him in the hospital and kills him.

Eli has seen Oskar being bullied and knows about his revenge fantasies. She encourages him to hit back, "harder than you dare." Oskar takes this advice and strikes the lead bully with a pole, injuring his ear. Eventually Oskar pieces together that Eli is a vampire. She confirms it, but insists that she and Oskar are kindred spirits. The difference is that Eli *needs* to kill, but Oskar only *wants* to kill. She again encourages him to respond in kind to his violent bullies. The next day, the bullies assault Oskar in the swimming pool, seeking vengeance for the ear injury. One of the boys declares his intention to either drown Oskar or stab him. While he holds Oskar's head underwater, Eli appears and dismembers the bullies. The film concludes with Oskar riding on a train with Eli, who is hidden from the sunlight in a box.[5]

Let the Right One In's queer themes are less overt than the last two films, but they are more than subtext. Oskar's parents are separated, and his father is implied to be in a relationship with a man. At home with his mother, Oskar is moody and withdrawn, but brightens when he goes to stay with his dad. His mother lives in a dreary apartment block, his father in a cozy cabin, and the scenes at the cabin are the only ones where Oskar can be said to be cheerful. Since he's so much happier with his gay father, Oskar might be predisposed to a positive view of queerness; at the very least, he has a normalized queer role model. Oskar himself is a social outcast, which aids his easy acceptance of the mysterious, nocturnal Eli.

Partway through the film, Oskar asks Eli if she wants to "go steady," to which she responds, "I'm not a girl." The wording is ambiguous, leaving Oskar and the viewer uncertain as to whether she means she is not a child, not female, not human, or some combination of the three. Even without clarity on this point, Oskar's response is blasé. He simply asks her again if she wants to go steady. Despite not knowing exactly who or what Eli is, Oskar is willing to accept her as a fellow outsider. Oskar later peeks at Eli while she is changing and gets a brief glimpse of her genital area. It appears to be scarred and perhaps stitched. The film lets the viewer draw their own conclusions about what, if anything, this signifies. (The source novel is much clearer on this point.) If Eli was born with male genitals and castrated—a prospect that would thrill Barbara Creed—then she might fit the bill as the older queer figure who initiates the protagonist into her ways. But this initiation never feels coercive or exploitative. To the contrary, Eli's influence on Oskar, helping him build his confidence to stand up to the bullies, seems to be a positive one. But like *Halloween Ends*' Corey, what starts as a confidence booster becomes, perhaps, a gateway into a life of murder.

As in *Thelma*, another queer Scandinavian horror film, the ending is ambiguous: Are Oskar and Eli escaping together to a better life, or has Oskar become the new Håkan, doomed to a life of human aging while doing the bidding of a perpetual 12-year-old? The character of Håkan, like Juan in *The Velvet Vampire*, is a human servant who lives with the vampire but does not seem to be an intimate partner. Oskar's innocent answers to Eli's questions about what exactly "going steady" would mean indicate that sex is, at this point, not on his mind. Does Eli change her mind about leaving without Oskar because she cares about him, or because she wants to use him? The swimming pool climax does not provide answers, but it does offer ample room for a trans reading. As noted above, for trans people the pool can be a site of both anxiety and redemption—of feeling vulnerable, or of feeling free to be oneself. Oskar is at the pool because he has joined his gym teacher's after-school fitness program, apparently to get stronger in order to face his bullies. But it's also the place where the bullies corner and nearly kill or maim him. If we remember that drowning is a means of vulvic death, then in the bullies' world of masculine aggression, by holding Oskar's head underwater they are feminizing him—putting him in his place.

Crucially, the viewer barely sees Eli during the pool sequence. The camera remains underwater, focused on Oskar's face, as the commotion happens above. We see a boy dragged across the surface, and then body parts begin to fall into the pool. The camera does not leave the water until Oskar does. The only glimpses we get of Eli are her arm lifting Oskar out of the water and two extreme closeups of her eyes. In the first she appears to give an intense stare; in the second she appears to smile, but in neither shot do we see enough of her face to get a reliable read on her expression. Eli delivers Oskar from the water in a symbolic rebirth, but what is he being reborn into? A future free from social exclusion with his new companion, or a lifetime of servitude in payment of this blood debt? The viewer does not know because Oskar does not know. This is a complex example of the threesome kill because, while Eli is there to literally hold his hand, Oskar does not do the killing. In yet another reprise of the *Cat People* scenario, we have a powerful, dangerous female figure elevated above a vulnerable figure in the pool. Oskar's passive role next to Eli's active one further queers traditional gender coding, as the swimming pool waters once again facilitate a renegotiation of identity.

The 2010 remake, titled *Let Me In*, relocates the setting from Sweden to Los Alamos, New Mexico. Eli is now named Abby, Oskar is now Owen, and Håkan is now Thomas, but the plot is broadly the same. However, *Let Me In* sacrifices much of *Let the Right One In*'s ambiguity, and many of the queer themes are missing. The subplot with Oskar's probably gay father is gone; all we get of Owen's father is a voice on the phone. There is no shot of Abby's genitals, and her deep masculine voice when in vampire form is the only suggestion that she may not have been assigned female at birth. The "going steady" scene's dialogue plays out differently. When Abby says, "I'm not a girl," Owen asks, "What are you?" and she replies, "I'm nothing." Owen thinks she is making a nonsensical excuse for not wanting to be his girlfriend, foreclosing on the possibility that he might not care about her sex.[6]

Owen stops short of Oskar's innocent willingness to accept Abby for whoever or whatever she is. This may weaken a queer reading of the character, but other things in the remake strengthen one. The nature of Owen's bullying is more overtly gendered and sexualized. In *Let the Right One In*, the bullies' favorite taunt is to call Oskar a piggy; in *Let Me In*, they call Owen a girl. The painful swimming pool experiences of those with gender dysphoria are evoked in an early locker room scene after gym class in the pool, when the lead bully Kenny says, "That's why he won't go swimming. He doesn't want everyone to see what a little fucking girl he is." Kenny then gives Owen a violent wedgie, similar to the ones I got from the bully at the YMCA

Chapter 9. Night Swimming Prohibited

In the 2010 remake of *Let Me In*, the swimming pool torment Owen (Kodi Smit-McPhee) receives from bullies is darker and more sexually charged than in the original.

day camp the summer between fourth and fifth grade. The nonconsensual wedgie is a veiled form of sexual assault. Since it's usually children who do it to other children, the implications are probably invisible to both assailant and victim—at least consciously—but the act of grabbing someone's underwear and forcing it between their buttocks is clearly an intimate violation. Likewise, the specter of sexual assault is present in all of Owen's bullying encounters. When Owen confronts the boys with a metal pole, Kenny threatens to "grab that stick and ram it right up your ass."

The final poolside confrontation is more chaotic and violent than in the original. Instead of merely cornering Owen in the pool, the bullies chase him into the locker room, drag him back to the pool and hurl him in. The frantic camera emphasizes Owen's near-nudity and his vulnerability to their physical overpowering. Whether the bullies' interest in Owen is truly sexual or whether they just equate feminizing him with domination, the outcome is the same. But their cruelty is no match for the monstrous-feminine Abby: the girl who cannot be dominated, who challenges gendered assumptions, if not gender itself.

Let Me In also offers a less ambiguous ending. Owen sees a photograph of Abby and a young Thomas, confirming that they were indeed children together. Thomas grew up while Abby didn't, and at some point he changed from her companion to her servant. This added detail encourages the interpretation that Owen is destined to be the next Thomas. Oskar may be heading for a brighter future, but Owen, it seems, is just trading one trap for another.

Not all queer swimming pool horror centers women, but the pool's female coding makes it uniquely suited to themes of non-normative female desire. Even when the pool is portrayed as a feminine space, though, it is not always an empowering one. Women may be looking at other women at the pool, but men are looking too, and thanks to cishet hegemony, they face far fewer barriers to acting on their desires. In the next chapter, we'll see the consequences of this privilege on the women they target.

CHAPTER 10

Skinny Dipping
Misogyny in Slashers and Gialli

> If teardrops could be bottled, there'd be swimming pools filled by models, told "a tight dress is what makes you a whore."
> —Billie Eilish, "idontwannabeyouanymore"

We've already seen our share of male horror villains motivated by entitlement and possessiveness, especially here in Part II: *Colossal*, *The Velvet Vampire*, *Les Diaboliques* and the rape-revenge films all feature men who believe it's their right to dominate the women in their lives. While no horror subgenre is a stranger to this dynamic, it's particularly common in the slasher and its spiritual predecessor, the giallo. Broadly speaking, both subgenres are known for misogynist messaging, but on the level of individual films they are just as likely to subvert those tropes as reinforce them. We'll now take a closer look at the two subgenres and how they approach the theme of male possessiveness. In doing so, we return to the pool as a site of the lustful gaze, particularly that of men directed at women. We'll meet the bathing beauties of the giallo and slasher canons, and try to reconcile their roles as subjects and objects.

The giallo wave, which crested in the 1970s, comprises a group of violent European murder mysteries that originated in Italy. The form was inspired by American film noir and the pulp crime stories of British novelist Edgar Wallace. Scholar Michael Mackenzie, in his thesis *Gender, Genre and Sociocultural Change in the Giallo: 1970–1975*, divides the films into what he terms "M-gialli" and "F-gialli," for films with male and female lead characters respectively, as well as a third category for mixed-gender ensembles.

Mackenzie argues that male protagonists in these films are generally active, and that "central women" (he avoids the term protagonist) are generally passive: "While the M-gialli present their male protagonists with an external problem to be solved in the shape of the murder investigation (which they may or may not accomplish successfully), in the F-giallo the central woman *is* the problem." That problem often takes the form of women who are challenging gender roles: Mackenzie writes of "the recurring depiction of women forsaking their conventional role as housewives and the resulting horrors that befall them." He later points out the double standard inherent in this presentation: "Whereas male individuality and autonomy

Chapter 10. Skinny Dipping 123

She looks familiar somehow: Lillian (Carroll Baker) makes an uninvited late-night visit to Arthur's (Michael Craig) pool in *The Fourth Victim* **(1971).**

are celebrated, female self-determination is demonised..., requiring male intervention to reassert the patriarchal *status quo* and save the central woman from her own vices."[1] It is not my intention to upend a survey of a whole subgenre with just two examples, but the gialli to follow represent more complicated gender dynamics than Mackenzie seems to acknowledge.

Eugenio Martín's *The Fourth Victim* (1971) opens with a woman dead in a swimming pool. Gladys was the third wife of rich businessman Arthur Anderson; when the police discover that Arthur's first two wives also died questionable deaths, and that Arthur made a fortune from the life insurance, there is an inquiry. Arthur is acquitted thanks to his maid, who testifies that she saw the late Mrs. Anderson attempt suicide on the day of her death. This does not allay police superintendent Dunphy's suspicions, and he begins to keep private tabs on Arthur. One night shortly thereafter, Arthur investigates a splashing sound outside and finds a beautiful woman helping herself to a swim in the pool where his wife died. She introduces herself as Julie Spencer, a neighbor. Despite his suspicions that she is a spy from the police or the press, Arthur and Julie begin a romance and soon she is the fourth Mrs. Anderson. By the end, we learn that Arthur was right to have misgivings: The woman who claims to be Julie Spencer is actually Lillian, sister of Gladys. Convinced that he murdered Gladys, she has set about to entrap Arthur into making an attempt on *her* life. The real Julie Spencer, who indeed lived at the neighboring estate, is a former psychiatric patient who murdered her philandering husband Frank. In the midst of the deception, Lillian finds herself falling in love with Arthur for real, no longer believing he killed her sister, and wants to end the ruse. Unfortunately, the real Julie is back and seems to be projecting her old personality onto Lillian, treating her as the Julie Spencer she claims to be and seeking vengeance for her husband's death. Julie takes Lillian on a boat into the lake and attempts to drown her like she did her husband, but she ends up drowning herself by accident.[2]

There are three drowning deaths (almost four) in *The Fourth Victim*. Returning to our understanding of drowning as an example—perhaps the preeminent example—of vulvic death, it makes sense that the killer is a woman. Indeed, gialli stand out from other forms of horror whodunit for their propensity to feature female murderers.[3] Most films in the genre give us ample room to read them as misogynist, and *The Fourth Victim* is no exception. Dunphy has a stereotypically shrill wife who is only interested in shopping. With annoyance, he tells her that Arthur is "the one and only man I admire," because he got rid of three wives and got rich doing it. The film's murderous figure turns out to be a woman, and a "madwoman" at that. Lillian, for her part, spends most of the movie being portrayed as nebulously untrustworthy, and indeed turns out to be a deceiver, but not in the way we're led to suppose. The film ends with a suggestion that Felicity the maid, who we know perjured herself at the trial, may have had something to do with the deaths of the previous Mrs. Andersons. *The Fourth Victim* has no shortage of unpalatable, sinful women, and it's easy to conclude that in the film's lens, they constitute a problem for our hero—this is an "M-giallo," after all.

But the character of Lillian poses a major challenge to this reading. She is motivated by a sense of justice, seeking to avenge her sister whose memory she feels the law has failed—but once she concludes that Arthur is not guilty, she wants to do right by him. She is clever enough to deceive both Arthur and Dunphy for most of the movie. At the climax, no man comes to her rescue; she survives by her own physical strength, gripping the side of the boat tightly enough to keep from being dragged under by the combined weight of a heavy anchor and Julie's body. If we look past her morally ambiguous femme fatale coding, in Lillian we find a virtuous, empowered female figure.

Julie's morality is more complex. She is a murderer, no doubt about it. But unlike many other giallo killers, she did not "off" her husband Frank for his money, or to cover up another crime, or for mere sadistic pleasure. She killed him because he humiliated and took advantage of her. He kept a veritable harem, and openly ridiculed her in front of them. (His flagrant infidelity reminds us of another drowned husband, Michel of *Les Diaboliques*.) The film implies that Frank's extravagant philandering drove Julie to madness. The psychic damage was so great that even after her stay in the institution, her identity splits in two, Julie the devoted wife and Julie the murderer. She conveniently projects the latter onto Lillian, who is pretending to be her. If we can't excuse her actions, we can at least have some compassion for a character who is so clearly ill.

Sex and death are intertwined in *The Fourth Victim*'s portrayal of the swimming pool. The film's opening moments show a glamorous blonde, in a white one-piece swimsuit and sunglasses, seemingly asleep on a pool raft as dreamy music plays. In closeup, the camera observes her tanned skin in the sunlight—not necessarily a leering gaze, but certainly an appreciative one. As the music grows a bit creepier, we see the woman's lit cigarette begin to melt the inflatable raft and she sinks into the water.

A moment later she is face down in the pool, dead, the raft a deflated piece of flotsam. The viewer's gaze is thus shifted from an erotic one to a morbid one in a way that will be replicated thematically throughout the film. The night he meets Lillian, Arthur is privately mourning Gladys by looking at slide projections of her swimming photographs. Upon hearing a splash, he goes outside to find Lillian, in an identical swim cap to Gladys' in the photos and a white swimsuit similar to the one Gladys died in. As he first glimpses her through the obscuring surface of the water, she may well be his wife back from the grave for a midnight swim. This is the first of the film's many identity slippages—Gladys to Lillian, Lillian to Julie, Julie back to Lillian—in a way reminiscent of *Taste of Fear* from Part I. We see a *Thelma*-like movement from the artificial confines of the swimming pool, where the mystery begins, to the natural lake, where it ends. The throughline that connects these bodies of water is the concept of feminine power—the power both to allure and to kill. Many things can be said about the women of *The Fourth Victim*, but they are definitely not passive. The way the movie's three blonde women's identities bleed into each other reveals the influence of Alfred Hitchcock films like *Vertigo* on the giallo genre.

Another Hitchcock riff, this time from *Psycho*, appears in the gender-bending reveal of the 1969 giallo *Naked You Die*, directed by Antonio Margheriti. The film opens with a nod to *Les Diaboliques* as a woman is drowned in a bathtub by an unseen assailant and the body is placed in a trunk to be transported by truck to the film's main location, a countryside boarding school for girls. The truck also carries a new teacher named Mrs. Clay, as well as a few other staff members. The school is nearly empty because of a holiday; we meet the remaining pupils in an early scene as they relax by the swimming pool. The students include Jill, an aspiring detective, and Lucille, who is secretly sleeping with Richard, one of the teachers. Lucille is about to turn 18, at which point she will inherit a fortune from her wealthy family. Her cousin Pierre is currently in charge of the trust, but she has been unable to

In *Naked You Die* (1968), Detective Gabon (Franco de Rosa) and his police colleagues help Lucille (Eleonora Brown) out of the pool after her narrow brush with death, while Inspector Durand (Michael Rennie) attends to Jill (Sally Smith).

reach him in advance of her birthday. A few students are murdered and the police arrive in short order. When Jill's offer to help with the investigation is rebuffed by Inspector Durand, she starts investigating in secret. As part of her plan, she strategically hides a walkie-talkie so that she can surreptitiously listen to police conversations. When another girl is murdered, this time in the shower Lucille had recently vacated, Lucille becomes convinced that the killer is targeting her. She tells Richard she wants to leave with him, and they make arrangements to meet at the pool. When the hour comes, Lucille is summoned to be interviewed by the police, so she sends another girl, Denise, to the rendezvous in her place. The killer attacks Denise and tries to drown her in the pool, but is stopped by Jill, who has followed her there. After a few more twists and turns, we learn that the person claiming to be Mrs. Clay is actually Lucille's cousin Pierre, who wants to murder her before she turns 18 and get the inheritance money. The real Mrs. Clay was the person we saw murdered in the prologue; Pierre brought the body to the school intending to leave it for the police to find and frame her for murder-suicide. Luckily, Inspector Durand shows up at the last moment, summoned through Jill's walkie-talkie, and fatally shoots Pierre.[4]

A closer look at the film's modes of violence—four stranglings, one drowning and one attempted drowning—reveals the killings' gender-coding. The only murder accomplished by blade is that of the killer's sole male victim: the gardener who is killed with one of his own sickles after he sees Cynthia's shower murder. Even the sickle, with its curved shape and inside edge, may be read as less phallic than most bladed weapons. All of the other vulvic attacks are performed on women, while Pierre is in the guise of Mrs. Clay. Only after being unmasked does he take out the more phallic knife and gun combo. Additionally, most of the attacks happen near water: the bathtub, the shower, the pool. Even Mrs. Clay's staged suicide involves her body being dumped in a lime pool, another wet space.

With respect to Michael Mackenzie, it's hard to claim that "female self-determination is demonised" in *Naked You Die*. Jill's efforts to step outside her prescribed role, to actively investigate the crimes even after being discouraged by the police, are rewarded rather than punished. Even if this is somewhat undercut by the ending that makes it clear she wants to be a cop's wife more than she wants to be a cop, she does save the day repeatedly with her quick thinking and concealed walkie-talkie. Even Lucille has more agency than the usual damsel in distress. Though most of her efforts involve trying to flee, at least she's not sitting around waiting to be a victim.

Once again, the boarding school pool is a site of shifting identities, and the pool itself is equally protean in its function. When we first see the pool, the film invites us to gawk at the young women lounging around it. Once night falls, the pool becomes a place of escape, a staging area for a nocturnal journey away from danger. When the killer appears, it turns into a site of violence. There are multiple cases of mistaken identity: Denise is almost drowned in the pool because the killer thinks she is Lucille; the same is true for Cynthia's murder in the shower. Like Julie-Lillian in *The Fourth Victim*, or Penny-Maggie in *Taste of Fear*, these women's identities are as variable as the ever-moving waters of the pool.

Mrs. Clay too is not the person, nor even the gender, she claims to be. As noted above, the twist is a nod to *Psycho*, and like that film, it can be read as transphobic. Certainly it is problematic to portray as inherently shocking someone whose sex does not match their gender presentation. But the nature of Pierre's plan is even more troubling. There is nothing gendered about his motive: He wants to kill Lucille so he can keep spending her trust money. But the way he goes about it—impersonating a woman, murdering multiple women using symbolically gendered means of murder, seeking to frame a woman for the crimes—is so convoluted and specific as to point to a deep misogyny that goes beyond mere greed. The misogyny, though, is clearly Pierre's and not the film's. Pierre seems to anticipate that framing a woman for the crimes will be easy because a patriarchal culture will not ask many questions, and the film's lens is critical of this point. After all, it's only through the intervention of a smart woman that Pierre's plan, rather than Lucille, ends up dead in the water.

Though lots of high-profile slasher movies feature female murderers, slasher killers on balance are less likely to be women than giallo killers. The stereotype is sometimes overstated, but it is true that more often than not (as with real-life serial killers),[5] slasher antagonists are men and their victims are women. In the last few chapters, we saw how murder in the queer horror film often represents rebellion against the status quo. In the average slasher, that equation is reversed: The murderer *is* the status quo, symbolic of the patriarchal world's violence toward women in ways both large and small. A representative example is Joseph Zito's *The Prowler* (1980). In a prologue set during World War II, a young woman named Rosemary breaks up with her deployed soldier boyfriend by mail. The next summer, she and her new boyfriend are murdered after their college graduation party; the killer leaves a rose as his calling card. Forty-five years later, the community is preparing to hold the first graduation ball since the 1940s killings, spearheaded by main character Pam. Sheriff Fraser is leaving town for the weekend, but his deputy Mark is staying behind to keep the peace. Mark, who shares a mutual attraction with Pam, is intercepted at the party by Pam's friend Lisa. They dance, which infuriates Pam. After Pam is chased by a prowler, she and Mark warn the partygoers, but Lisa has already gone to a nearby pool, telling a drunk boy named Paul that he can join her when he finishes throwing up. Lisa swims alone in the pool before being attacked by the prowler, who slits her throat in the water. At the end of the film, the killer is revealed to be Sheriff Fraser, the young man who was dumped by Dear John letter back in the '40s. The revival of the graduation dance triggered his memories of his shattered romantic hopes, and he decides that since he could not have love, no one else should either.[6]

Lisa, for the "crime" of flirting with multiple men and being sexy in public, becomes a target for Fraser's rage. This rage is rooted in an old-fashioned disregard for women's agency in their romantic lives. Lisa, in a bikini at the pool, fits the

For the crime of embracing her sexuality, Lisa (Cindy Weintraub) gets a different kind of embrace from *The Prowler* **(1981).**

profile of a sexually free woman who threatens the order of patriarchal control. Similar motives for romantically frustrated killers can also be seen in the early slashers *He Knows You're Alone* (1980) and *My Bloody Valentine* (1981), as well as a watershed series that confronts the dynamic head-on and in explicitly feminist terms.

In the classic slasher canon, the *Slumber Party Massacre* franchise is a rarity: Each entry is written and directed by women, and the films are known for feminist takes on genre tropes. In the first film, Amy Holden Jones' *The Slumber Party Massacre* (1982), high schooler Trish invites her friends Kim, Jackie, Diane and Linda to a slumber party while her parents are out of town. A recently escaped murderer, Russ Thorn, stalks them at school, first killing a telephone repairwoman and then attacking Linda with a large power drill. Unaware of Linda's disappearance, the other four girls party at Trish's house while Valerie, a neighbor, babysits her younger sister Courtney across the street. Two boys, Neil and Jeff, show up to spy on the girls through the window and end up being invited in after they sabotage the fuse box. When Russ makes his presence known by killing the pizza deliveryman, the teens try to get help but Jeff and Neil are quickly killed, followed by Jackie, Kim and the girls' gym coach, who has come to investigate. Wielding a machete she found in the garage, Valerie chases Russ out of the house to the pool. She cuts off the tip of his drill bit (it lands in the water), then severs his hand and slashes his abdomen. He falls into the pool, apparently dead, as Valerie and Courtney embrace. After Russ emerges from the pool and attacks Valerie, Trish comes out of the house with a kitchen knife, and the three girls work together to defeat Russ, impaling him on the machete.[7]

Every *Slumber Party Massacre* film is haunted by the threat of male intrusion into female spaces. This plays out on a variety of scales, from the prying eyes and

Russ Thorn (Michael Villella), perpetrator of *The Slumber Party Massacre* (1982), wields his drill in the climactic poolside confrontation.

party-crashing of Neil and Jeff to the driller killer invading the girls' locker room; from the drill bit penetrating locked doors to the killer's weapons entering women's bodies themselves. The film aligns these violations not to equate them, but to show that they exist on the same spectrum. Mary, the telephone repairwoman, is first seen from behind and below through the eyes of the leering Neil and Jeff. Being an object of their gaze marks her symbolically as a target, and she is murdered immediately after the encounter. John Kenneth Muir writes that this scene "points out that field of vision—what characters perceive and don't perceive—is an important part of the slasher format."[8] In this case, once the boys have shifted their gaze away from Mary, she literally ceases to exist. They walk away, unaware of the encounter's violent outcome. Out of sight, out of life. Neil and Jeff later watch through a window as the slumber party girls change clothes, in a scene that is repeated in each of the film's sequels. The window, the titillating scene beyond, and the boys who feel entitled to stare are just as significant to the *Slumber Party Massacre* ethos as the extravagantly phallic drill which has become emblematic of the franchise. The drill is less interesting for how it mimics a penis than for how it mimics the penetrating male gaze. The sexually frustrated killer expresses his desire in visual terms: "You're pretty," he tells the gym coach. "All of you were very pretty." Like the peeping boys who never considered the implications of their nonconsensual gaze, he follows this line with the timeless mantra of the entitled rapist: "You know you want it."

To this end, the film leverages the pool's social function as a place where young women's bodies are on display. When she corners Russ poolside, Valerie is taking the battle to its most symbolic terrain. If the drill represents the killer's gaze as much as it represents a phallus, then by cutting off its tip, Valerie is rejecting being treated as something to look at. Beyond just castrating the killer in classic Carol Clover style,[9] she is also emasculating his eyes. When the drill bit lands in the water, and Russ himself follows it moments later, the pool's feminine power is reclaimed. The film subverts the Final Girl tradition by featuring three survivors, each of whom played a part in vanquishing the killer. This community of women, united by their victimization at the hands of maleness, mounts a mutual poolside defense against its tyranny.

One of those survivors, Courtney the kid sister, returns as the protagonist of 1987's *Slumber Party Massacre II*, directed by Deborah Brock. Now a high school senior, Courtney plays rhythm guitar in a rock band with her friends Sheila (bass and lead vocals), Amy (lead guitar) and Sally (drums). Sheila's dad has just bought a new condo near a desert golf course, and the band plans to spend the weekend there rehearsing for an upcoming gig. Courtney, who suffers recurring nightmares of the Driller Killer incident, decides to take advantage of a weekend without parents and invite her new sweetheart Matt to the retreat. They arrive at the new development, parts of which are still under construction, to find most of the neighboring houses uninhabited. On the night they arrive, the girls drink champagne, which results in a giggling dance party. Two of them end up topless in a shower of feathers from a torn pillow.

Sheila's boyfriend T.J. and his friend Jeff, who have also been invited, show up a day early and spy on the girls through the window before sneaking in the back door to startle them. That night, Courtney has another nightmare about the Driller Killer, who is now a 1950s-styled rockabilly greaser. In the morning, T.J. teases her about her hangover and throws her in the pool. In the water, she has another vision of the killer, loses consciousness, and needs to be rescued. After this incident, she begins seeing bizarre things, climaxing in a vision of a pimple on Sally's face ballooning into a facial abscess that explodes, killing her. Since Sally cannot be found, the group calls the police, whose ridicule is validated when Sally returns from an unannounced trip to the store. Matt, who arrived in the middle of the Sally incident, surprises Courtney with a birthday cake and they begin to make love. The killer from Courtney's dreams appears, wielding a spiky electric guitar with a giant drill bit on the end. After a few failed attempts to flee, everybody ends up slaughtered but Courtney, who finally defeats the Driller Killer at a construction site by setting him on fire with a welding torch.[10]

Slumber Party Massacre II doubles down on the theme of male intrusion. In addition to the sex-mad boys who enact a repeat of the original's window peeping scene, we have condescending cops, uncaring neighbors and a new version of the Driller Killer who challenges the girls' validity as rock musicians. Ever since Chuck Berry lifted guitar licks from Sister Rosetta Tharpe (which the Beach Boys would later lift from *him*[11]), it was clear that the power structure would assimilate everything about rock'n'roll that was worth assimilating. Being an all-girl rock band has never been as simple as thumbing your nose at the establishment and jamming out some riffs. This was true even in the 1980s, the decade when the Go-Go's became

Chapter 10. Skinny Dipping 131

In *Slumber Party Massacre II* (1987), T.J. (Joel Hoffman) prepares to throw Courtney (Crystal Bernard) in the pool while her bandmates Amy and Sheila (Kimberly McArthur, in chair at left) and Juliette Cummins) look on disapprovingly.

the first (and so far only) rock band of exclusively female players and songwriters to chart a #1 album—but still had to deal with music industry sexism and skeptical male critics.[12] It's unsurprising, then, that the *Slumber Party Massacre* series' "boys won't let girls have nice things" thesis manifests here as a hyper-masculine rockabilly death-dealer wielding a weaponized electric guitar. His black leather wardrobe and spiky, blood-red guitar contrasts the defiantly feminine presentation of the girl band: pastels, bright-colored instruments and Sally's pink drumsticks. In one of Courtney's visions, the Driller Killer delivers the line, "Rock'n'roll will never die, baby!" declaring his intention to reassert male dominance over the music.

At the same time, the film acknowledges the importance of appearances to performers, particularly female ones. The pimple on Sally's face that erupts into a ghastly abscess in Courtney's imagination literalizes the adolescent fear of acne as a life-ending affliction. Even as the girls try to reclaim rock'n'roll, they cannot escape being objects of the audience's gaze. In Sally's case, a bad zit equates to actual death.

Like in the first film, the murderer is not the only male figure accustomed to getting his way. *Slumber Party Massacre II*'s other representative of male entitlement is T.J., and some of his dialogue could just as easily come from the killer's mouth. T.J. enters the first pool scene by cannonballing into the water with a blowup sex doll left at the house by Sheila's brother. Though its intention may be innocent, deliberately splashing water on someone is on the same spectrum of assault as throwing someone into the pool, which T.J. does moments later. When the women complain about being splashed, T.J. says, "You girls are so uptight." Then, in reference to the previous night's dance party when the girls removed their tops due to sprayed champagne, he says, "It looked to me like they were into it last night." This last line is directed at the blowup doll, a sexually available facsimile of a woman who never says no—or says *anything*, for that matter. Is this sentiment, presuming to tell women what they have permission to consent to, really that different from the Driller Killer's line, repeated from his predecessor Russ, "You know you want it"?

Speaking of consent, as previously mentioned, a man throwing a woman in the pool should be construed as a form of sexual assault, or at the very least an assertion of dominance. T.J.'s behavior is especially egregious, since he takes hold of Courtney with the promise of helping her with her hangover. Given this violation of trust and rough treatment at the hands of a man, it's no surprise that she has another attack while in the pool. The film's ending, where Courtney appears to wake up in a psychiatric institution while the killer's drill emerges from the floor, invites the interpretation that the whole film took place in Courtney's subconscious as a PTSD episode. If so, we can revisit the psychoanalytic point of view that reads the pool as a womb. By being forced into it, Courtney is being born into possible futures that the killer, chasing her through the empty frames of half-built houses, refuses to let her live.

Adolescent girls, the *Slumber Party Massacre* films say, need spaces where they can experiment with being a little silly, a little naughty, a little sexy, without the intrusion of men who might expect them to make good on whatever promise they perceive in that behavior. The series' killers, like the title character in *The Prowler*, are motivated by a sort of blanket misogyny, a refusal to let women self-actualize into anything but objects of desire. We'll now look at two slasher films whose killers, though their impotent angst might be generalizable, focus it on specific individuals, thus embodying less metaphorical versions of male possessiveness.

In the opening moments of Howard Avedis' *Mortuary* (1982), psychiatrist George Parson is bludgeoned by an unseen killer and drowned in the swimming pool at his coastal home. Some time later, a teenager named Greg accompanies his friend Josh to steal tires from Josh's former workplace, a mortuary owned by Hank Andrews. They stumble upon an occult ritual involving Hank and several other townspeople. Josh is killed by a cloaked figure with an embalming instrument. It turns out that Greg's girlfriend is the murdered doctor's daughter Christie. The next night, Christie sleepwalks out to the pool deck, where she is attacked by the hooded figure. Christie's mother Eve says it was probably just a dream. Greg tells Christie that Eve was among the attendees he saw at Hank's black mass.

Hank's eccentric son Paul has been trying awkwardly to flirt with Christie, with little success. After several more odd events and attacks by the killer, Eve tells Christie that Paul was a psychiatric patient of her father's and that he had been obsessed with her. The killer turns out indeed to be Paul, who kidnaps Christie and almost embalms her alive back at the mortuary, only to be interrupted by his father Hank, whom he murders. Paul then takes Christie to the warehouse where he has gathered the corpses of his victims to witness a wedding ceremony between him and Christie. Greg appears and helps Christie defeat Paul.[13]

Chapter 10. Skinny Dipping 133

A bad day at the pool: Dr. Parson (Danny Rogers) catches the business end of the killer's bat in the opening scene of *Mortuary* **(1983).**

Parent-child relationships take center stage in *Mortuary*, and we are back in *A Nightmare on Elm Street* territory where the swimming pool gestures toward the secrets a town's adults are keeping from their children. Eve and Hank are part of a secret occult group that seems to include many of the town's grownups. (This is a theme we'll see a lot in Part III.) But the cult subplot, complete with a seance to contact George's spirit, proves to be a red herring. Paul's murder spree is motivated simply by his infatuation with Christie. Nonetheless, the older generation's secretiveness is significant, since Paul's targets are the parental figures who stand in his way. He begins with Christie's father, who sought to keep them apart. He later kills Christie's mother for telling her about his psychiatric treatment, and he then kills his own father Hank, when he tries to stop Paul's rampage. He murders each of them for not keeping their mouths shut about his mental health struggles; they can keep their own secrets, but cannot seem to keep his. Paul feels entitled to a romance with Christie, and believes it would happen if there weren't so many people "against" him, to use his language. What Christie wants is never something he considers. This disregard for consent is contrasted with the mature portrayal of Greg's romance with Christie. In one scene when they are about to make love, Christie says, "Wait a minute," and Greg obligingly stops. "I haven't said yes yet," she says. Though it is a small, playful moment, it demonstrates *Mortuary*'s awareness of consent issues.

In the final scene, Paul gathers the bodies of all four parents for a makeshift marriage ceremony. The tradition of the bride's father "giving her away" carries connotations of ownership, of the passing of an asset from one man to another. The consent of the woman, again, is secondary. Since Paul could not get George's blessing to marry Christie, he removed the obstacle by killing him. When he drowns George, using his own pool against him, Paul is asserting dominance, symbolically saying that the water-woman belongs to him now. By attacking Christie next to the same pool while she sleepwalks, he is furthering his claim to the territory. If the pool represents the female body, Paul wants to leave no doubt about whom Christie's belongs to.

A variation on the male slasher killer motivated by possessiveness over a woman can be seen in *All the Boys Love Mandy Lane* (2006), directed by Jonathan Levine. High schooler Mandy is the object of desire for several boys in her grade. In a prologue, she and her misfit friend Emmet attend a pool party at the house of a popular boy named Dylan. While standing on the roof of his house overlooking the pool, Emmet talks to Dylan about the latter's infatuation with Mandy. Saying he needs to do something bold to distinguish himself from the other boys who want her, Emmet encourages the drunk Dylan to jump off the roof into the pool. Dylan does so, but misses the water and fatally lands on the concrete deck. Nine months later, Mandy, who seems to have ended her friendship with Emmet, accepts an invitation to a weekend party at a remote ranch belonging to the father of a boy named Red. Once they arrive, the competition is on among several of the boys to be the one to bed Mandy. One by one, the partygoers are murdered by an unseen killer, eventually revealed to be Emmet, who has followed the group to the ranch to get revenge for his bullying and ostracization. Emmet chases Chloe, the last surviving teen, into the arms of Mandy, who stabs her to death, revealing her collusion with Emmet in the massacre. Mandy and Emmet discuss their plan to commit mutual suicide after the murders were finished. But Mandy decides to back out, and kills Emmet after a struggle.[14]

Mandy Lane's character, a deliberately enigmatic figure, is a critique of the male gaze. The viewer is given no insight into her personality, nor any revealing dialogue. None of the boys who lust after her know anything about her as a person, nor do they particularly want to know. Even Emmet, the one character who seems to know her on a deeper level, does not understand her. After collaborating with him on the killing spree, she rejects him when it becomes apparent that, like the other boys, he was motivated by infatuation with her.

Emmet's speech to Dylan on the rooftop, and Dylan's receptiveness to it, reveal the self-centeredness of this superficial point of view. In between high-angle shots looking down at Mandy, Emmet tells Dylan, "She's looking at you right now, waiting to see what you do." The poolside Mandy is merely an object of desire, and as Dylan takes Emmet's speculation about her frame of mind at face value, the viewer is encouraged to do the same. The film asks us to accept Mandy as our protagonist without questioning what she is all about. Dylan's accident underscores the limitations of this perspective. By slasher movie standards, Emmet's motive is a common one: revenge, in addition to the male entitlement we've been dissecting in this chapter. By contrast, Mandy is a blank slate, and the reveal of her villainy catches us off-guard—because, like Dylan at the swimming pool, we jumped into something we did not understand.

Emmet (Michael Welch, right) talks the drunken Dylan (Adam Powell) into leaping before he looks in the prologue of *All the Boys Love Mandy Lane* **(2006).**

Cishet men who feel entitled to a woman's love and go on killing sprees when rejected is, sad to say, not a far-fetched idea. The online incel, or "involuntary celibate" ideology, in which men disparage women for not having sex with them, was linked to the deaths or injuries of 110 people in North America between 2014 and 2023.[15] Sexual frustration has been noted as a motivating factor for roughly one-third of mass shooters in the U.S. since 1966.[16] Of course, this behavior is much older than the creation of the term "incel." As long as women have been able to say no, there have been men who have taken it as a reason to enact violence.

The theme has been common in slasher movies since at least 1980's pool-less *He Knows You're Alone*, about a jilted lover whose ex becomes engaged to another man, so he sets out to murder every bride-to-be he can find.[17] With that in mind, we're finally ready to tackle the last word in swimming pool slasher films: Boris von Sychowski's *The Pool* (2001).

The Pool opens with a young woman named Catherine, who is cooking dinner for her boyfriend while on the phone with her mother. If we're paying attention, we'll hear her make passing reference to an ex whom she dumped because "he gave me the creeps." The new boyfriend never makes it inside; Catherine finds him murdered in his car. The skull-masked killer chases Catherine through the house with a machete, kills her and tosses her body into the swimming pool.

After this prologue, we are introduced to the main plot: The senior class at an elite international high school in Prague has just finished final exams. Gregor, the *de facto* leader of a friend group of wealthy teens from all over the world, has planned a secret graduation afterparty at an indoor water park. Among the attendees are his girlfriend Sarah, Sarah's friend Carmen, another friend of Sarah's named Mike who has just been dumped by his own girlfriend, and Frank, who makes an unsuccessful pass at Sarah. To break into the water park, Gregor enlists the help of Martin, a former classmate with a criminal past. Martin is reluctant but Gregor convinces him with a promise that he can hang out at the party with Mel, one of the friend group whom Martin has a crush on. Once inside, the group begins drinking at the bar and carousing in the facility's multiple pools. One couple goes to a secluded pool to have sex, but the boy gets stabbed and the girl gets sliced open by a machete thrust from beneath into the waterslide; she collides with the blade, legs spread. After discovering the bodies, most of the group members try to leave, but they are locked in. Meanwhile, Martin and Mel are about to have sex, but when he goes to get a condom, the killer chases Mel through the locker room and kills her by shoving his machete through the bathroom stall door. When Martin learns what happened, he suggests trying to crawl to freedom through the building's air ducts. The killer manages to murder Martin and Mike by stabbing them through the ducting from below. Soon, only Gregor, Sarah and Carmen remain. Believing Gregor to be the killer, the girls knock him out and lock him in an upstairs room. Carmen also tells Sarah that she and Gregor have cheated together. Carmen swims to freedom through the water duct, but the killer stabs her at the exit. Back inside, the killer approaches Sarah and reveals himself to be Frank, telling her that he embarked on this murder spree because she and the other girls rejected him. Gregor breaks out of confinement, he and Sarah battle Frank, and Carmen, having survived the attack, appears and shoots Frank. He dies in the swimming pool.[18]

The Pool takes place in an extravagant setting, with its pools, waterfalls, fountains and waterslides. It depicts the adolescent pool party with all its attendant excitement, anxiety and frustration. The illicit party takes place outside the purview of adults, and bacchanalian pleasures abound. Everyone is either getting laid, trying to, or wishing they could. In this wet and wild environment, group dynamics bubble to the surface. Carmen, a sexually free young woman, trades a flash of her breasts for a beer, and later dances seductively with a boy whom she tells, "Look, but don't touch." Mike is not so subtly carrying a torch for Sarah, but seems to have been friend-zoned. Two of the other boys, Diego and Chris, are openly hostile toward each other, but we never learn why. Carmen feels compelled to come clean to Sarah about her infidelity with Gregor. The pools, ever-present in the background even when they're not being utilized, stand in for everyone's desires, secrets and anxieties. Into this soup of teenage drama, Frank sticks his machete and stirs. What Carol Clover called "the killer's phallic purpose"[19] is more intrusive in *The Pool* than any other slasher movie I've seen—and that's saying something. Frank seems obsessed with thrusting his machete through barriers: the underside of a waterslide, a locker room door, bar shelves, air ducts. Every murder is manifestly about this long blade of death and what it does inside the human body.

Frank's character is fragile male sexual frustration embodied. In an early scene when Chris picks Sarah up and tries to throw her in the pool, Frank raises his beer can in a salute as he watches. The gesture displays his approval of male physical domination over women, of not taking no for an answer. Some of Frank's statements in his climactic villain speech are eerily similar to the words of Elliot Rodger, the incel-inspired mass murderer who killed six people and injured 14 in Isla Vista, California, in 2014.[20] Frank: "Women are so cruel. You just take whoever you want, and when you've had enough you spit them out again." Elliot Rodger: "Why do women behave like vicious, stupid, cruel animals who take delight in my suffering and starvation?"[21] The only part of the scenario that rings false is when Sarah incredulously asks, "You did this massacre just because you weren't treated right?" If being a woman in the world hadn't already taught Sarah how unsurprising that motivation really is, maybe she could have learned from slasher movies.

Part III

A Dip in the Labor Pool

The Pool as a Site of Social Segregation

Introduction

> I think that the idea of having a cube of water just for a few people is like having a slave.
> —Lucrecia Martel[1]

> When I wake up, I'm in America where Dorothy Dandridge once emptied a pool with her pinkie.
> —Lauren K. Alleyne, "Variations in Blue"

This may seem comical coming from somebody who has just written 50,000 words about swimming pools and is about to write 50,000 more, but the truth is that pools do not have to be complicated. Fill a hole with water; hop in to have fun, exercise or cool off. Invite the neighborhood. But in reality, swimming pools in the U.S. have been fraught with social tension since at least the early 20th century. Historian Jeff Wiltse's *Contested Waters: A Social History of Swimming Pools in America* charts the pool's shifting significance, from progressive reform efforts to improve the physical and moral hygiene of the poor, to middle-class fitness fads, to civil rights battlegrounds, to symbols of wealth and leisure, and back to reform efforts focused on forestalling crime and civil unrest by keeping the inner cities cool in the summertime.[2]

I promise this is the last time I'll break my no TV rule: "The Bewitchin' Pool" (1964), the final episode of the original *Twilight Zone* series, traffics in the show's common theme of a magical return to an idealized rural American past ("A Stop at Willoughby," "Once Upon a Time," "Of Late I Think of Cliffordville"). In the episode, directed by Joseph M. Newman, a wealthy couple tells their two young children that they plan to divorce. Upset, the kids dive together into the backyard pool, swim to the bottom and—from the parents' perspective—seem to disappear. In fact, they have escaped through a magic portal to the riverside country home of a kindly matriarch, Aunt T., who presides over a community of children who have all been transported from unloving homes.[3] The closing narration sells the episode as a cautionary tale for parents—perhaps against getting divorced, but certainly against treating your kids like nuisances. On one hand, For parents, the idea of your children disappearing before your eyes in a pool is a frightening one (as we learned in *House*, which might have been inspired by "The Bewitchin' Pool" as well as another

Part III—Introduction

Sport (Mary Badham) and Jeb (Jeffrey Byron) get an invitation from the other side courtesy of Whitt (Kim Hector), who emerges from the depths of "The Bewitchin' Pool" (*The Twilight Zone*, 1964).

Twilight Zone episode, "Little Girl Lost"). It plays on fears of pool drowning and child abduction. On the other hand, the episode spends less time on the parents' confusion than it does on the joy and wonder of escape for the children. Despite the narration referring to a "gingerbread house," recalling "Hansel and Gretel"'s witch, the episode portrays Aunt T.'s domain as a place of love and simplicity. In doing so, it suggests an understanding of affluent urban life as cold and loveless, while rural life, though humble, is more authentic and warm. The fact that the kids enter through the pool and exit into a bucolic, Huck Finn–esque river drives home the point through the natural-artificial contrast we looked at in Part I. The opening narration wryly belittles the pool by calling it "a backyard toy for the affluent." We're back to the pool as both portal and border, and we haven't seen the last of the urban-rural dimension of the class divide.

Most of the films we've examined so far have dealt with class in some way, but the remainder of the book will focus on the ways that pools symbolize and reproduce structures of inequality. To do so, we'll have to start paying attention to whether a film's pool is public, private or residential. I've touched on this before, particularly in *Poltergeist* and *Cannibal Man*, but in Part III it becomes key to our analysis. As Christopher Brown and Pam Hirsch write in *The Cinema of the Swimming Pool*, whether a pool is private or public "is a central consideration in virtually every film that features one."[4]

As a kid, I never paid much attention to the distinction. I swam in public pools when we lived in town, the Yacht Club pool when we moved to the 'burbs, and in our backyard pool for the brief time we lived in a rented house. I suspect this is true for many North Americans who, like me, grew up upper middle-class and white. Not so for everybody else.

It's easy to think of the swimming pool as an inherent status symbol, but it was not inevitable that it should become one, nor did it happen by accident. The private pool's reputation as a totem of luxury is a direct result of the social forces that changed it from an uncontroversial public utility to a highly divisive space. Municipal pools in the late 1800s were largely considered hygienic, and were built in poor areas to compensate for substandard public sanitation. The pools were segregated by gender, but they were colorblind. As the 20th century dawned and swimming for fitness became more popular with the middle class, wealthier people began appearing in pools. There was no racial strife.

Between the World Wars, the influence of these more genteel crowds prompted city governments to make the swimming pools co-ed. Not coincidentally, they also started racially segregating them. Mostly this is attributed to white men's nervousness about white women being in states of undress around Black men. By the late 1940s, the struggle to racially integrate public pools was creating both civil unrest and legal victories for groups like the NAACP. Many cities, rather than integrate, decided to simply close their pools, or cut funding and allow them to fall into disrepair. But this move may not have been necessary, because by the mid–1950s, white people with the means to do so had already joined private swim clubs or built backyard residential pools.[5] All of which makes me wonder if the pool club in my neighborhood, which sells $1000 memberships and trumpets having been around since the early 1920s, knows exactly what they're bragging about. Simply put, the private pool as shorthand for "the good life" has everything to do with America's legacy of bigotry and exclusion.

Nor can any of these segregation-era factors be dismissed as relics of the past. In June 2018, a 15-year-old Black boy was invited to a private community pool in Summerville, South Carolina, by a friend who lived in the neighborhood. A white woman, Stephanie Sebby-Strempel, harassed the boy and his friends, telling them they "did not belong" and hitting the teenager in the face.[6] A viral video showed Sebby-Strempel swiping at the camera, calling the kids "little punks," and threatening to call the police, earning her the social media nickname "Pool Patrol Paula." She was charged with assault and resisting arrest for body-slamming and biting the deputies who came to her house after the incident. She ended up with a $1000 fine and no jail time.[7]

With this in mind, the luxurious infinity pool in Deon Taylor's *Traffik*, released that same year, takes on more significance than its minor role in the plot would suggest. As the film opens, investigative journalist Brea is celebrating her birthday. Her boyfriend John, a specialty auto mechanic, takes her for a weekend getaway at a swanky mountain house provided by John's friend Darren. During a gas stop, Brea and John, who are Black, are harassed by a white biker gang. In the gas station rest room, a distraught-looking woman approaches Brea and says something cryptic about the Fourth of July. Later, at the house, Brea and John swim and make love in the scenic patio infinity pool overlooking the valley. Darren and his girlfriend Malia arrive unannounced, spoiling John's plans to propose. The sound of an unfamiliar cell phone ringing from Brea's purse leads them to discover a phone that the woman in the bathroom had secreted into it. Remembering the Fourth of July clue, Brea manages to unlock the phone and finds an array of photos of sex-trafficked women. The woman from the rest room shows up to ask for the phone back, and it's soon revealed that members of the trafficking group, which includes the biker gang, have accompanied her. They kill her for failing to retrieve the phone, then terrorize the group in the house. The two men end up dead, the two women abducted and drugged. At this point we learn that a sheriff's deputy, Sally Marnes, is working with the traffickers, allowing them to operate with impunity. Brea wakes up in a cavern where the trafficked women, including Malia, are being kept. With Malia's help, she turns the tables on her captors and escapes. The tunnel is beneath the gas station, which acts as a way station for the trafficking operation. She makes her presence known and calls her editor in the city on a purloined cell phone. Sally arrives first and handcuffs her. The FBI shows up, arrests Sally, and frees the captive women.[8]

The gas station confrontation between John and the biker begins as a series of microaggressions. While admiring the classic car John is driving, the biker asks him if he is a ballplayer. When John says that he rebuilt the car himself, he asks if he learned those skills in the prison auto shop. The casual stereotyping is the biker's way of racially taunting John without coming right out with it. When John says he doesn't want any trouble, the biker claims that *he* is the one being profiled, saying John assumes he is up to no good based on his appearance. At this point, John has done nothing to offend the biker other than merely exist as an affluent-looking Black man with a nice car and a pretty girlfriend. All of this happens before the gang finds out that Brea has the cell phone. While the gang's subsequent violent actions are taken to protect their illegal business, the gas station harassment scene makes it clear that Brea and John are targets for the crime of thriving while Black.

With this understanding, the Black couple enjoying the opulent mountaintop house can be seen as an act of defiance. The fancy car is a status symbol; so is the pool. With their aquatic lovemaking and poolside lounging as R&B music plays on the stereo, Brea and John's Black bodies are occupying a space that white America spent decades doing its best to keep them out of. This is the America of Migos' "Bad and Boujee" (2016), where Black people exhibiting the trappings of bourgeois material success is an explicitly political act. Simply by using the pool in the first place, John and Brea are defying a stereotype. The widespread belief that Black people can't—or don't—swim comes from several sources: hack comedians, misunderstandings about Black women's hair, and the sad reality of Jim Crow keeping Black folks out of pools, establishing a generational lack of water competency.[9]

Obviously, any movie that deals with modern-day slavery and features racial violence by white people toward Black people is countenancing the U.S.'s legacy of white supremacy, but *Traffik* wants to make sure its point is not missed. By making the password to the slaver's phone 070476, ironically known as Independence Day, the film is acknowledging the centrality of forced Black labor to the country's birth and founding. Furthermore, it reminds us that slavery and Black subjugation have never gone away. The role of state agents in perpetuating them is embodied by Sally, the corrupt deputy. Sally's attempt to absolve herself reifies the status quo: By facilitating sex slavery, she says, she is no worse than anyone else who participates in supply chain economics. "Everything is trafficked," she tells Brea, acknowledging the inherent exploitation of capitalism. "I'm just a part of a system that already exists." It's the same buck-passing logic that has enabled generations of white people to look the other way from systems of oppression that keep, and have kept, Black people in prison, in underserved schools, in substandard housing … and out of swimming pools.

Racial discrimination is not the only thing that has excluded people from pools. Class, employment, geography, housing status, physical ability, neurodivergence, political affiliation, perceived involvement with stereotyped subcultures—pretty much every factor that can contribute to the construction of in-groups and out-groups, including the gender and sexuality concerns we've already discussed, has been wielded as an instrument of poolside segregation. In such spaces of tension—between welcome and unwelcome, between public and private, between spoken and unspoken—we can always expect to see horror cinema thrive.

Chapter 11

Swimming Pools, Movie Stars

Los Angeles and Secret Societies

> I play film star with my child and jump with her fully dressed into the swimming pool, because we've read they do this here.
> —Liv Ullmann, *Changing*

> In the fountains, pink champagne, someone carving their devotion in the heart-shaped pool of fame.
> —Siouxsie and the Banshees, "Kiss Them for Me"

The intersection of the film industry, swimming pools and the occult is almost a synonym for Southern California. Before the Civil Rights–era backyard pool boom in the rest of the country, the residential swimming pool was known as the province of Hollywood elite. Movie star mansions boasted ostentatious pools as far back as the 1920s.[1] Art historian Daniell Cornell writes, "The fact that so many Californians aspired to have their own pools may be attributable to the number of celebrities whose glamorous image was reinforced by poolside photographs at their own homes."[2] After the residential pool became more affordable, the stage was set for Southern California to become the nation's swimming pool capital. In 1961, *The Los Angeles Times* reported that the region had more pools than any other.[3] These days, the southland still flaunts its pool fetish despite California's ever-increasing water shortages. In 2020, Los Angeles County, according to its sustainability office, imported almost 60 percent of its water from thousands of miles away.[4] For the swimming pool, L.A.'s climate is a double-edged sword: warm enough to make pools appealing, dry enough to make them wasteful.

If there's one thing SoCal *doesn't* have a shortage of, it's people living unconventional lifestyles. Since its frontier days, the region has attracted dreamers, believers, outcasts, weirdos, opportunists and swindlers. From the Moneyan Institute to the Manson Family, Jim Jones' People's Temple to the Source Family to the Church of Scientology, a whole host of communes, cults and alternative religions have called Los Angeles home. That's just the ones that operate in the open. And what of the longstanding rumors of occult activity in Hollywood chambers of power? As *The Los Angeles Times* puts it, "No other community on the face of the globe has given rise to half as many mystic, philosophical, psychological, occult, consciousness-raising, therapeutic and alternative creeds as 20th century L.A."[5]

Writing for *The Atlantic* in 1946, Carey McWilliams opined, "Migration is the basic explanation for the growth of cults in Southern California."[6] It's a place where transplants are as common as natives, and many move there seeking a better, or at least *different* life. For migrants chasing entertainment industry stardom, the pool represents the glamor of the dream as well as the danger of the reality, and what it might take to achieve it.

Although it isn't strictly a horror film, when we talk about Hollywood, swimming pools, madness and murder, we have to talk about director Billy Wilder's *Sunset Blvd.* (1950). It follows a down-on-his-luck screenwriter, Joe Gillis, who gets drawn into the warped world of faded silent film star Norma Desmond. What starts as his scam to milk Norma for money by helping her with a screenplay evolves into a co-dependent relationship wherein Joe is basically a kept man. Meanwhile, Norma is trying to engineer a show business comeback, unaware that she is completely forgotten. When Joe has finally had enough and packs his bags to leave, Norma shoots him in the back and he falls dead into the swimming pool.[7]

"The poor dope," narrates Joe, addressing his own dead body, "he always *wanted* a pool." This famous line hinges on the swimming pool's status as totem of success and object of aspiration in the Hollywood mythology. The line continues: "In the end, he got himself a pool. Only the price turned out to be a little high," implying an understanding that this dream's attainment comes at a cost. Even before it cost Joe his life, the pool cost him his honor, his relationship with fellow writer Betty and, depending on how you interpret the sexual nature of his arrangement with Norma, perhaps his dignity. As Joe delivers these lines in narration, the camera is positioned underwater, looking up at his floating body. The visual language of this low-angle shot indicates that we are being shown the scenario from a non-standard, antithetical perspective. Accounting for the reflective nature of the water's surface, we are literally through the looking-glass. This iconic underwater shot has been quoted so many times, when a film wants to show what the world looks like on the other side of the mirror, that I'm going to add another term to our pool horror lexicon: the "Joe Gillis shot" (no pun intended).

Although the film never fully commits to horror, gothic elements are plain in *Sunset Blvd.*'s plot and setting. Norma's decaying mansion, as gloomy as it is grand, is all long shadows and buried secrets. Both the house and the people in it are hiding things. A huge oil painting rises to reveal a projector screen—an illusion on top of an illusion. The roof of Joe's first bedroom leaks, letting in the rain. Norma's butler Max is actually her ex-husband, a renowned film director. Her fan letters are forgeries. Borders of space, identity and time are blurred and permeable. What appears to be an intimate relationship between Norma and Joe is actually one of deceit and bondage. The pool is a place not of leisure, health and vigor, but of death. Like so many films about Hollywood, *Sunset Blvd.* is obsessed with artifice, suggesting that

Chapter 11. Swimming Pools, Movie Stars

In the iconic underwater shot from *Sunset Blvd.* (1950), Joe Gillis (William Holden) learns about the flip side of Hollywood glamor.

the purveyors of movie magic have become so skilled that they have lost the ability to distinguish reality from illusion.

Starry Eyes (2014) approaches these concepts from the other end. Instead of an irrelevant ex-star trying to claw her way back to the top, this film, directed by Kevin Kölsch and Dennis Widmyer, shows us an aspiring starlet willing to do whatever it takes to get there. Struggling young actress Sarah auditions for a part in a film called *The Silver Scream* with a notorious but mysterious horror production house called Astreus Pictures. Disappointed after the initial audition, she punishes herself in the bathroom by pulling out her hair in a self-harm ritual. The casting director witnesses the episode and asks her to repeat the behavior in the audition room. This earns her a callback, at which point she quits her job at a Hooters-like tater tot restaurant.

At the callback, Sarah is asked to strip nude for the camera. She is invited to meet the producer, whose sexual advance she rebuffs—but she later changes her mind and submits to him. After her second encounter with the producer, which seems to include something more than sex, Sarah gets sick and her body begins to decay. She grows irritable and violent, resulting in her murdering several of her friends. She ends up being buried alive in a ritual by an occult group that includes the Astreus Pictures personnel, and emerges as a hairless, flawless, movie-star-perfect version of herself. She returns home and murders her roommate before donning a gown, wig and jewelry, admiring herself in the mirror. *Sunset Blvd.*'s iconic final line is not spoken, but heavily suggested: Sarah has completed her movie star metamorphosis, and is now ready for her closeup.[8]

Sarah's friend group of aspiring actors and filmmakers spends their free time lounging by the apartment complex pool and planning how to break into the entertainment industry. Echoing many of the films from Part II of this book, *Starry Eyes*' pool sets the stage for Sarah's eventual transformation into an object of desire. But in Hollywood style, the pool itself is an object of desire as well. Floating around, hatching film ideas, taking and posing for photographs, Sarah's friend group is rehearsing the perceived behavior of Hollywood bigwigs.

Just as *Sunset Blvd.*'s underwater photography shows the dark side of the dream, the shots from below Sarah's frolicking friends give a view from the other end. By portraying the desperation of playing the field, the degrading nature of auditions, and the overall vulnerability of show business aspirants, *Starry Eyes* shows the glamorized film industry as a labor market like any other—an especially exploitative one, in fact, where even the bit players are petty and backstabbing (in Sarah's case, literally). Near the film's end, Sarah's roommate Tracey violates her trust by divulging that Sarah agreed to exchange sex for the movie role. Erin, Sarah's frenemy, needles her: "Did you actually suck some old producer's cock for a role in a movie called *The Silver Scream*?" The comment is a dig, but it also implies that the exchange might have been acceptable if it were a more prestigious film with a less mockable title. In this world, it's not about whether you sell out (or engage in "prostitution," to use Erin's word), it's about what you get in return.

Speaking of *The Silver Scream*, before he solicits Sarah for sex, the producer calls the script his "love letter to this town. Ambition: the blackest of human desires." He adds, "You cut through the fog of this town and you get desperation." Sarah's ordeal is an exaggeration of the sacrifices made by aspiring actors desperate for fame. Sarah is an easy target for exploitation. We don't see or hear anything about her family; it's reasonable to conclude that she moved to L.A. from somewhere else and only has a tenuous, *ad hoc* support system. She is anxious and vulnerable, ambitious but self-doubting, and engages in self-harm behavior. The Astreus cultists refer to her upcoming "metamorphosis" into a movie star. This ends up being literal, as she is reborn after shedding her old skin at the ritual's completion. It's the cutthroat Hollywood story taken to its logical conclusion: Instead of cosmetic surgery, she undergoes occult transformation; instead of drifting away from the friends she deems to be holding her back, she murders them.

Putting an even finer point on the glamor industry's superficiality and its secret darkness is Nicolas Winding Refn's *The Neon Demon* (2016). Like *Starry Eyes*' Sarah, *Neon Demon*'s protagonist Jesse is new to Hollywood, and seemingly uprooted, with no connection to her family. At a shoot, makeup artist Ruby takes Jesse under her wing and introduces the 16-year-old to her friends Gigi and Sarah, both models.

Another staging of the *Cat People* shot, as Jesse (Elle Fanning) claims the high ground over Ruby (Jena Malone) in *The Neon Demon* (2016).

Seemingly overnight, Jesse goes from obscurity to landing a contract with a prestigious modeling agent and being chosen over Sarah for a big-time fashion show. When she suspects that a woman is being harmed in the motel where she is staying, Jesse calls Ruby for help, and Ruby invites her to stay at a mansion where she claims to be house-sitting. The jealous Ruby, Gigi and Sarah attack Jesse and, after a chase, push her into the mansion's empty pool, killing her. Then they bathe in her blood and consume her body. Some time afterward, Gigi and Sarah are doing a poolside shoot at another Hollywood house when Gigi begins to retch. She goes into the bathroom and vomits up Jesse's eyeball before stabbing herself with a pair of scissors, saying, "I need to get her out of me." Sarah watches this happen, eats the regurgitated eyeball, and goes back to resume the shoot.[9]

The Neon Demon mounts its satire of the modeling industry with even less subtlety than *Starry Eyes*. The earlier film critiques the way Hollywood chews ingenues up and spits them out, but in *The Neon Demon* it happens literally. However, while *Starry Eyes* implicates the older, male Hollywood establishment and its lewd gaze, Refn's film seems to blame women for their own exploitation. *The Neon Demon*'s villains, the secret cabal of industry insiders who practice occult subjugation, are a group of envious women seeking to destroy Jesse for the crime of being younger, fresher and more alluring. In pitting women against each other rather than against patriarchy, *The Neon Demon*'s gender politics are more *Cat People* than *Slumber Party Massacre*.

Accordingly, we get two *Cat People* shots in the film's swimming pool climax. In the first, Jesse stands on the diving board, towering over Ruby in the empty pool, and delivers a speech acknowledging the power she holds, and foreshadowing her fate: "I know what I look like…. Women would kill to look like this." The low-angle shot from the bottom of the pool emphasizes her superior position, suspended in midair wearing a long gown, reminiscent of *Jennifer's Body*'s levitation scene. The second *Cat People* shot reverses the roles after Ruby pushes Jesse into the pool. The camera again shoots from below, this time at Ruby looking down upon the girl she has just murdered. "The fog of this town" has been cut through, and Ruby has reasserted her power with the blunt tool of violence.

After the murder, we cut to a shot of Ruby in a bathtub, covered with Jesse's blood, an image that evokes the legend of Elizabeth Báthory's youth-restoring blood baths.[10] It's implied that *The Neon Demon*'s villains use Jesse's blood, and perhaps that of others, to renew their beauty and competitive edge in the modeling world.

All of this is preceded by a bedroom encounter between Ruby and Jesse that starts as a case of misread signals and escalates into sexual assault. We are back in the realm of the lesbian vampire and Barbara Creed's notion of the asexually reproductive "archaic mother."[11] The occultists Gigi, Ruby and Sarah prey on younger women, not to reanimate them in their own image like *Suspiria*'s Helena Markos, but rather to steal their youth and beauty. The empty pool where Jesse dies doesn't just represent the emptiness of Jesse's dreams of fame; it's also a stand-in for a barren womb. There is no nurturing of the next generation, just the older one clinging to power. Ruby is Mrs. Li from *Dumplings*, aborting what would have been her stepchild and eating it to stay young. The scene then changes from an empty pool to a full one where Gigi goes into symbolic labor, staring into the swimming pool, at the corrupted water of the womb. After she expels Jesse from her body, cutting herself open in a mock Caesarean, and dies in the process, Sarah re-consumes the eyeball and returns to the pool, assuring us that the cannibal cycle will continue.

Ti West offers a twist on the theme of occult Hollywood sacrifice in *MaXXXine* (2024), a direct sequel to his 2022 film *X*. The year is 1985, and Maxine Minx, the lone survivor of a massacre in rural Texas six years before, has made it to Hollywood. Having earned stardom in the adult film industry, she sets her sights on mainstream fame. After a tour de force audition, she lands the lead role in a new, buzzy horror movie. A serial killer known as the Night Stalker has begun murdering young women in Hollywood and branding them with occult symbols. The most recent victims all seem to be people Maxine knows. Meanwhile, an unknown person is blackmailing Maxine with video evidence of her involvement in the Texas murders. It turns out that the killer and the blackmailer are the same person: Maxine's estranged father Ernest, a well-known Christian televangelist. Ernest has come to Hollywood to rescue his daughter from show biz's corrupting influence, including "Satanic" movies like the one she is starring in. He assembles a group of followers from the parents of kids who have run away to Hollywood, and begins making a documentary about his crusade. For the climax of his film, he stages an exorcism with Maxine tied to a palm tree next to the swimming pool of a lavish Hollywood hills estate. The police arrive in the nick of time and engage the group in a shootout. Maxine frees herself from the tree, but is pulled into the pool by one of Ernest's robed followers, who fell in after being shot by the cops. She stabs the cultist to death with a switchblade in an underwater struggle, and follows Ernest as he escapes into the hills. She finds her fallen father, wounded by police, and blows his head off with a shotgun.[12]

MaXXXine weaves the 1980s Satanic panic together with ongoing conversations about the morality of the entertainment industry into a story of religious hypocrisy. Though ostensibly soldiers for Christ, Ernest and his followers with their robes and rituals are indistinguishable from Hollywood cults as seen in films like *Starry Eyes*. As much as Ernest decries Hollywood's sinfulness, he himself is a performer, as both a preacher and TV personality. Like everyone else in L.A., he is trying to make a movie. He chooses the swimming pool as the site of Maxine's exorcism, not just because it symbolizes show business life, but also because it looks good on camera. He is evidently aware of the performance, too: After delivering a fire-and-brimstone speech, he momentarily drops the act and looks at the camera, as if to ask if the take was good.

In a film like *MaXXXine*, rich in allusions to movie classics, it's hard not to detect an ironic echo of *Sunset Blvd.* when the cops shoot Ernest and he falls into the pool. The viewer is tempted to repeat the line about the poor dope who always wanted a pool—and with that comes the recognition that this is the same ruthless ambition he bequeathed to his daughter Maxine. We next see her demonstrate her own gumption when the cultist pulls her into the pool and she must fight her way out of it—a symbolic struggle to make it through the mire of everyone else's ambitions and rise to the top of a male-dominated field that is, in this case, literally cutthroat. When Maxine tells her father, "You gave me exactly what I needed" before shooting him, she's talking about two things. First, the positive press that stopping the serial killer will bring her, accelerating her career and making her movie a hit. But she's also thanking him for the values he taught her, ruthless pursuit of your goals and letting nothing stand in your way. Whether it's for Jesus, in self-defense, or for the sake of a bravura performance, neither father nor daughter stops at murder.

Joel Schumacher's *8MM* (1999) offers a more grounded, realistic depiction of the corrupted Hollywood dream. Hired to investigate the provenance of an apparent snuff film, private detective Tom Welles follows the trail of a runaway named Mary, who went to Los Angeles hoping to become a movie star. The search leads him to a sleazy pornographer with the evocative name Eddie Poole. Tom follows Eddie to a porn shoot at Eddie's home, only to be chased by a goon whom he tackles and knocks into the dirty water at the bottom of a disused swimming pool. Like his namesake, Eddie embodies the promise and peril of the Hollywood dream—in reality, it's a pit of filth. Near the film's end, confessing his part in luring Mary to her death, Eddie says, "I told her everything she wanted to hear. How she was gonna be a big star, how she was gonna make a lot of money, and all the rest of the bullshit." The last time we see Eddie's pool, it is completely empty; all Mary's hopes for Hollywood success have been drained away.[13]

Daniell Cornell points out how the aspirational movie-star life complicates the distinction between private and public space, and this fluid border is reflected in

Framed between the dream of the L.A. skyline and the reality of its empty promises, Eddie Poole (James Gandolfini) needs to leave town in a hurry in *8MM* (1999).

residential architecture that "elides any boundary between the public space ... and the private grounds." Cornell also references the post–World War II Palm Springs resorts, which created spaces where "the glamour of visiting celebrities could be reinforced without requiring that they be continually performing their public personas."[14] A distinctive feature of L.A. living for the less privileged is the apartment complex with a swimming pool at its center, as depicted in *Starry Eyes*. Striking a balance between public and private, this style of pool serves a few different functions. It allows working-class people, many of them employed in the film industry in less visible support roles, a version of movie star poolside leisure. Orthogonally, these pools create community by design. The pool-centric complex's architecture, with outward-facing apartment doors and windows arranged around the perimeter, amounts to a reverse panopticon where the pool area becomes a communal space that everyone needs to pass through on the way to their homes, and which everyone in the complex may observe at any time. Whether or not they work for "the dream factory," Los Angelenos are assumed to have both public and private personas—and just like with celebrities at a resort, you don't always know which one you're getting.

The made-for-TV movie *The Apartment Complex*, directed by *Poltergeist*'s Tobe Hooper, aired on Showtime on Halloween 1999. Stan Warden, a graduate student in psychology, lands a manager job at a quirky complex called Wonder View Apartments. While cleaning the filthy pool, he dredges up the dead body of the last manager, Gary Glumley. Although nothing seems to suggest foul play, Stan finds himself a suspect in a nonsensical murder investigation. Meanwhile, he gets to know the complex's eccentric inhabitants, including a paranoid ex-spy, a movie stuntwoman and a police psychic. Stan starts to fall for a resident named Alice, despite the fact that she has a psychotically possessive boyfriend, Morgan. In the manager's apartment, which is stuffed with Glumley's possessions, Stan finds a journal where Glumley wrote about fearing that the man in apartment 9 wanted to kill him. Stan is later unable to find the journal again for the police. In another episode, a package arrives addressed to a unit that doesn't exist. While Stan's back is turned, a giant python slithers out of the package and disappears. Later, Stan knocks Morgan out in a fistfight and, while Stan is otherwise occupied, the snake reappears and nearly constricts Morgan to death. The police arrive and arrest Stan for the murder of Glumley and the assault on Morgan. The residents visit the police station bearing what appears to be Glumley's suicide note, as well as the news that Morgan has awoken in the hospital and is not pressing charges. Freed from jail, Stan returns to his apartment and is assaulted by a man who turns out to be Glumley: He murdered apartment 9's resident and switched identities with him. Glumley seals Stan inside a waterbed to drown him, but the residents come to his rescue. In the final scene, Stan and the residents celebrate the happy ending by re-opening the swimming pool. The residents reveal that they faked Glumley's suicide note and, insisting that Stan be the one to inaugurate the newly cleaned pool, push him into the water.[15]

In keeping with the Los Angeles setting, many of *The Apartment Complex*'s residents work on the periphery of the film industry. The building's owner Dr. Caligari, whose name alludes to a classic horror film, bills himself as "plastic surgeon to the stars." Another character works as a body double and has appeared onscreen standing in for various stars. This theme of appearances and shifting, superficial identities culminates in the reveal that the body in the pool was not Glumley but another man dressed in his work overalls. Glumley remarks that he knew nobody would recognize him in his disguise as the man in apartment 9, because in his professional capacity he was essentially invisible. This echoes some of the dialogue about Mary, the victim in *8MM*, whom several characters refer to as a disposable person that nobody would miss.

Stan, too, is not allowed to forget his position. The complex has recently been through several, interchangeable managers, and the residents make sure Stan knows it. The police insist on interrogating him at the bottom of the empty pool, and in the end, the residents insist on pushing him into it. He is accepted as part of the community, just so long as he remembers his place: Stan is the man who cleans the pool.

Early in the film, a homeless man named Chett says that the complex's pool is "the only one of its shape in the western hemisphere." Later, a police crime scene technician remarks that the pool is the deepest one he has ever seen. Squatting at the center of the off-kilter complex, defying reason with its geometry, the pool is symbolic of the confusing contours of the systemic hierarchy Stan finds himself subject to. He is literally in over his head in the Kafkaesque bureaucratic nightmare of an investigation. In the end, Glumley tries to kill Stan the same way he killed apartment 9's unnamed inhabitant: by drowning him in the waterbed, a swimming pool microcosm and symbol of luxury in the incongruously dilapidated confines of the manager's apartment.

When Stan mistakes him for a resident, Morgan declares, "I don't live in this dump," yet he is always there. Chett similarly does not live there, yet he seems to be able to come and go as he pleases. In his closing narration, Stan says that he has decided to write his psychology thesis on "a common human habitat and its effect on group psychology." By sharing a certain amount of space, the residents' individual lives combine into a whole. Despite the locked gate, the Wonder View Apartments collapse the distinction between public and private space, just like the pool at their center.

Another group of L.A. residents is not what they claim to be in *1BR* (2019), which also explores the pool-centric apartment complex and how it shapes community. In David Marmor's film, a newcomer to L.A. named Sarah (please do not be confused by all the Sarahs in this chapter) becomes the newest resident of Asilo del Mar Apartments. Estranged from her father, she has moved to L.A. hoping to work as a costume designer in the movies, but takes an office job where she is routinely exploited and humiliated by her middle-management boss. At the complex, what seems to be a tight-knit community of otherwise normal people turns out to be a cult. Drugged and imprisoned, Sarah undergoes a brutal, prolonged initiation designed to break her will. They send a message to her only friend in town, a co-worker named Lisa, ending the friendship, and they force Sarah to turn away her father when he visits to attempt to make amends. After Sarah is accepted into the cult, they hold an open house to recruit their next inhabitant. Lisa shows up, applies for the apartment and is accepted. During her initiation, the strong-willed Lisa manages to break the cult's hold on Sarah. Sarah kills cult leader Jerry and escapes the complex, only to discover that all the apartments in the neighborhood are owned by the same cult.[16]

Sarah, *1BR*'s protagonist, and Sarah the protagonist of *Starry Eyes* share more than a name. Both young women are estranged from their families, emotionally vulnerable, and ambitious to work in the film industry but naïve about its realities. This constellation of traits makes them prime targets for cult exploitation. The cult in *1BR* uses real-world tactics of psychological torture, deliberately isolating Sarah from family and friends, and attempting to subsume her individual identity into the group.[17] Once again, the swimming pool provides a gathering place for the community: Sarah's acceptance ceremony into the cult and her final confrontation with the group before escaping both happen poolside. In the same way her dreams of working in the movies clash with her humiliating office job, the apparently easygoing communalism of the pool area contrasts the reality of restrictive social control practiced by the cult.

Hollywood, land of illusion, presents itself as a magic meritocracy, obscuring a system of capitalist exploitation where those in power have a thumb on the scale. The characters in this chapter are being sold dreams: glamor, wealth, healing, a new start, a supportive community. Over the course of their films, they realize that what they thought was freedom is really another trap. Deceived by performers and expert manipulators, taken in by public personas, these characters experience the reveal of reality as a shock, like a splash of cold swimming pool water in the face.

CHAPTER 12

Suburbed, Othered, Submerged
Outsider Status in the Teen Horror Film

> Don't let the chlorine in your eyes blind you to the awful surprise that's waiting for you at the bottom of the bottomless blue, blue, blue pool.
> —The B-52s, "Private Idaho"

More Americans live in suburbs than anywhere else: as much as 69 percent, depending on how you define the 'burbs, but no less than 55 percent.[1] Although they are quickly diversifying, the suburbs are still thought of as predominantly white spaces, and with good reason. As I mentioned in the Part III introduction, the growth of the North American suburbs correlates to white flight from cities in response to civil rights inroads made by Black people. In the search for segregated swimming opportunities, suburbanizing whites brought their backyard pools and private swimming clubs with them.[2] In 1947, when developers broke ground on the first Levittown in New York, considered the prototype of the modern suburb, the occupancy covenant explicitly forbade non-white residents. This discrimination had the teeth of the state, too: The Federal Housing Administration only granted mortgages to racially segregated housing developments, stating in its underwriting manual, "If a neighborhood is to retain stability, it is necessary that properties shall continue to be occupied by the same social and racial classes." The Supreme Court outlawed these covenants in 1948, but according to historian Kenneth T. Jackson, Levitt "publically [sic] and officially refused to sell to blacks for two decades after the war."[3]

The growth of the 'burbs is also intertwined with another major shift in American life: the birth of teen culture. Though suburbs have existed as long as there have been cities, the modern era of American suburbia started with the post–World War II baby boom. Between 1944 and 1950, single-family housing starts rocketed from 114,000 to an all-time high of 1,692,000, a growth of almost 1500 percent in just six years. By 1955, more than 75 percent of those new houses were part of suburban subdivisions.[4] Military personnel returning from the war were having an unprecedented number of babies, and they needed housing for their new families. At the same time, the emerging Baby Boomers were creating the first truly distinct youth culture. The term "teenager," first used to describe a marketing demographic in the

1940s, became an all-encompassing identity with its own music, television and movies that sought to distance itself from the culture of the boomers' parents.[5] Part of this media landscape was the horror film. What is generally thought of as the first teen horror film, *I Was a Teenage Werewolf*,[6] was released in 1957—the same year Daisy and William Myers became the first Black couple to move into Levittown, Pennsylvania, and had crosses burned on their lawn.[7] It's not much of a stretch to say that American suburbia, the swimming pool as exclusionary status symbol, and the teen horror film would not exist without each other.

The suburbs try to balance the communal accessibility of a city with the countryside's spacious serenity. Those who appreciate them see this in-betweenness as an asset. To those who are critical of the 'burbs, it imparts an uncanny, liminal quality. The endless avenues of identical houses give an unsettling feeling of conformity, courtesy of the American mass-production juggernaut. It seems, despite the millions of people who live there, that disdain for the suburbs is the more popular position, at least among those who create art about them. Because of the 'burbs' neither-fish-nor-fowl essence, in this chapter we'll return to the indeterminacy of Part I and the atavism of Part II when we unpack the symbolism of the suburban pool.

Especially for teens, whose development depends on the ability to socialize, the built environment of the suburbs encourages alienation. This begins with physical design. Cul-de-sacs minimize through-traffic, discouraging non-residents from using suburban streets to get somewhere else. The distances between destinations make walking impractical, and public transportation is sparse, isolating people in personal automobiles. Those who cannot afford their own cars are probably not living in the suburbs anyway, since building ordinances ensure that every house caters to a similar income bracket, unlike traditional neighborhoods where dwellings of different socioeconomic classes can sit side by side. Furthermore, single-use zoning laws prohibit the mixing of commercial and residential properties, demolishing the tradition of the neighborhood corner store and similar gathering places.[8]

While the suburbs are designed to distance people physically, in theory they should unite people socially. After all, as outlined above, subdivisions both select for and reinforce homogeneity. Movies that criticize suburban life usually feature an outsider figure, a character who defies the values of conformity and capitalist consumption. They are *in* the suburbs, but not *of* them. Often the film's protagonist, this figure's out-group status can result from something inherent—social class, sexuality, neurodivergence, race—or because the character has visibly aligned themselves with a counterculture, like heavy metal or geekdom. We've already met some of these characters, like the witches of *The Craft* and *The Rage: Carrie 2*, and the queer-coded antiheroes of *A Nightmare on Elm Street Part 2* and *Halloween Ends*. Since the beginning of the form, teen horror films have exploited the fear of not fitting in. Adolescents who don't struggle socially are terrified of these characters; those who do struggle socially are terrified *for* them. The swimming pools in these films embody Kristeva's

Bill (Billy Warlock) finds out the consequences of making waves in *Society* (1989).

border: They delineate who belongs and who doesn't. Pools are suited for this since, as status symbols, they rely on exclusivity. An outsider character emerging from a pool threatens the symbolic order, and by falling or being pushed into one—like Stan in *The Apartment Complex*—they are reminded of their place.

One of the best-known horror satires of 1980s class conformity is Brian Yuzna's *Society* (1989). Our protagonist, Bill Whitney, is the adopted teenage son of a wealthy Beverly Hills family. He is mistrustful of his family but does not quite know why. Due to a scheduling conflict, he is unable to attend his sister Jenny's debutante party. A few days later, Jenny's ex-boyfriend David tells Bill that he too is suspicious of the family, so he hid a microphone in Jenny's earring. He plays Bill the tape of the coming-out party, which seems to include orgiastic sex and murder.

Bill gets a surprise invitation to a party hosted by Ted Ferguson, alpha male of the rich high school crowd, whom he heard his sister discuss having sex with on the tape. At the party, Bill confronts Ted about what he heard, and Ted confirms Bill's fears before pushing Bill into the pool. Later, Bill is drugged by his family and taken to the hospital, where his death is faked. He escapes and returns home to find a party in progress with all of the community's wealthy people. It's explained to Bill that his family, along with the rest of the elites, are non-human creatures who can deform their bodies into all sorts of grotesque shapes. Since Bill, a human, was adopted into the family, he can never truly belong. The creatures feed on humans, leaving their bodies sapped of life, and engage in a process called "shunting" where their bodies temporarily fuse into an amorphous knot of flesh. With the help of two friends, Bill narrowly escapes being eaten.[9]

Society's subtext is not difficult to decipher. The rich view themselves as a different breed from the commoners, and feed off the poor's vitality to sustain their own indulgent, amoral lifestyles. They are so homogeneous that they seem at times to converge into an undifferentiated blob. At Ted's party, he throws Bill into the pool saying, "You make waves, Whitney, you're going to drown." The scene capitalizes on the pool as a longstanding site of social exclusion. Even if we don't know the history detailed at the start of this chapter, the scene still resonates thanks to our acculturated understanding of the pool as a status symbol.

On a more universal level, *Society* speaks to the adolescent fear of being left out. Most of us can relate to the paranoid suspicion of being surrounded by people who know something we don't, that everybody is laughing at us behind our backs. This fear is extra potent for teenagers. Adolescence is about figuring out who you are in relation to others, which makes the social stakes feel high. Anecdotally, neurodivergent kids are particularly susceptible to this feeling, struggling to understand social nuances that seem intuitive to everyone else. Moreover, young people are indeed at the mercy of mysterious forces they cannot control—they're called adults. The relationship between youths and grownups is often one of mutual bafflement. For teens, adults—just like the rich in the eyes of the poor—might as well be a different species. Whatever Bill does, however hard he works, he will never be part of Society, because he was not born into it. For him, the plunge into Ted's pool is not just a class rebuke, it is an anthropological one. It reduces him to an atavistic other, a lower life form more suited to an aquatic habitat—a reminder that the difference between him and those around him is flatly irreconcilable.

We find similar dynamics in another teenage paranoia film: *The Faculty* (1998), directed by Robert Rodriguez. Explicitly inspired by *Invasion of the Body Snatchers*, it takes place at a suburban Ohio high school where an alien life form has started to infect the staff. The malevolent parasites hijack their hosts' bodies and absorb their personalities. As the aliens work their way through the faculty and start to usurp the student body, a group of teenage outcasts manages to avoid being infected: Stan, the football captain who has recently decided to quit the sport; his girlfriend Delilah, head cheerleader and school newspaper editor; Casey, a shy and nerdy photographer who has a thing for Delilah; Zeke, a drug-dealing juvenile delinquent with a sharp intellect; antisocial goth girl Stokely, a science fiction aficionado with a secret crush on Stan; and transfer student Marybeth, who arrives the same day the aliens start to take over. When Casey finds an alien on the football field, he brings the apparently dead creature to science teacher Mr. Furlong for examination. Furlong drops the creature into a fish tank, where it springs back to life. The students deduce that the aliens are aquatic beings, who can function on land but need plentiful water to survive. When they return to Furlong's room to find him infected, they learn in the ensuing fight that they can kill the aliens through rapid dehydration by injecting them with Zeke's homemade drug "skag," which is mostly caffeine. Using Stokely's knowledge of science fiction, they postulate that there must be an alien queen, and if they find and kill her, the rest of the infected people will return to normal. Minus

Comfortable in her waterborne element, the alien queen reveals her true form to Stokely (Clea Duvall, left) and Casey (Elijah Wood) in *The Faculty* (1998).

Delilah, who has become infected and fled, they head to the high school armed with skag. After Stan is infected, Marybeth reveals herself to be the alien queen. Morphing into her monstrous form, she chases Casey and Stokely into the school's swimming pool. The creature drags Stokely into the pool and infects her. Back in human form, she tries to talk Casey into giving up. Casey kills the queen by injecting her with the last dose of skag. With the death of the queen, all the survivors again have their old personalities. Stokely, who no longer dresses in alternative style, is dating Stan, and Casey is dating Delilah.[10]

A pool that is part of a public school might seem like a corrective to the accessibility problems we've been discussing. Sadly, the expense of maintaining pools and the extra insurance they require mean that only the most affluent districts can afford them.[11] Since most school districts in the U.S. are funded by area property taxes, the wealth of a public school tends to mirror the wealth of its community.[12] As we've discussed, suburban areas are not known for socioeconomic diversity, so the high school pool in *The Faculty* reproduces broader social inequities.

The scene where Stan tells his football coach that he no longer wants to play is staged poolside, accompanied by the splashing sounds of swimming practice. Stan is surprised by how casually Coach Willis receives the news. As Delilah says, the star quarterback quitting the team is a major social transgression. The lane dividers in the pool stand in for the borders of high school propriety that Stan is violating by refusing to "stay in his lane." Coach Willis should know this too, and the nonchalant reaction from the normally loud and aggressive coach is Stan's first tipoff that something is amiss.

As I mentioned in reference to *Shock Waves*, a fish tank is a scaled-down version of a pool's artificial environment. Although it's the alien that gets dumped in the science classroom's fish tank, the human kids are the real guinea pigs. High school students often feel like test subjects, thrown together from disparate social groups and backgrounds into one place and forced to make it work. Compulsory public education, after all, is a 20th-century social experiment. When the fight with the infected Furlong shatters the fish tank, it signals that these kids are ready to break free from their prescribed roles.

Each kid represents a different social archetype. Delilah speaks to this directly when she calls Casey "that geeky Stephen King kid." Stokely is the goth girl who revels in being an outcast. Zeke is the bad boy. Stan has made himself an outsider by quitting the team, and Delilah, both cheerleader and journalist, mixes brains with superficiality in a way that creates dissonance when she shows up with glasses and unstyled hair. These five characters all embody different ways a high schooler can gain outsider status. Marybeth, it would seem, is the naïve newcomer who hasn't yet found her clique. In a way this is true, but the alien queen is more conniving than naïve, and seeks not to join a clique, but rather create one by force. She sets herself in opposition to the rest of the kids as the ultimate conformist, delivering a villain speech about the pleasure of renouncing individuality and joining the hive. The resonances with alternative teenagers' opposition to suburban conformity are obvious, and yet the queen's message is tempting because it promises an end to the loneliness of exclusion. As theorist Alexandra West puts it, "In essence, everything that is both wonderful and awful about being a teenager is done away with in favor of blind allegiance."[13]

The Faculty takes the suburbs' tendency to alienate teenagers and makes it literal. Zeke tells Casey, "The only person in this school who's an alien is you." At another point, Stan protests, "I'm not an alien, I'm discontent." The language varies, but the message is clear: These characters swim against the current, and the alien menace is an exaggeration of the homogeneity many adolescents struggle with. Notably, the weapons that defeat the aliens are the same illicit stimulants Zeke peddles in the parking lot. Bourgeois alienation leads lots of young people to self-medicate with drugs. Zeke refers to his drug dealing as "doing my part to the deconstruction of America." (Another '90s teen horror film where slackers use drugs to defeat the monster is the pool-less *Idle Hands* from 1999.)[14]

When the alien queen pulls Stokely into the pool, she is forcing her into the place the social world has prescribed for her. As she morphs back into human form, a naked Marybeth swims across the pool in another example of the transforming woman predator, similar to the overhead swimming shot in *Jennifer's Body*. The pool again functions as symbolic womb, with the alien queen as Barbara Creed's archaic mother, reproducing asexually by infecting Stokely underwater. In a movie where parents and other adults are not to be trusted, the alien mother takes on an especially abject character.

The film's coda seems to undermine its overall message. Yes, the characters have

A TV, a pool and gold chains—what more could a man want? Stanley (Gerrit Graham) shows off his "pleasure dome" in 1986's *TerrorVision*.

learned to live as truer versions of themselves, but in Stokely's case, apparently being truer means dressing in pastels. Immediately after we see the new Stokely, the film cuts to a closeup of a butterfly, emphasizing that we are meant to understand her transformation as a beautiful one. This implies that the only reason to dress in goth style is to keep others at arm's length out of a fear of being vulnerable. Moreover, with everything returning to normal, presumably all the "normal" problems that existed before the alien invasion are still there. Things have changed for the individual characters, but the status quo has not. But maybe this ending is more realistic than the kind of film that tears everything down and starts anew. For most of us, the best we can hope for is to equip ourselves to cope with the world. After all, those black painted lane lines on the pool's bottom aren't going away any time soon.

Another pool-transforming, human-mimicking alien is loose in the suburbs, and it's up to the counterculture kids to intervene—but this time we're in the world of Ted Nicolaou's *TerrorVision* (1986). As the film opens, the Putterman family is getting intermittent reception from their new satellite television antenna, until it's hit by what appears to be lightning, strengthening the signal. The parents, Stanley and Raquel, are going out to meet a couple of fellow swingers. Their daughter Suzy has a date with her metalhead boyfriend O.D., and their young son Sherman joins his ex-military Grampa in front of the television to watch an Elvira-esque horror host named Medusa. Unbeknownst to them, the satellite receiver is picking up signals from a distant planet, where an alien named Pluthar is trying to warn them about a dangerous entity transported to Earth through an energy beam. The monster emerges from the television and eats Grampa, causing Sherman to flee. The parents bring the swinging couple, Spiro and Cherry, back to their house and Sherman tries to tell them what has happened, but Raquel locks him in the basement. The monster finds its way into Stanley's fancy indoor swimming pool via a poolside television screen. The creature emerges from the pool to consume Cherry, Spiro and both parents. Suzy and O.D. return home to Sherman and encounter the monster, which seems about to kill them until O.D.'s studded leather gloves remind it of its caretaker on its home planet. After the three kids learn that the creature can be placated with food, they call Medusa in an attempt to arrange a television appearance. By the end of the film, though, the alien has consumed everything around it—including O.D., Sherman, Suzy and Medusa—and is heading for the TV station so it can beam itself into even more homes.[15]

As a satire, *TerrorVision* is only slightly subtler than *Society*. The apparatus that beams the hungry beast from its home planet is referred to as a garbage disposal, literalizing the idea that TV pumps "trash culture" into our households. Stanley brags to anyone who will listen about how much he paid for his hideous decor—he clearly has more money than taste. Obsessed with the trappings of success and leisure, he shows off his new satellite antenna and the poolside TV in his "pleasure dome."

From the TV, and later the pool, into this garish monument to '80s excess comes a creature that literally does nothing but consume. It loves junk food, rock music and TV. It eats five adults without hesitation, but recognizes something about O.D.'s heavy metal gauntlets that it finds soothing. "He looked right at my studs and cooled out," O.D. observes. "This dude's into metal!" The monster, an outcast on its own planet, is drawn to the counterculture signifiers of the leather-clad O.D. and the colorful-haired Suzy. The kids, though, are not immune to the influence of trash culture. "Next to food and music," Suzy says, "[TV] is mankind's greatest invention." Nevertheless, their early scenes with the monster are cheerful and fun; it's not until they start planning to exploit the alien for financial gain, proving themselves as crassly capitalist as the parents, that the monster turns on them.

In the final scene where the swimming pool appears, the kids find it full of alien gunk, the water too polluted to see through, and Sherman fires a rifle into the pool. He's aiming at a potential unseen monster hiding in the murk, but he's also shooting at the pool itself, the symbol of excess whence a creature emerged to threaten the hyper-consumerist order with a taste of its own medicine.

Heavy metal culture, 1980s-style, rears its shaggy head again in 1986's *Trick or Treat*, directed by Charles Martin Smith. Bullied high schooler Eddie "Ragman" Weinbauer is a devoted fan of Sammi Curr, a rock hero from his hometown. He learns at the start of the film that Curr has died in a hotel fire. Ragman visits Nuke, the local metal radio DJ, who consoles him by giving him a studio acetate disc, the only copy of Curr's final record. At school, a student named Leslie, whom Ragman has a crush on, invites him to an after-hours party at the indoor swimming pool. Ragman goes to the pool party in street clothes looking for Leslie, but does not find her. Instead, the popular kids pick him up and push him into the pool with a weight in his backpack so that he sinks to the bottom. Leslie, arriving late, dives in and

Street clothes at the pool party: Metalhead Ragman (Marc Price) is used to looking out-of-place in *Trick or Treat* (1986).

saves him. Ragman leaves humiliated, vowing revenge against both the bullies and Leslie, believing she was in on the prank. Back at home, a backmasked message on the Sammi Curr acetate seems to address Ragman directly, instructing him to bait a trap. The next day, he goads the bullies into chasing him along a booby-trapped route. A spilled mop bucket causes one of them to slip and fly through a door. Thinking Ragman is hiding in the teachers' lounge, the bullies burst in and spray a room full of teachers with fire-extinguisher water. Later, following Sammi's instructions from the haunted record, Ragman lures the bullies into the woodshop, where a lathe spontaneously turns on and almost kills Tim, the lead bully. After a demon summoned by the record injures Tim's girlfriend, Ragman starts to regret ever playing the record. When Sammi names Leslie as the next target, Ragman tries to neutralize Sammi by smashing his record player. The undead rocker, who is now able to travel through electronics and radio signals, escapes. Ragman and Leslie rush to the radio station to stop Nuke from playing the deadly tape at midnight. Along the way, they discover that Sammi, as a ghost of electricity, is vulnerable to water, so Ragman lures Sammi into his car and crashes it into the river, killing the rocker and saving the day.[16]

The scene where Tim and his entourage push Ragman into the swimming pool mirrors *Society*'s pool-pushing scene. These characters are being punished for treading where they shouldn't. Invitation notwithstanding, they flouted the unspoken rule that certain social lines are not to be crossed. We get a Joe Gillis shot from Ragman's point of view, looking through the water at the popular kids looming over him on the pool deck. Between these social tiers is a gulf of worlds. Like *Society*'s Ted who warns, "You make waves, … you're gonna drown," *Trick or Treat*'s Tim taunts, "Hey, metalhead, you're in the shallow end!" But the bullies are shallow too, since they victimize Ragman based on his style and appearance. Like O.D. in *TerrorVision*, whose leather and studs align him with the alien, Ragman's metal signifiers affirm his outsider status. In *Trick or Treat*'s world, clothing is important. The bullies mock Ragman by putting on the clothes they find in his locker, including his denim vest. At the pool party, he is the only one in street clothes, further marking him as part of the out-group. The bullies use this difference against him when they put the weight in his backpack. Later, when Ragman turns the tables on the bullies, the woodshop lathe snags Tim by his preppy necktie.

As in *The Faculty* and others, *Trick or Treat*'s swimming pool is part of a larger water motif. Ragman's interactions with the bullies seem to cluster around water. They steal his clothes when he is in the locker room shower. After they push him in the pool, Ragman vanquishes one of the bullies with a mop bucket and tricks the others into hosing down the teachers' lounge. Sammi later emerges into a bathroom through a shower radio and is almost defeated by a flushing toilet, exposing his own water weakness. This vulnerability references heavy metal's reliance on electricity in the form of guitar amplification and distortion. Like the hungry beast of *TerrorVision*, Sammi can travel through mass media signals, a nod to the '80s anxiety about harmful messages amplified by popular culture and beamed into our homes. The dirtiness associated with heavy metal is also evoked in the names of Ragman and Sammi Curr, redolent of poverty and stray dogs. Immersing them in water is a literal way of "cleaning them up." On yet another level, the occult being's sensitivity to water recalls the old practice of "swimming a witch," discussed in Part II. In several ways, *Trick or Treat* uses water to police the boundaries between worlds—social, cultural, natural and supernatural.

"The song remains the same," Ragman says in his opening narration, a reference to Led Zeppelin. "Total conflict. Them against us." While sympathizing with the outsider, *Trick or Treat* is ultimately critical of this social war footing. Sammi's old school friend Nuke (another significant name, suggesting a kind of warfare there's no coming back from) cautions Ragman against following in Sammi's rageful, aggrieved footsteps. The water motif links Sammi's aggression to that of the bullies. By the end, Ragman has learned the error of that approach and instead tries to bridge the water gap through his romance with Leslie, a rebuke of "total conflict" and an embrace of integration. But unlike *The Faculty*, *Trick or Treat* does not suggest this integration must come at the expense of the counterculture Ragman holds dear. In the film's final moments, Ragman takes to the airwaves and says, "Wake up, sleepyheads," before playing a heavy metal song as the credits roll. By realizing he can still rock without burning the world down, the metalhead has finally made it out of the shallow end.

David Irving's *C.H.U.D. II: Bud the Chud* (1989) broadens its critique from preppy high schoolers to the adult representatives of American conservative hegemony. As the film opens, the U.S. military is discontinuing the C.H.U.D. Project, a

The zombie horde of *C.H.U.D. II: Bud the Chud* (1989) try to escape the swimming pool trap set by a clever group of teenagers.

Shock Waves–like experiment in creating undead super soldiers. Colonel Masters, who has become attached to the project, rescues the last C.H.U.D. and hides it in a suburban medical storage facility. When three mischievous teens, Steve, Kevin and Katie, lose their science teacher's anatomy cadaver, they replace it with a body stolen from the storage facility, which turns out to be the C.H.U.D., nicknamed Bud. Shocked back to life with a hair dryer in the bathtub, Bud wanders away and starts zombifying the townspeople. As the zombie horde grows, the military hunts the teens and both groups hunt the C.H.U.D.s. Everyone converges at the high school's Halloween dance, where the zombies attack the assembly. The teens lure the zombies into the school's swimming pool, flash-freeze them in the water, and destroy them with electricity.[17]

As in *Piranha*, the monsters of *C.H.U.D. II* are the results of a military experiment gone out of control, and we get a human villain in the form of an officer trying to clean up the mess. The film takes jabs at military ideology, both the principle of "might makes right" and the hypocritical reverence for vaguely defined "traditional" values. We see how cartoonish conservatism flows downstream from the likes of Colonel Masters—who resents the Geneva Convention for putting a hitch in his bio-warfare giddyup—to suburban patriarchs like Steve's dad, who is offended by the idea of his son not working in the family construction business and gripes about modern cosmetics because *his* mother never used them. At one point, a man sits in a barber chair and reminisces about the good old days when people didn't lock their doors. The monologue quickly becomes absurd: "My dad, he used to take all of our valuable possessions and put them out in the street every night before he went to sleep; they'd be there the next morning." All the while, he lacks the awareness to realize that the barber is a zombie. This exchange is intercut with scenes of Colonel Masters talking about how "kids have to be taught respect for authority." He discusses how his father would have beaten him if he had skipped school like the teens they are looking for. In the conservative mind, the past is both an idyllic time when all was peaceful, and a time when war crimes went unregulated and children lived in fear of whipping by tyrannical parents.

C.H.U.D. II's satire of the "new equals bad" mindset reaches its zenith when, for all their bluster and resources, the military proves ineffective at stopping the zombies. It's up to the scrappy teenagers to save the day, and their weapon of choice is the swimming pool. Teen horror films of the '80s often feature what John Kenneth Muir calls "the character archetype of useless authority."[18] It taps into a common teenage feeling of betrayal by those who came before them, and the growing realization that adults are not necessarily competent merely because they hold authority. By saving the day with the help of the public school swimming pool—symbol of both carefree youth and the non-warfare allocation of public resources—these goofball kids give a decisive counter-argument to the idea that the younger generation has nothing to offer.

A similar swimming pool climax does not go so well for the young people in David Robert Mitchell's *It Follows* (2014). In the Detroit suburbs, college student Jay lives at home with her mother and high-school–age sister Kelly. After she sleeps with her new boyfriend for the first time, he drugs her and she wakes up strapped to a wheelchair in an abandoned building. He explains that by having sex with her, he has made her the target of an entity that will follow her until she passes it to someone else. In human form—sometimes a stranger and sometimes a loved one—the entity slowly but ceaselessly walks toward its target, whom it will murder if it manages to make contact. Jay and Kelly, along with their friends Paul, Yara, and Greg, drive to a faraway lakeside hunting cabin to buy some time. When the monster arrives and almost kills Jay, she flees in a panic and crashes Greg's car into a cornfield. While Jay is recovering in the hospital, she has sex with Greg and thereby passes the curse to him. (He doesn't believe in it.) Greg's overconfidence gets him killed when the monster, mimicking Greg's mother, breaks into his bedroom and murders him. Paul, who has had a crush on Jay since childhood, hatches a *C.H.U.D. II*–esque plan to lure the entity into the water at a defunct public swimming pool and electrocute it with household devices. The plan fails when the entity arrives in the form of Jay's absent father and starts throwing the appliances at her rather than following her into the water. The friends manage to push the figure into the pool and Paul shoots it in the head, enabling Jay to get away, though we know from an earlier scene that a headshot is not sufficient to kill the entity. Later, Paul and Jay have sex, and the film ends on a shot of the pair walking hand in hand at dusk, with an out-of-focus background figure following.[19]

It Follows is one of just a handful of films in this book to feature multiple pools, and the only one with an above-ground pool. The above-ground variety is an

Chapter 12. Suburbed, Othered, Submerged 167

Before it all goes wrong, Jay (Maika Monroe) enjoys the simple pleasures of her above-ground backyard pool in *It Follows* **(2014).**

economical solution for homeowners who want a backyard pool on a budget. They tend to be smaller than in-ground pools, lack their variety of depth and shape, add less value to a home, and many people think they look tacky.[20] They suggest a household whose reach exceeds its grasp in terms of social status, that aspires to a life of leisure but doesn't quite have the means to achieve it. This mirrors *It Follows*' primary setting, in a fairly humble suburban community that looks luxurious only in contrast to the blighted urban locales around it.

It Follows exploits the symbolic link between water and sexuality that we covered in Part II. The first time we see Jay, she is floating in her above-ground pool, under the clandestine gaze of the neighbor boys, who show up later to spy on Jay in the bathroom. In another scene, Jay sees a boat on the lake and enters the water while undressing. Perhaps she is contemplating seducing those aboard to pass the curse to them, though the point is left ambiguous. Finally, it's revealed that Paul and Jay shared their first kiss as children at the public pool, the memory of which sparks the idea to try to defeat the entity there. But inasmuch as the film is about sex, it's as part of a larger theme: the death of childhood and the recognition of mortality. It's here that the borders—between urban and suburban, public and private, teens and adults—all intersect at the swimming pool.

The post-industrial wasteland of 2010s Detroit figures prominently in the film. The plot-catalyzing sexual encounter between Jay and her boyfriend happens at a large abandoned building. Later, in an attempt to track down the boyfriend, the group travels to a rundown house he rented under an assumed name, passing several derelict dwellings. The trip to the public pool is similar. As Yara reminisces on how she was never allowed to travel past a certain point on the map ("Where the city started and the suburbs ended"), they drive by row after row of dilapidated houses. The contrast of the public pool in the city with Jay's suburban private one reminds us of bourgeois white abandonment of urban areas, and the supposed reasons for it. Suburbanites want to raise their children in neighborhoods they deem "safe." In Jay's first appearance in the film, the camera tilts upward from a closeup of sidewalk gutter debris to a voyeuristic long shot through a backyard fence of the young woman preparing to swim. Echoing *Sunset Blvd.*'s opening shot, this visual communicates that the suburbs' safety is both illusory—the 'burbs have their dirt as well, but are a bit better at hiding it—and comes at a social cost: the cloistered backyard pool vs. communal public space.

Suburban parents want to protect their kids from what they see as a world full of hazards, symbolized by the booby-trapped public pool, surrounded by mundane objects that threaten electrical death. But those hazards are inescapable. Death follows each of us steadily; the question is not if it will reach us, but when. In the film's final shot, Jay and Paul have grown up, accepted the inevitability of death, and decided to make the best of the time they have left, even as the sun goes down over a suburb they'll never look at the same way again.

Like *C.H.U.D. II*, *It Follows* is critical of reflexive nostalgia. There are two photographs on Jay's bedroom mirror: a photo of her and Kelly with their father as children, and a photo of Jay smiling in the swimming pool. The film leverages the nostalgia many people associate with pools. It knows that nostalgia is never entirely painless, because the happy memories are inextricable from the bittersweet ones, two pictures sharing space on the same mirror. It's not specified if Jay's dad is dead, but he's definitely not in her life. In the swimming pool climax, when death appears personified in the form of Jay's father, the circle is complete. Jay knows you can never go backwards; in trying to do so, you just might run into the entity that strides inexorably toward you.

The idea of vanquishing the monster in a swimming pool goes back almost to the birth of the teen horror film—as far back as 1962 with Arch Hall Sr.'s *Eegah!*. While driving through the California desert, teenager Roxy almost hits a giant caveman, somehow survived from prehistory. She tells her father Robert and her boyfriend Tom, a musician, about the incident. Robert goes in search of the caveman by helicopter; when he fails to return, Tom and Roxy journey into the desert after him. The caveman, named Eegah, kidnaps Roxy and brings her to his cave, where he is also keeping Robert prisoner. Tom comes to the rescue, helping father and daughter escape. Eegah follows the trio back to civilization, arriving at a suburban backyard swimming pool which he treats like a watering hole, perplexed at the taste of the chlorine, until he is frightened away by the arrival of a domestic dog. He wanders to a hotel, where a confrontation ends with two men thrown into the swimming pool. Roxy and Robert attend a party at a house where Tom and his band are playing next to the backyard pool. Eegah arrives, interrupting a fistfight between Tom and another young man over who gets to dance with Roxy. Eegah beats up several partygoers, picks up Roxy, and is about to leave with her when the cops arrive. He rips out the pool ladder and threatens the cops with it, but they shoot him and he falls dead in the pool.[21]

The teens of *It Follows* (2014) don't have as much success as the ones in *C.H.U.D. II* at luring the monster into a pool trap. From left: Keir Gilchrist, Maika Monroe, Olivia Luccardi.

Like *C.H.U.D. II*, *Eegah!* critiques adult dismissiveness of teenage culture and reckons with the specter of American military might. Most of the action takes place deep in the desert, a locale that recalls the sites of American nuclear weapons tests in remote parts of New Mexico and Nevada. The idea that the age of nuclear weapons would send civilization "back to the Stone Age" was a common one during the cold war.[22] In *Panic in Year Zero!*, another horror film from the same year as *Eegah!*, a nuclear attack collapses civilization to the point where a middle-class suburban American family is reduced to battling other survivors for resources and living in a literal cave.[23] By the same token, U.S. military aid could help bring friendly nations "into the twentieth century." Mid-century Americans believed the power of the state gave it a monopoly on time itself.[24] Modern housing, transportation infrastructure and the other trappings of civilization, including swimming pools, were imbued with a moral dimension by virtue of being new.

But as in *C.H.U.D. II*, this elevating of the new does not extend to teenagers and their cultural practices. In a spirit of good-natured generational culture clash, Robert makes wry jokes at the teens' expense. He decries their music as unlistenable, and the lyrics as indecipherable. To him, their dancing looks like fighting. Into this dynamic the film throws a literal caveman, personifying both the threat to modernity posed by nuclear war and the perceived gulf between the younger and older generations. "He's from another age," says Robert of Eegah, "another eon." Eegah speaks in an unintelligible tongue and does not possess the social discernment to handle conflicts without violence. Both of these are exaggerations of the criticisms Robert levels at teenage culture in all its perceived savagery.

Rather than socioeconomic status or membership in a counterculture, the teenagers of *Eegah!*, like *C.H.U.D. II* and *It Follows*, earn their outsider status simply by being teenagers. Their very youth makes them part of the out-group, and this is especially pronounced in *Eegah!*, made in the early years of a postwar teen culture that seemed positively alien to adults. Unlike in *C.H.U.D. II*, it's not the plucky teens that kill the beast in the swimming pool; it's the forces of law and order, who show up just in time to save the day. But rather than being categorically monstrous like the C.H.U.D.s, Eegah is more like King Kong: a misunderstood figure whose attraction to a woman is mistaken for aggression because of his inability to communicate. Roxy is left devastated at the end of the film, not by Eegah, but by the police whose shoot-first show of force, like the bombs that irradiated the desert, left a confused outsider dead in the pool—a reminder of what we stand to lose if we keep demonizing what we don't understand.

Chapter 13

The Stepford Dives
Manufactured Perfection at the Pool

> Actually a pool is, for many of us in the West, a symbol not of affluence but of order, of control over the uncontrollable.
> —Joan Didion, "Holy Water"

In the last chapter, characters' suburban alienation is a byproduct of the built environment, not an intended feature. Some films, though, take the legacy of racial covenants and other forms of suburban segregation to its logical extreme, with communities whose architects literally play God. These films exploit the same paranoia as *Society* and *The Faculty*, but rather than raising questions of identity, they touch on something more fundamental: doubts about the nature of reality itself.

Because fascist regimes tend to be contradictory among or even within themselves, Umberto Eco set out to identify the features that "allow fascism to coagulate around" them, which he calls "Ur-Fascism" in an essay of the same name. The first feature he lists is the "cult of tradition," followed by its attendant "rejection of modernism."[1] Fascism gestures toward some point in the past, sometimes defined and sometimes fuzzy, when things were perfect, and posits that culture's goal should be to return there. Today in America, fascist thought seems to romanticize the 1950s and early 1960s era, with its postwar prosperity, well-defined gender roles and putative "safety." Three films in this chapter, released in three different decades, all depict a unilaterally male-driven fascist desire to recreate the supposed perfection of the Eisenhower years. Another shows us a budding authoritarian's early attempts to remake the world around him with the help of advanced technology. Despite its inherent contradictions, the hi-tech regression approach has precedent: As Eco points out, "Nazism was proud of its industrial achievements."[2] The 1950s, as we've already noted, saw the rise of both the modern American suburb and the backyard swimming pool. Both innovations owe their existence to technological strides forward in cheap materials and efficient construction. Why not use modern technology, then, to facilitate the return to a hallowed time in the past?

Based on Ira Levin's novel, Bryan Forbes' *The Stepford Wives* (1975) struck such a nerve that its title spawned a colloquial term for a woman who slavishly, and seemingly soullessly, embodies the 1950s subservient domestic ideal. In the film, photographer Joanna moves with her husband Walter and their two children from Manhattan to the suburban community of Stepford, Connecticut. She soon notices that all the women there are submissive and vacuous, except her new friend Bobbie, another recent arrival. The town's men all belong to the secretive Stepford Men's Association. At a fancy poolside party, a neighbor named Carol, who has recently been in a car accident, seems dazed and keeps repeating the same phrase. Carol later comes to Joanna's door to apologize, saying that she was drunk, but Joanna and Bobbie still think something is amiss. Researching the other Stepford women, they learn that they were all once leading lights in the women's liberation movement and did not become 1950s-style housewives until after moving to Stepford. When Joanna returns from a trip and discovers that Bobbie has, seemingly overnight, become another bland domestic, she follows her psychiatrist's advice and makes plans to leave town. At home, Joanna's children have disappeared and Walter tries to physically restrain her. She escapes to Bobbie's house and, in an altercation, stabs Bobbie, who begins to malfunction like Carol did earlier, revealing herself to be a robot. She goes to the Men's Association looking for her children, but finds only Dale, the association's leader, who explains that the town's men have been replacing their wives with robotic replicas to ensure domestic bliss. Joanna flees and runs into her own unfinished android doppelgänger, who strangles her to death with a nylon stocking.[3]

The setting where Carol begins to malfunction, a bourgeois garden party gathered around a swimming pool, reflects both the aspirations of the neighborhood's architects and the potential pitfalls of their approach. As waiters in white jackets mill around serving hors d'oeuvres, nobody is actually using the pool. In fact, nobody in the film is ever seen swimming. For the characters as well as the viewer, the pool is a symbolic backdrop. The Stepford Men's Association wants wives who are beautiful and compliant without the complexity of actual humans, just as they want the status symbol of an attractive swimming pool without the untidiness of swimming. The pool, like the women around it, is there to be looked at. The phrase Carol repeats, "I'll just die if I don't get this recipe," carries some irony. She has already died, and it is not her, but rather the replicant that replaced her, who treats hors d'oeuvres recipes with such life-and-death importance. The Carol-bot's malfunction results from a minor car accident which knocked something loose in her hardware. If the perfection Stepford prizes is tenuous enough to be jarred awry by a fender-bender, how sustainable is it? The whole town tiptoes around the perimeter of a metaphorical swimming pool, where one small misstep could send them tumbling in, breaking the surface of the illusory ideal.

Along with its connotations of wealth and domestic pleasure, *The Stepford Wives*' pool is also coded as a site of identity disruption. Like some other films we've looked at which use pools in conjunction with mirror motifs, the film plays with the concept of doubling. Each Stepford wife exists in two versions: the ungovernable human one, and the predictable android one—Kristeva's "clean and proper" body.[4] When Joanna enters Bobbie's house expecting to find the former version and

Chapter 13. The Stepford Dives 173

Ted (Joseph Sommer) leads the malfunctioning Carol-bot (Nanette Newman) away from the swimming pool before she can cause more trouble in *The Stepford Wives* (1975).

instead encounters the latter, she responds by violating the clean and proper (synthetic) flesh with a kitchen knife. Mirroring the imposition of male will upon the female form, she penetrates the Bobbie-bot with a phallic weapon that is coded for feminine use in a feminine space. Later, when Joanna comes face to face with her own robot double, it murders her by strangulation—vulvic death—with a symbol of feminine beauty, the nylon stocking. Joanna's reclaiming of her agency has proven short-lived, no match for the Men's Association's fascist power.

The Stepford Wives birthed three made-for-TV sequels and a 2004 remake. In between *Revenge of the Stepford Wives* (1980) and *The Stepford Husbands* (1996), both pool-less, director Alan J. Levi's *The Stepford Children* (1987) shifted the focus to the Connecticut community's rebellious teenagers, resulting in a film that could easily have fit into the previous chapter. Attorney Laura Harding moves to Stepford with her husband Steven, who had lived there earlier in life with his now-deceased first wife. Accompanying them are their teenage children: David, an athlete, and Mary, a counterculture music lover. In an early scene, Kenny, a wild-haired, surly Stepford teen, is browbeaten into a fishing excursion with his father. Some members of the Men's Association—including the high school principal, football coach and sheriff—join them on the lake, restrain Kenny and inject him with a hypodermic. The next time we see Kenny, he is a clean-cut paperboy. On their first day at Stepford High, David and Mary expect to meet some other edgy kids, but are shocked to find the school seemingly populated by nothing but boring do-gooders. All except Lois, a fellow newcomer whom David soon starts dating. Meanwhile, as Steven re-integrates into the Men's Association, Laura befriends Lois' free-spirited, motorcycle-loving mother Sandy. Like Joanna in the first movie, Laura is unsettled by the uptight conformity that seems to pervade the whole town except her one friend, another recent transplant. At the high school, this conformity manifests as an obsession with excellence and propriety, along with a strange resistance to Laura's efforts to start a parent-teacher association. When Sandy's personality changes overnight into a Stepford wife, Lois becomes suspicious. The next day at school, as Mary is engaged in diving practice, men behind a hidden wall collect video recordings and biometric data as the gym coach hectors her to keep diving. Soon thereafter, Mary returns from a shopping trip with her father changed into a perfect Stepford teen. Laura digs up the grave of Steven's first wife and finds an android. Learning that Steven has taken David on another "shopping trip," she goes to the Men's Association where she finds the real Mary, not yet murdered. David arrives, crashing a motorcycle through the window which causes an explosion that destroys the building.[5]

Two of the Stepford children are prepared for their android replacements while in water. Kenny is abducted on the lake with his father, and data for the Mary-bot is collected from Mary while she is diving. Both scenes have a gendered element. Kenny's father admonishes him to stop fussing with his hair, a feminine-coded preoccupation. Mary's coach tells her to "find your spot, keep your head down and your legs together"—conservative commands to a rebellious teenage girl, disguised as diving advice. This implied encouragement of self-effacement and modesty, though, is contradicted by the film's visual language. In the diving scene, our first view of Mary is through monitors, one video and one thermal. The camera then pans over to a view of her through a window as a voice recites data about her body temperature, surface moisture, lung capacity, biochemistry and other metrics. It's only after another cut that we see Mary on the diving board, unmediated by the gaze of the Men's Association. Mary protests that she feels ill, but the coach keeps barking orders at her. While his words insist that a girl should keep her "legs together," the scene's construction leaves little doubt that the Men's Association is only interested in Mary's body, not her personhood.

A similar contradiction occurs at the high school's Parent's Night, when Steven tries to soft-pedal Laura's public challenge to the Stepford way by saying, "She's in a bit of a time warp. She tends to linger nostalgically in the bygone days of protest and rebellion." The remark typifies a Baby Boomer tendency to disavow the 1960s counterculture's progressive values after the country's conservative turn in the Reagan years. As author Jay McInerney puts it, Reagan's ascendancy "seemed to mean that the sixties were finally over."[6] Anyone can see the bald absurdity of Steven's statement: It is Stepford, not Laura, that is in a time warp. Its big band–listening teens don't even know how to dance to rock music. This evokes another one of Eco's fascist hallmarks: the use of Orwellian double-speak.[7] In Stepford, 1960s-style rebellion is a "time warp," whereas a lifestyle that apes an even earlier time is the way things are supposed to be. When you redefine terms to suit your purposes, you can force people to do things—from diving into a pool all the way to giving up their lives—and reframe it as being for their own good.

Olivia Wilde's *Don't Worry Darling* (2022) is an homage to *The Stepford Wives*, with the 20th-century fear of replacement by mechanical machines traded for 21st-century paranoia about digital ones. Alice is a housewife living with her husband Jack in a company town called Victory, founded by Frank, the head of the company. The time period is not specified, but it appears to be the early 1960s. The women are forbidden from entering the desert which surrounds the town, and likewise discouraged from asking questions about the company where all the men work. A housewife named Margaret recently broke the former rule and lost her son as a result. At a poolside party at Frank's house, Margaret declares, "We shouldn't be here." When Alice witnesses a plane crash in the desert and attempts to help, she finds herself at Victory Headquarters, where she touches the window and has strange hallucinations that linger even after she wakes up at home as if nothing happened. Later, Alice sees Margaret commit suicide on the roof of her house, but afterward everyone denies that Margaret is dead. While watching one of Victory's propaganda videos advertising the swimming pool, Alice has a vision of herself being pulled under the pool into a black abyss. She becomes increasingly suspicious that Victory is not what it seems, until Frank privately confirms that she is on to something, and says that he welcomes her challenge. At a dinner party, Alice attempts to convince her guests that their memories are being manipulated, but Frank succeeds in making her look unwell and drunk. After being subjected to shock therapy by Frank's henchmen, Alice remembers her and Jack's real life in the 21st century. Jack, it turns out, was one of dozens of men recruited online by Frank into the Victory Project, a virtual reality simulation of an idyllic midcentury community. The women, drugged and without their consent, are plugged into the simulation permanently. After Jack admits the truth, Alice kills him in a quarrel and flees into the desert. With Frank's minions in pursuit, she reaches Headquarters and puts her hands on the window again, seeking to unplug from the simulation.[8]

Don't Worry Darling was filmed on location at Canyon View Estates, a Palm Springs, California, development built between 1962 and 1965 in several phases, each of which consisted of a group of tract houses arranged around a communal swimming pool.[9] The midcentury modern style was made possible by industrial advances allowing greater availability of materials like steel and concrete. The design of the houses, with their floor-to-ceiling windows, clean lines and open-concept interiors, evokes a midcentury vision of the future.[10] This retrofuturist aesthetic is consistent with Frank's rhetoric, which is full of references to "pushing forwards" and rejecting the status quo, while in reality the entire project is designed to revert to an older status quo the men prefer. "We crave order," Frank says repeatedly. His world is a future yearning for the past that yearned for the future.

One of those midcentury modern architectural elements, the floor-to-ceiling window, becomes a major motif. Designed to let in an abundance of light, and to afford a view as expansive as the ports of a starship, these windows are nonetheless a hindrance to privacy. Several exterior shots frame Alice through one of these

Shelley (Gemma Chan) gathers the Victory residents around the swimming pool to hear her husband's speech in *Don't Worry Darling* (2022).

windows, on display like an animal in a terrarium. They resonate with Alice's paranoia, the omnipresence of surveillance, and the notion that her life is not her own. This is made explicit in a scene where Frank, standing in front of a mirror, watches Alice and Jack have sex in his house.

The mirrored windows of the Headquarters building only show Alice the version of herself that Victory wants her to see, until she touches them, at which point she is able to see through to another reality—like her namesake in Lewis Carroll's *Through the Looking-Glass, and What Alice Found There.* Later in the film, Alice is at home cleaning a window when she hallucinates the wall behind her pushing forward, contracting the space and crushing her against the window. The house has become a prison, and the window a barrier, providing a view but not an escape. On the other side of a full-length mirror in a dance studio, she sees a vision of Margaret, who smashes her head against the glass but fails to break it—a visual metaphor for how Margaret got a glimpse of the truth but was not able to free herself. In another scene, Alice awakes from the vision of being pulled underwater to find herself pressed against one of her house's windows, linking the glass imagery with the swimming pool imagery. Like the pool's surface, the windows both reflect and distort. This tension between transparency and reflection reminds us how human perception can be exploited. What should be private—like Alice's sex life—is out in the open, and what should be transparent—the true nature of the Victory Project—is opaque.

Like *The Stepford Wives*, the film also plays with doubling. There are two Alices: the "perfect" one in the simulation, and the 21st-century one, messy and struggling but real. The mirror, rather than showcasing duality, obscures this truth. It can only be seen by going through the looking-glass—by passing the surface of the pool into the darkness beneath.

Another recurring symbol is the black-and-white footage of 1930s-style synchronized female dancers. Alice sees visions of them each time she touches the Headquarters window, and has flashbacks of them while watching a burlesque dancer at a company party. It is revealed that looped footage of the dancers is being projected onto the canopy that surrounds Alice's unconscious body in the real world. The dancers also appear, this time in color, under the film's end credits. Although they are not seen in water, they wear matching two-piece swimsuits, and their coordinated movements are reminiscent of Busby Berkeley's famous choreographed swimmers in the 1933 film *Footlight Parade*.[11] (The same set piece is evoked at the climax of *The Rocky Horror Picture Show*.) The dancers are likewise connected with the Victory women's own geometric movements at the dance class where Alice has her vision of Margaret trying to break the mirror. The latter footage is repeated in a late-film montage after Alice's shock therapy, when her memories of the real world force themselves back into her consciousness. The images are intercut with an overhead shot of Alice swimming alone across a vast blue stretch of pool as a woman's voice intones, "There is grace in symmetry; we move as one."

The dancers' old-fashioned style evokes an archaic female ideal, and their blonde wigs suggest the whiteness that Frank's fascist order presumes to be optimal. Their coordinated movements imply not just conformity, but also the expectation that Victory's women "dance for the man," colloquial for self-debasing subservience. In the same party scene with the burlesque dancer, Jack is instructed by Frank to dance for his promotion, which he dutifully does—a reminder that authoritarian patriarchy humiliates men as well as women. In the hypnotic audio recording that lulls the unwilling women into the simulation, Frank instructs, "Allow your consciousness to sink into this world," though the word "sink" can also be heard as "sync." Alice's brainwaves are syncing with the computer program, even as social expectations require her to synchronize her life's rhythms to Victory's regressive norms.

As in *The Stepford Wives*, Alice gets her first clue that something is wrong from a fellow housewife behaving strangely at a poolside party. Margaret, who is Black, is an outsider in this manufactured midcentury suburban milieu. Alice and Jack are also set up as outsiders early in the film when we learn, in another poolside scene, that they do not want children. Thus both Margaret and Alice are objects of Eco's Ur-Fascist "fear of difference."[12] Despite Frank's exhortations to reject the status quo, every attempt has been made to ensure conformity among Victory's residents, down to implanting each with one of a handful of falsely remembered backstories. More Orwellian doublespeak: Frank's alternate reality comes complete with a confusing language where rebellion actually means sameness, where progress means moving backward, and where freedom means confinement. In addition, Frank has created a cult of personality around himself. "You're lucky to even know who he is," one character says in an early scene. Victory's residents practically worship him as a deity, and in this case the comparison is literal: Frank has created not just the neighborhood, but the very reality they inhabit. The men's voluntary self-delusion and willingness to live in a simulation is resonant with our modern world at the dawn of the post-truth era, when a powerful, charismatic man can flagrantly lie, and masses will accept it as truth simply because they like his style.

Like *Revenge* and *The Velvet Vampire*, *Don't Worry Darling* uses the incongruous symbol of the swimming pool in the middle of the desert to evoke the idea of an oasis, an escape from everyday reality where ordinary rules do not apply. Whether as a symbol of wealth and privilege (*Revenge*), or colonial conquest (*The Velvet Vampire*), all are examples of human technological dominance over nature—at least temporarily. *Don't Worry Darling* ends on a hopeful note when Frank's wife stabs him to death in front of the swimming pool. If Frank is the Father of All, maybe his wife Shelley is Mother Nature, asserting at the point of her kitchen knife that no emperor may reign forever.

The Stepford Wives, its sequels and its spiritual daughters feature women whose correct suspicions that something is wrong with the world around them are dismissed as paranoia or hysteria. Whether it is overindulgence in alcohol (*The Stepford Wives*, *Don't Worry Darling*), overpermissiveness (*The Stepford Children*), overzealous progressivism or general "irrationality," men can find no shortage of excuses for not taking women seriously. All are subjected to an inordinate amount of scrutiny. Whether it is to gather programming data for their robotic doppelgängers, to remind them that their lives are not their own, or simply to treat them as objects of desire, women in these films are perpetually under the male gaze. The manufactured fascist projects they inhabit seek by turns to observe, other, infantilize and control them—and at every juncture, there is a swimming pool there to serve its symbolic function.

We'll close this chapter with a very different kind of film where an entitled male character uses technology to remake the world around him. If Donny the teenage hacker from *Assassination Nation* were the protagonist of a film, it might look a lot like Pascual Sisto's *John and the Hole* (2021). Thirteen-year-old John lives in an affluent suburb with his parents and older sister. While flying a drone through the woods near his house, he discovers the huge concrete pit of an unbuilt bunker. Seemingly out of nowhere, John decides to drug each of his family members and imprison them in the hole for several days with no explanation, bringing them food while he goes about life on his own. He drives his father's car, withdraws money from the ATM, orders food, plays video games, goes to tennis practice. He invites his online gaming friend Peter to visit for a few days, saying his family is away. Peter shows him a game in the backyard swimming pool that involves submerging yourself in water until you almost lose consciousness, at which point you supposedly see the Virgin Mary. A family friend comes to visit and becomes suspicious. She later returns with the police, but John hides. Eventually, John becomes bored and lonely enough to lower a ladder so his family can exit the hole. They find John floating motionless, face down in the swimming pool. They rush to him, fearing the worst, but he is alive and well. As the film ends, the family eats dinner together, reunited as if nothing happened.[13]

Newly freed from their concrete pit, Laurie (Taissa Farmiga) and Bradley (Michael C. Hall) fear the worst when they see John (Charlie Shotwell) floating in a different kind of concrete pit in *John and the Hole* (2021).

John and the Hole leaves many things unexplained. Chief among them is John's motive for imprisoning his family. He does not do anything outrageous with his newfound freedom. Essentially, he carries out a mundane life. John's mother recalls him asking her what it feels like to be an adult. He was disappointed by her answer: It doesn't feel much different than being a kid, just with more responsibility. His disappointment may stem from feeling adrift in his current life and hoping that being an adult would bring more fulfillment, so he decides to try it out. In the same conversation, the mother remembers John asking her why the water in the swimming pool did not "feel like real water." Again the pool's artificiality echoes the perceived fakeness of bourgeois suburban life as a whole. Indeed, John's experience of the world is highly mediated. He sees the woods around his house through the camera of his drone. At one point, he uses a virtual reality headset. He plays a tennis video game with Peter, even though he is proficient at actual tennis. His dialogue with Peter is insincere, full of the foul-mouthed adolescent boy bravado typical of online gaming culture. Peter is, apparently, his only friend, and he mainly interacts with him online. Nothing of real emotional significance is ever said between them.

True to its era, *John and the Hole* examines the crisis of entitlement and ennui that engulfs privileged white boys. John is a future Frank from *Don't Worry Darling*:

He feels entitled to tell people where and how to live, and his familiarity and comfort with digital worlds might one day inspire him to create the most immersive one possible—one where being a middle-class white man is not (what he perceives to be) a liability.

John wants to experience something real, to *feel* something—but his acculturation has never taught him how. This is why Peter's drowning game appeals to him. Supposedly, at the point of asphyxia, you have a religious experience. Maybe this is the way to overcome his anomie, to fix whatever he feels is broken in him—to feel "real water" in the pool. This could be why, after his experience living on his own falls flat and he sets his family free, the first thing he does is try the pool game again. John's blank face when his family pulls him out of the water, and the business-as-usual ending, suggest that the pool has failed to deliver on its Freudian promise of rebirth.

John is a different kind of disaffected suburban youth from the ones we looked at in the last chapter. He is not alienated because of a subculture he aligns himself with, a lower-class birth family, generation gaps or gendered expectations. John's outsider status comes from a deeper, more existential place. He feels he does not belong in the world at all. Nothing excites him, nothing feels genuine—the "hole" of the title can be read as the hole within John that he cannot figure out how to fill. Like the other men in this chapter, he is ready to sacrifice his family on the altar of his own self-will. This leads him to seek transcendence in extreme places—in a concrete pit, inside a VR headset, and at the bottom of the swimming pool.

CHAPTER 14

Skimming the Gene Pool
The Ghost of Eugenics

> I want to say that the pool is for anyone; we all share the water. And yet, it seems impossible to escape the confines of our bodies, or the histories that they evoke.
> —Elizabeth L. Rogers, "Public Swim"

> Swimming isn't a sport. Swimming is a way to keep from drowning.
> —George Carlin, *Playin' with Your Head*

During the Progressive Era (roughly 1890–1920), two American social movements popularized two different meanings of the word "fitness." The physical culture movement promoted bodily health and physical strength as key to mental wellness, moral rightness and responsible citizenship. At the same time, the eugenics movement sought to "cleanse" the gene pool by dictating who should and should not have children.[1] Eugenicist tactics ran the gamut from mass-media promotion of some types of bodies as more desirable than others, all the way to anti-miscegenation laws, forced sterilization and calls for genocide—all based on the notion of various groups' "fitness" to reproduce. The popularity of the American eugenics movement served as a model for the ethnic cleansing ambitions of an up-and-coming German politician named Adolf Hitler.[2]

The concurrence and mutual influence of the two movements meant that the twin meanings of "fitness"—athletic and reproductive—became conflated in the public understanding. The assumed alignment of physical capability, mental health and morality slipped easily into the desire to control human breeding based on those factors, especially when both movements were championed by luminaries like U.S. President Theodore Roosevelt.[3] The same era that saw widespread civic initiatives to build public swimming pools and encourage their use—according to Jeff Wiltse, both to reform the poor and to enervate the affluent[4]—also saw the birth of cinema and the rise of the horror film, depicting monstrosity through the visual language of abnormal bodies.[5] This intersection created a lineage of horror films bound up in the question of who deserves to reproduce, which continues to this day. Often these films feature a symbol of both physical fitness and reproductive anatomy in the form of the swimming pool.

In *A Cure for Wellness* (2016), Hannah (Mia Goth) returns to the underground aquifer where her life began as she experiences her menarche.

Gore Verbinski's *A Cure for Wellness* (2016) directly addresses both schools of thought. A young man named Lockhart is sent by his employer, a New York finance firm, to a wellness center at the foot of the Swiss Alps to retrieve the company's CEO, Roland Pembroke, despite his stated intention to stay there. The institute, run by Dr. Volmer, is built over an ancient aquifer said to have healing properties. After an auto accident strands him at the secretive facility, Lockhart realizes that Volmer has no intention of letting him leave, with or without Pembroke. He meets a young patient named Hannah, toward whom Volmer behaves paternally. Lockhart pieces together the history of the place: Two hundred years ago, a baron, obsessed with the purity of his bloodline, attempted to have children with his sister, but the babies kept being born with deformities. Seeking a "cure" for these incest-related birth defects, the baron started performing heinous experiments on the townspeople, distilling their life essence into the aquifer water and leaving them desiccated husks. The baroness eventually conceived a non-deformed baby, but before the child could be born, the townsfolk retaliated, aborting the fetus and throwing it in the aquifer, then burning the castle to the ground. The present-day sanitarium is built on the castle ruins. The climax reveals that Volmer is the baron and Hannah is his daughter, who survived being thrown in the aquifer. Both of them have lived prolonged lifespans thanks to the "cure." When Hannah wades into an underground swimming pool and has her first period, Volmer decides that it is time to father the next generation. Hannah fights back with Lockhart's help, killing the baron and burning down the sanitarium.[6]

A Cure for Wellness' look and feel are old-fashioned by design, frozen in time like Hannah and the baron. In an early scene, an executive at Lockhart's company asks, "Who the hell takes the waters in the 21st century anyway?" "Taking the waters" was a fad that was largely passé even 100 years prior. In the 18th and 19th centuries, wealthy people traveled far and wide to undergo treatment at thermal springs and other facilities with supposedly healing waters.[7] Much of the "hydropathy" developed during this period has since been proven to be pseudoscience.[8] Undeniably, at least part of the fashion for taking the waters was a lark for the wealthy. In the film, the sanitarium's clientele is rich and powerful, and most of them seem to have been healthy when they entered. It's implied that they are happy to believe themselves sick and to submit to treatment, even if the treatment is hurting them rather than helping. As it turns out, Volmer is subjecting his clients to the same experiments he performed on the peasants centuries ago, extracting their life force to distill it into "the cure."

A Cure for Wellness points out the eugenics movement's hypocrisies. You would expect the baron, whose philosophy of physical perfection viewed abnormal bodies as undesirable, to see a preponderance of birth defects as a signal that having children with his sister was a bad idea. Instead, believing without evidence in the superiority of a "pure" bloodline, he treats it as a problem to be solved. He's on the right track, he thinks, it's just a matter of ironing out some details. His iron, in the grand tradition of aristocracy, flattens the common folk.

The film draws several parallels between water and birthing. It bears kinship to other films we've examined, about the prolonging of youth, but instead of *Dumplings'* folk magic or the occult vampirism of *The Hunger* and *The Neon Demon*, the longevity is extracted through scientific means from the aquifer itself, a mythical fountain of youth. "Life on this planet first came from water," Volmer declares, before comparing the isolation tank Lockhart uses to a return to the womb. A turning point comes when Hannah experiences her menarche in the pool which, like the rest of the sanitarium, is fed by the aquifer. She cycles her reproductive blood back into the same surrogate womb she emerged from after being torn from the natural one. Like the eugenicist family tree, it is a closed system. This archaic womb is a source of life for a chosen few—Volmer's bloodline and his collaborators—and death for everyone else. In true eugenicist fashion, the baron ordains himself with the power to decide who should reproduce and how. Despite all the birth defects that resulted from his experiments, the only monster he created in the process was himself.

Not every horror film is as critical of eugenicist thought as *A Cure for Wellness*. As noted above, the genre has a longstanding tendency to equate outward disability with inward corruption. For an unreconstructed take on horrific birth, we'll turn for the last time to the *Nightmare on Elm Street* franchise. The fifth installment, *A Nightmare on Elm Street: The Dream Child* (1989), directed by Stephen Hopkins, focuses on the circumstances of Freddy Krueger's birth. In series lore, depicted in flashbacks, Freddy was the product of a gang rape carried out against Amanda Krueger, a Westin Hills Psychiatric Hospital staff member, when she was accidentally locked in

Only one way down: Freddy Krueger transforms the diving platform into a giant claw to ensnare Yvonne (Kelly Jo Minter) in *A Nightmare on Elm Street: The Dream Child* (1989).

with the inmates. In *The Dream Child*, Alice, the Final Girl from the previous film, is pregnant and the film focuses on the parallels between her pregnancy and Amanda's. On the night of their high school graduation, Alice's friend Yvonne, a swimmer, hosts a pool party; the guests include Dan, the father of Alice's baby. He leaves to meet up with Alice, but Freddy kills him on the way. Later, alone in the pool complex, Yvonne dozes off in the hot tub and climbs the high dive in her dream. The diving platform morphs into a gargantuan version of Freddy's claw, pushing her off. As she hurtles toward the water, the pool suddenly empties, echoing the anti-drug PSA I mentioned in the preface, which launched the same year.[9] Rather than going splat, she falls through a puddle of dirty water in the cratered surface and emerges in a dream version of the asylum where Freddy was born. Freddy holds Yvonne hostage to distract Alice, who has entered this dream world in search of Amanda.[10]

The two pools—a wholesome one that transforms into a dirty one—represent the two pregnancies the film focuses on. Alice's pregnancy is the "clean and proper"[11] version, while Amanda's is portrayed as evil and ungodly. Freddy is sometimes called "the bastard son of a hundred maniacs," which is self-evidently sensationalist. Regardless of how many men participated in the gang rape, only one of them is Freddy's sire. The nickname implies that the collective madness of all the rapists was consolidated in the child. In reality, no matter what illness Freddy inherited from his biological father, his being a murderer was not preordained. That his birth resulted from gang rape is traumatic enough, and does not need to be amplified. The characterization betrays a regressive understanding of not only genetics, but of mental illness and sexual assault as well.

As in the 2010 remake, we see the familiar image of pool as portal: a character enters the pool in one reality and emerges in another. In this case, Yvonne leaves the world of Alice's wholesome birth story and enters the world of Amanda's perverted one. Freddy's ultimate goal is to possess Alice's baby and be reborn into the waking world. If he can change the circumstances of his birth, he can have another chance at life. The pool is one of several aquatic images in the film symbolizing the leaky border between these realities, and between two kinds of birth: the "fit" and the "unfit."

Like *A Cure for Wellness*, 1983's *The House on Sorority Row* features a doctor whose experimental fertility treatment results in a misbegotten child. Mark Rosman's film begins with a prologue where Dorothy Slater undergoes a difficult labor under the supervision of Dr. Nelson Beck. The baby's fate is not specified. Many years later, Dorothy is a sorority house mother with a contentious relationship with the sorority sisters. She refuses their request to keep the house open after the end of the semester so they can host a graduation party. The frustrated girls plan a revenge prank: They steal Dorothy's cane and force her at gunpoint to wade into the disused swimming pool to retrieve it. The gun, which they think is loaded with blanks, actually contains a live cartridge, and they accidentally shoot and kill her. Panicking, with party guests about to arrive, the girls decide to hide Dorothy's body in the pool. Later, when the pool lights are turned on, the body is gone, leading the girls to conclude that Dorothy survived. Meanwhile, an unseen figure is murdering partygoers with Dorothy's cane. In the latter part of the film, Dr. Beck shows up to deliver some backstory: Desperate to have a child, Dorothy took an experimental and illegal fertility drug that resulted in a child born with physical and intellectual disabilities. Her son Eric lived in the attic, and is now out for revenge after seeing his mother murdered by the girls.[12]

In a clear homage to *Les Diaboliques*, a body that disappears from a disused pool prompts speculation that the victim is still alive. But the power dynamics on display are less about gender than about class. On a basic level, the condition of the pool represents Dorothy's womb, underused and "unclean." But the girls' relationship to the pool also stands for their relationship to the house in general, and by extension to Dorothy herself. The sorority sisters are all able-bodied, wealthy and white, embodying the American eugenicist ideal. One of them is off to law school in the fall, one is going to work for an airline—they will be replaced by another group of able-bodied, wealthy white undergraduates, and Dorothy will remain, hiding her disabled child in the attic like an embarrassment. As in *Taste of Fear*—another film that riffs on *Diaboliques*—a dirty pool with a disappearing corpse is a stand-in for a character's abnormal physicality, a violation of the "clean and proper." Also, like Penny in that earlier film, Dorothy's identity is inextricable from her disability as far as those around her are concerned. Dorothy's cane becomes both the subject of the girls' prank and Eric's primary weapon, symbolizing the way Dorothy's family is othered by physical disability and relative lack of privilege. When the cane is thrown in the pool, like when Penny falls wheelchair and all into hers, literal and symbolic otherness collide.

The girls from *The House on Sorority Row* (1983) take the prank too far: Vicki (Eileen Davidson) pulls a gun. From left: house mother Dorothy (Lois Kelso Hunt), Liz (Janis Ward), Morgan (Jodi Draigie), Jeanie (Robin Meloy) and Katey (Kathryn McNeil).

Dorothy closes the house every year on Eric's birthday, to celebrate it without the girls around. Believing her to be a spinster, assuming no boundary between her professional and personal lives, the girls think Dorothy does this merely to spite them, leading to the cruel prank that results in Dorothy's death. The relationship is typical of privileged people with domestic servants; working-class women hired to take care of wealthy kids either make arrangements for the care of their own children, or leave them to look after themselves. The sorority sisters do not know that Dorothy has her own family, and it's not clear if they care. Even the job title "house mother" elides the possibility of Dorothy having a biological family of her own. She is only a "mother" as it pertains to the comfort and privilege of the girls on sorority row. As far as they are concerned, she is derelict in this duty. She doesn't even take care of the pool.

More birth defects and class disparities show up in *Fever Dream* (2021), directed by Claudia Llosa. The film unpacks the relationship between two mothers: wealthy Amanda and small-town resident Carola. Amanda rents a vacation home in Carola's village. Carola has a son named David, whom she is reluctant to talk to Amanda about. We eventually learn that as a young boy, David drank contaminated river water and was taken to a local witch doctor, who saved him through a process called "transmigration," which placed half of David's spirit into another body. The procedure halved the effect of the toxins and saved his life, at the cost of David's body now playing host to another soul. Carola believes her son is a stranger living in her house. Amanda is skeptical, until her daughter Nina falls ill and needs to undergo the same procedure. Meanwhile, Amanda begins to notice that the town is full of children with visible deformities. "Very few children are born normal here," David confirms. It turns out that the birth defects, and the poisoning of the local water that leads to Amanda's hospitalization and eventual death, result from the constant spraying of pesticides in the agrarian community.[13]

The swimming pool at Amanda's vacation house is a recurring image in the film, underscoring the glamorous image Amanda has of Carola. Even though she works as a horse farm accountant, she dresses and acts like a cosmopolitan woman of leisure. Amanda has difficulty reconciling these two views when she sees Carola lounging poolside. The pool, with its deceptive reflections, represents the two sides of Carola, like the twin souls that exist in David and Nina's bodies after the transmigration procedure. As she watches Nina playing in the pool, Amanda privately calculates what she calls the "rescue distance": how far she can allow Nina to stray while still being close enough to save her from danger. The pool, despite its attendant risk of drowning, represents safe water, because the danger is plain to see. The other water, the town water poisoned with pesticides, is the dangerous water, because the peril is invisible. How can she rescue her child from disaster she doesn't even know is lurking?

Like the baron in *A Cure for Wellness*, the agriculture industry in Carola's town treats the peasants as disposable, flooding the area with pesticides for profit's sake without considering their damage to the populace. As Carola points out, the wealthy visitor Amanda has the privilege of being able to leave, while Carola and her family have no choice but to stay. Surfaces are deceptive: Carola's upscale fashion sense does not save her from the industry that is strangling her community; David's physical normalcy does not make him healthier than the deformed local children; the seemingly peaceful river is not safer than the artificial pool. *Fever Dream* roundly disproves the eugenicist point of view: A poisoned gene pool is the result of external forces, not inherent, and its effects go much further than skin deep.

At the start of director Rodo Sayagues' *Don't Breathe 2* (2021), we learn that Norman Nordstrom, the blind ex–Navy Seal who was the villain of the first film, is now our protagonist. Norman is attempting to live peacefully, operating a plant nursery in the house he shares with a young girl named Phoenix, who believes herself to be his daughter. Norman has told Phoenix that her mother died in a house fire. One night, a group of men attacks the pair in their home. The group's leader, Raylan, announces that he is the girl's biological father. They leave Norman for dead, trapped in the burning house, and take Phoenix to the city. In a partially abandoned apartment building, Raylan, who was just released from prison, tells the girl that her real name is Tara. She also meets her mother Josephine, who was badly injured in a house fire and is in a wheelchair. We learn that Raylan and Josephine are meth dealers, and the fire was the result of a lab explosion. They also reveal why they sought her out: Josephine needs a heart transplant, and the donor must be a blood relative. The girl is strapped to a table for a black-market organ extraction, but Norman, who

Phoenix (Madelyn Grace) embraces the dying Norman (Stephen Lang) near the derelict pool at the end of *Don't Breathe 2* (2021).

survived the fire and tracked them down, cuts the power to the building before the procedure can begin. One by one, Norman defeats Raylan's henchmen, culminating in a confrontation at the derelict building's empty pool. The girl is handcuffed to Josephine's wheelchair, and when Josephine is killed in the struggle, the wheelchair pulls her into the pool, despite her efforts to sever her dead mother's arm before they can fall together. After a fight, Norman defeats Raylan, gouging out his eyes with his bare hands. The still-living Raylan gets the drop on Norman, wounding him. The girl stabs Raylan with a machete and he falls into the empty pool, finally dead. Norman apologizes to the girl and obtains her forgiveness before succumbing to his wounds. The girl escapes to a better life at an orphanage, introducing herself as Phoenix, the name Norman gave her.[14]

Speaking practically, it's hard to separate Norman's character from his portrayal in the first *Don't Breathe*, which in traditional horror fashion uses disability to signal internal corruption. It's a bold choice by the sequel's filmmakers to try to turn the first film's evil sexual assaulter into a sympathetic protagonist, but since I believe that sequels should be considered on their own terms, I will confine my analysis here to his portrayal in *Don't Breathe 2*.

Don't Breathe 2 is dominated by disability narratives. As scholar Seth Hadley has observed, the *Don't Breathe* films embrace the social model of disability, which holds that disability is not an inherent condition, but rather a relationship with a built environment that is difficult to live in with a certain kind of body or brain. When Norman turns out the lights on his foes, creating a dark battleground where he now has the upper hand, this shows how the built environment can be remade to blind people's advantage.[15] On the other side of the disability politics coin is wheelchair-bound Josephine, who conforms to the stereotype of disabled person as burden to those around them. The film portrays this relationship in ways both literal—she tries to murder her daughter to steal her heart—and symbolic. In the scene where Phoenix is handcuffed to the wheelchair as it inches toward the pool, the girl is literally shackled to her mother's disability. She tries to sever the connection, thereby disfiguring her mother further, but can't keep from being dragged down with her.

The difference between Norman and Josephine—disability as superpower or burden—might be due to how they acquired their disabilities. Norman's blindness is the result of a war wound, while Josephine was injured by the smoke from her burning meth lab. Like the corporate agriculturalists of *Fever Dream*, Josephine poisoned her community in the selfish pursuit of profit. Thus, despite resulting in a rather muddled politics, the characterization may have more to do with personal responsibility than physical ability.

The climax's setting, an empty, dilapidated pool, is consistent with the film's worldview. The specter of civic decay haunts the film's locations. Everybody is broken, sick or struggling. Phoenix finds salvation not in her intact two-parent home, but rather in an orphanage. There is no room in this world for cleanliness, fitness or recreation, the three traditional functions of the apartment pool. Instead it sits empty and yawning, an open grave waiting for an occupant. In the end, it finds not one occupant, but three: Raylan, Josephine and Norman, all of whom lived and died by the sword.

Raylan proves that he is Phoenix's biological father by displaying a heritable trait: a lock of white hair they share. Early in the film, Phoenix asks Norman, "Did I get my white hair from you or from mom?" interrogating the role of genetics in determining personhood. People with disabilities, congenital or otherwise, were victimized by eugenicist thought as much as people of minoritized ethnic groups.[16] In the same way that *A Cure for Wellness* and *Fever Dream* critique the eugenicist obsession with exteriors, *Don't Breathe 2* calls genetic determinism into question. The family that matters is not the people with whom you share blood, the film says, but rather the people who truly care for you, as emphasized in the film's final moments, when the girl chooses the name Phoenix.

In Part I, I mentioned Angela M. Smith's argument that the horror film, while it may use disability for shock value, balances sensationalism with an assumed audience compassion for "embodied vulnerability."[17] This chapter's films do not beg much sympathy for the disabled people they portray. Most of them lean more toward revulsion. Even *Don't Breathe 2*'s Norman is violent and physically imposing at best, and if the character's history is taken into account, homicidal and sadistic at worst. All of these films, though, grapple with the legacy of eugenicist thought—with the ethics of policing human reproduction and the relationship between physical ability and social viability—through the well-understood symbol of the pool and its place in public life. In the words of scholar Shannon L. Walsh, progressive era physical culture was "both radically democratic (methods were accessible to all) and fundamentally exclusionary (some bodies were assumed to be beyond correction)."[18] The progressive-era passion for building municipal pools was part of the attempt to democratize fitness, but the other kind of "fitness" was inherently undemocratic. Historically, proponents of exclusion have not been known to break their stride for a little thing like complete lack of evidence for their claims. If the underclasses are not courteous enough to treat their own inferiority as a foregone conclusion, those in positions of power may go even further, as in *A Cure for Wellness* and *Fever Dream*, and quite literally poison the well.

CHAPTER 15

Life Guards

Interlopers and Home Invasions

> He stole a Rolls-Royce and drove it in a swimming pool.
> They took a clean-cut kid and they made a killer out of him.
> —Bob Dylan, "Clean Cut Kid"

> I was tempted by the devil in this deep blue swimming pool,
> until the devil's makeup ran.
> —Duran Duran, "I Believe/All I Need to Know"

"One of the most common boogeymen featured in 1990s horror films," writes John Kenneth Muir, "is the dreaded 'Interloper.' This invading villain may be defined as a person (and often a woman) who deliberately interferes with the affairs of another." In a typical interloper film, the protagonist opens the door a crack and the villain muscles their way in and takes over their entire life. Muir notes that every aspect of the victim's life is ultimately threatened by these "boogeymen," up to and including identity itself.[1] This chapter focuses on the interloper narrative's class and gender dimensions, because very seldom are the interlopers on the same social footing as their victims. Wealthy characters and their families are often menaced by an unscrupulous working-class villain who sees an opportunity to improve their lot in life. Also, as Muir points out, the interloper is more likely than other types of horror villains to be a woman—due in part to the interloper's tendency to use sexual seduction, and in part to women's assumed preeminence in the domestic sphere. Thus the interloper film, in its typical form, reverses the usual power dynamics. In the real world, men are more likely to victimize women, and rich people are more likely to victimize poor people (at least in the domestic realm, where these movies live) than vice versa. Interlopers actively use cops, courts, government and other institutional machinery against their victims, exploiting legal loopholes and filing fraudulent reports. In a world where unreported sexual assaults are 15 times more common than false accusations,[2] and where a landlord can evict a tenant for calling the police on an abusive partner,[3] these films can seem like projection—a nightmare of class warfare tactics being turned around the other way.

Because of the class divide these films frequently present, and because inter-

Snake in the garden: Interloper Violet (Jaime Pressly) turns on the poolside temptation in *Poison Ivy: The New Seduction* (1997).

lopers often use seduction to infiltrate their victims' lives (there is lots of overlap with the erotic thriller), swimming pools function as both symbols of affluence and sites of sexuality. A good example is *Poison Ivy: The New Seduction* (1997). In a prologue to Kurt Voss' third entry in the *Poison Ivy* series (which for simplicity's sake I'll call *Poison Ivy III*), we meet Violet and Ivy, the young daughters of a housekeeper named Rebecca, who works for the Greer family. Violet and Ivy treat the Greers' daughter Joy as a third sister, until Catherine Greer fires Rebecca for sleeping with her husband Ivan, a wealthy banker. Eleven years later, the now-adult Violet returns to the Greer household and reconnects with Joy. Joy invites Violet, who works as a waitress and says she is saving up to attend community college, to stay in her deceased mother's old bedroom. After Joy's fiancé Michael and his yuppie friends insult her with classist microaggressions at a late-night pool party, Violet takes revenge by seducing Michael. Violet later seduces Joy's father Ivan after skinny-dipping in the pool. Eventually, Violet murders both Michael and the new housekeeper Mrs. B after both threaten to expose her, as well as Ivan when he tries to evict her. Violet wants Joy to carry out a suicide pact with her, but the two women struggle and Violet ends up falling to her death down the house's grand staircase.[4]

Violet is a typical interloping temptress. Like her sister Ivy from the first film, she not only seduces her target family's patriarch, but also seeks to replace the mother, living in her bedroom and wearing her clothes. *Poison Ivy III* also demonstrates a common blind spot in this subgenre: Ivan makes a deliberate choice to sleep with Violet, whom he has known since she was a child and he was a full-grown adult, but somehow the blame is still placed on Violet for this indiscretion. Ivan is shown to have a history of infidelity—with Violet's mother, no less!—but at no point is the film critical of his part in the tryst with Violet. There is a rape-culture tendency to portray sexy women as predatory, and the men who fall for them as helpless victims of their wiles. Ivan, it seems, could not help himself, and in the film's lens, Violet bears the full responsibility for leading him astray.

Almost every time the film portrays a sexual encounter, it involves the Greer family's swimming pool. The film's opening image is an establishing shot that pans across the pool, setting up the opulence and simmering sexuality of the scenario. The pool boy arrives at the house with the skimmer sticking out of his car, a phallic foreshadowing of his assignation with Rebecca. Later, Violet endures microaggressions about waitressing and community college by Michael's ivy-league friends while lounging poolside. This leads to her decision to seduce him. The second time Violet and Michael have sex, it happens next to the pool. Violet gives Michael cocaine to reignite his drug addiction, which lowers his inhibitions, and also sets the stage for Michael's firing from his prestigious internship at Ivan's bank. Finally, Violet's dalliance with Ivan begins when she swims naked in the pool while he watches.

Violet, the daughter of a domestic servant, is a working-class conniver, adept at recognizing and exploiting people's flaws—Ivan's promiscuousness, Michael's drug addiction, Joy's insecurity. She wants the good life, represented by the pool, but is also able to see through the prosperous family's deceptive surface to the liabilities beneath. She represents the bourgeois male fear of a working-class woman who is more clever and crafty than she appears—and the chaos that can result if she manages to outsmart the men around her.

Another aquatic seductress surfaces in 2002's *Swimfan*, directed by John Polson. Protagonist Ben is a reformed delinquent whose drug use and thievery landed him in juvenile hall, where he discovered a passion for swimming while cleaning the facility's pool. Now a high school senior and champion swimmer, he is being eyed by college scouts and has a healthy relationship with his adoring girlfriend Amy. All of that changes when a new student, Madison, sets her sights on Ben. She seduces him in the school's pool after hours, and does not respect his boundaries when he regrets the infidelity and wants to remain friends. Madison's psychotic possessiveness escalates from cyberstalking to spreading rumors to falsifying drug test results to get him kicked off the team, all the way to framing him for murder. One day, Ben dives into the pool and finds the floating dead body of his friend Josh, bludgeoned with a baseball bat that was planted in Ben's locker. Finally, Madison runs Amy off the road in Ben's truck, landing Amy in the hospital. Ben tricks Madison into confessing on camera and she is arrested, but she escapes custody, kidnaps Amy, and pushes her into the pool handcuffed to a wheelchair. Ben is able to rescue Amy and pull Madison into the pool, where she drowns.[5]

Like *Poison Ivy III*'s Violet, Madison uses the wet, unclothed atmosphere of the swimming pool as a tool of seduction. In keeping with the woman-blaming tendency noted above, the guilt for the infidelity is placed squarely on Madison's shoulders.

Also echoing *Poison Ivy III*, like the ivy-league banker Michael, Ben has a history with drugs which Madison exploits to thwart his life ambitions. Frequently in these films, physical and financial harm is not bad enough for the well-to-do victims; the interloper may also seek to destroy their futures. Professional reputations are often in jeopardy, and in getting Ben kicked off the swim team, Madison is blocking Ben's way out of the hole he dug himself with his poor choices earlier in life.

Fittingly, the film's climax brings us back to the high school pool, site of the original transgression. It is no longer a sexy place, nor does it represent Ben's quest for a better life; all that is left is a primal struggle against death. The image of a character falling into the pool while handcuffed to a wheelchair recalls a similar scenario in *Don't Breathe 2*. Like Phoenix in that film, Amy shackled to the wheelchair is an innocent who is made to pay for the misdeeds of another. Also like Phoenix, Amy is rescued by the film's flawed protagonist using the skills of the lifestyle he is trying to leave behind. Ben calls upon his lockpicking ability, a relic from his thieving days, to save Amy from drowning. In traveling to the bottom of the pool, he also travels back to his old life before swimming, stripped of everything but the will to survive.

The dangerous seducer of the erotic interloper thriller is not always a woman. In James Foley's *Fear* (1996), a rough-and-tumble working-class man named David infiltrates the lives of the wealthy Walker family when he begins a relationship with 16-year-old Nicole. After David's psychotic jealousy rears its head when he beats up Nicole's platonic friend Gary for hugging her, he responds to Nicole's attempts to break things off with increasingly violent behavior. David and his gang lay siege to the Walker house, where after a long struggle Nicole's father Steven finally throws David to his death through a window.[6]

Steven's conflict with David is portrayed in primeval terms. The younger, macho David is a threat to Steven's masculinity and ability to look after his family. This is made clear when Steven comes home to find David and his friends lounging around the pool with Nicole and Steven's wife Laura. As Steven watches, David teasingly throws Laura into the pool and jumps in after her. As we discussed in Part II, a man throwing a woman in the pool is never as playful as it seems. It is an implicit gesture of sexual dominance, and Steven is just as bothered by Laura's good-natured reaction to it as by the act itself. David is well aware of this dynamic. When Steven confronts him near Nicole's school, David points out that Steven's dislike of him is rooted in his "inadequacies": his worry that he is losing control over his daughter and his wife. David says, "I also know you ain't keeping up your end of the bargain with the missus. 'Cause if you were, she wouldn't be all over my stick."

David, it turns out, has been lying about his past, claiming he comes from an intact family when in fact he grew up in foster care. He is also concealing criminal activity, as it seems that he and his gang run a drug operation. Most filmic interlopers are deceptive in this way. Violet in *Poison Ivy III* lies about going to community college, Madison in *Swimfan* conceals that her ex-boyfriend Jake is in a coma that she caused. Despite all the evidence that David is not who he claims to be, Steven's multiple attempts to get the police involved are unsuccessful. Muir notes this as a common feature of the interloper film: "[A]ll attempts at police intervention in these films are utter failures. Victims must take care of interlopers without benefit of help from authority."[7] When the class disparity is taken into account, this element emerges as another projection of bourgeois insecurity. Policemen's hands are always tied in these movies. In the real world, if a rich architect called the cops on an adult, working-class, demonstrably untruthful man who was having sex with his 16-year-old daughter, it's highly unlikely that he (the architect) would be rebuffed.

The typical interloper film seems to take place in a world where rich men are easily victimized by women, the poor, or both. In *Poison Ivy III*, Violet causes the classist Michael to lose his bank internship, thereby bringing him closer to her social level. *Swimfan*'s Madison uses the legal system against Ben, leveraging his past as a juvenile delinquent to cast suspicion upon him for the assaults on Josh and Amy. Spreading rumors to smear reputations, exploiting legal loopholes, making fraudulent claims of criminal activity, playing the game of "it's your word against mine; which are they going to believe?"—these tactics are much more likely to be employed by the rich against the poor, or by men against women, than the other way around. Describing a technique called "accusation in a mirror," an anonymous Rwandan genocidaire wrote that successful propagandists "impute to enemies exactly what they and their own party are planning to do."[8] Along the same lines, the interloper movie is often a subconscious expression of the bourgeois fear that one day, the poor might treat them the way they treat the poor.

Not every interloper movie casts a person from a minoritized group as the villain. The interloper rogue's gallery has more than its share of privileged white men. But even when this is the case, class consciousness bubbles to the surface of the swimming pool in sometimes unexpected ways.

Ben of *Swimfan* is not the only former delinquent turned competitive high school swimmer whose future in the sport is threatened by a 2000s interloper. The same situation befalls Michael Harding, whose family is targeted by the titular villain in Nelson McCormick's 2009 remake of *The Stepfather*. The villain, who spends most of the film going by David Harris, has a pattern. He seduces single mothers and marries them, infiltrating their households in an attempt to have a picture-perfect family. When things go wrong—when the family does not conform to his ideal, or when he is in danger of being exposed—he murders the family, changes his appearance, and moves to another town to start again.

The film focuses on David's relationship with the recently divorced Susan Harding. She has a young son and daughter as well as a teenage son, Michael, who attends military school due to some bad behavior in school. By the time Michael comes home from school and meets David at a backyard pool party, David and Susan are already engaged. Michael is suspicious of the charming but secretive David, even after David does him a favor by convincing the high school athletic director to let him participate in the summer swim program, a first step in getting him enrolled back in his

The title character (Dylan Walsh) in *The Stepfather* (2009) weaponizes the swimming pool against the nosy Jackie (Paige Turco) for prying into his affairs.

home school. Meanwhile, David has been disapprovingly watching Michael's amorous behavior with his girlfriend Kelly in the backyard pool. Over the course of the film, David kills various people who threaten to expose his lying or his murderous past, like a neighbor who recognizes his face from *America's Most Wanted*, and Michael's father, who catches David in a lie about his background. David briefly works as a real estate agent for Susan's sister Jackie, but quits when asked for a photo ID. This makes Jackie suspicious. When David gets word that she plans to hire an investigator, he goes to her house and drowns her in the pool. Things come to a head when Michael finds his father's dead body in David's basement, leading to a fight where the two fall together off the roof of the house. Michael wakes from a coma to learn that David survived the fall and is still out there somewhere.[9]

Like in *Swimfan*, the pool and the sport of swimming represent Michael's ambitions to improve his life. He keeps a large photo of a swimmer above his bed. Many scenes find Michael and Kelly in or around the pool, discussing their hopes and plans for the future. Swimming is Michael's ticket out of military school and back to his home, where he does not need to be separated from his family or from Kelly. David gives Michael this opportunity, but while they want the same thing, they want it for different reasons. David does not really care about Michael's wellbeing, he simply believes that the family cannot be perfect if they are separated. In this regard, David has a lot in common with the fantasy suburban architects of *The Stepford Wives* and the abusive patriarch of *The Woman*: He is interested in the appearance of perfection, regardless of how healthy it is underneath. This is evident in the scene where David admonishes Michael for getting frisky with Kelly in the pool. "A young man should be more discreet with his affection," he says. "People might get the wrong idea about her."

The pool is a powerful symbol for both Michael and David, but in different ways. David is interested in checking boxes, and the pool signals both material success and domestic tranquility. When he comes home and suspects that Michael and

Kelly are snooping around, his fears are assuaged when he looks out the window and sees them swimming in the backyard pool, just like they are supposed to be. He later drowns Jackie, literally weaponizing the pool to maintain the illusion of perfection. Michael is more interested in what happens inside the pool, about the struggle and work that moves you forward into the future. David looks at the surface of the pool, while Michael sees through it. This contrast is demonstrated in a Joe Gillis shot where Michael and Kelly embrace underwater and Michael looks up to see a distorted image of David standing on the pool deck, looming over him. The staging emphasizes the gap between the two characters' points of view.

The Glass House (2001) offers a more realistic portrayal of class dynamics than the standard interloper film. Directed by Daniel Sackheim, it follows the sister and brother pair of Ruby and Rhett Baker, who lose their parents to a car accident and are placed under the guardianship of a pair of family friends. Erin Glass, a physician, and her husband Terry, manager of a transportation company, are a childless couple living in an opulent Malibu home. The teenage Ruby starts to become suspicious soon after moving in. Despite the size of the house, the siblings are forced to share a bedroom. The Glasses take them out of private school without a good explanation, and blatantly lie to a social worker. Terry leers at Ruby and behaves inappropriately when he sees her swimming in the house's pool. Ruby is skeptical that the drugs she sees Erin injecting are really for diabetes as she claims. Ruby's investigation reveals that the Glasses orchestrated her parents' deaths. They are after the siblings' trust fund money because Terry is deeply in debt to a loan shark and Erin has a serious drug addiction, which ends up ruining her career.[10]

Along the way, Ruby tries several times to appeal to authority, including the family lawyer, the social worker and the police, but she is rebuffed each time—a more realistic example of the interloper film's useless authority trope, as it's easy to believe that these authority figures would not take a teenage girl's word over that of a respected doctor or successful businessman. The Glasses' motive, too, is consistent with the film's themes. Rather than poor people seeking to infiltrate the lives of the rich, this film's villains are wealthy but in debt, seeking to maintain their lavish lifestyle by any means. They still have all the outward markers of material success, but they are in danger of losing them. Like much of high society, they are asset-rich but cash-poor.

The swimming pool does not play a large role in the plot of *The Glass House*, but it is frequently seen in the background. The film's title has multiple meanings. It is a pun on the family's surname, but it also describes the home itself, a modern building full of floor-to-ceiling windows. As I noted in reference to *Don't Worry Darling*, these windows offer the appearance of openness, but also rob people of their privacy. The Glasses, like many other villains described in this book, maintain an exterior as placid as the surface of the pool. In almost every scene set on the house's main floor, we can see through the walls to the pool in the background, a constant reminder of the sheen of affluence, but also of the place where Terry implicitly threatened Ruby

The quietly menacing Terry (Stellan Skarsgård) helps Ruby (Leelee Sobieski) out of the pool in *The Glass House* (2001).

with sexual violence. It underscores the tenuous situation the siblings are in, where putting a foot wrong could land them in harm's way. The Glasses, though, are in their own kind of hole—serious debt—and the last meaning of the title refers to their own peril. The life they have built around themselves is too fragile to sustain for very long—and when it shatters, everyone is in danger of being cut.

A more violent sister subgenre to the interloper film is the home invasion movie. Indeed, many interloper films, like *Fear*, transform into home invasion scenarios at the end. The only difference between the interloper and the home invader is that the latter is more blunt, never disguising their intentions to usurp and pillage your life—or at least, not disguising them for long. At the dawn of the 1980s, a film was released that set the stage for the Reagan-era class war horror that was about to unfold. Ruggero Deodato's *House on the Edge of the Park* (1980) is indebted to *The Last House on the Left*, but charts its own course through the tangle of resentment and domestic envy that characterized class struggle at the end of the 20th century.

It opens with the main character Alex accosting, raping and murdering a young woman in a park. We then get into the main plot, which finds Alex and his friend Ricky closing up the garage where they work when a rich couple, Tom and Lisa, arrive complaining of car trouble. After Ricky fixes the problem, Tom invites them to a party at a friend's house. They arrive at the opulent home and meet the rest of the friends: Gloria, Howard and Glenda. A dynamic quickly emerges: Ricky, who is established as "slow," is being ridiculed by the yuppies, but does not realize it. Alex recognizes the humiliation and becomes resentful, a frustration that is compounded by Lisa's sexual teases toward him. The yuppies make Ricky perform a striptease and take all his money by cheating in a poker game. Alex, infuriated by his friend's treatment, pulls out a razor and threatens the partygoers. Howard fights back, but Alex pummels him, throws him into the backyard pool and urinates on him. After incapacitating Howard, Alex tries to get Ricky to rape Gloria, but Ricky can't go through with it when he sees how scared she is. Alex ends up sexually assaulting all three women himself. The rest of the film unfolds as a tense home invasion scenario, with Alex holding the yuppies hostage despite intruding neighbors and an escape attempt. Gloria seduces Ricky during the latter incident, which gives him the gumption to stand up to Alex; he ends up disemboweled for his trouble. When the rich folks finally manage to turn the tables, Tom gets a hidden gun and shoots Alex before revealing that the woman Alex killed in the opening scene was Tom's sister. The whole scenario has been an elaborate revenge scheme. Another gunshot from Tom sends Alex sprawling into the pool, where Tom, Gloria and Howard take turns shooting him until he dies.[11]

Venus Flytrap (1987) is a spiritual successor to *House on the Edge of the Park* with a plot so similar that some consider it a remake.[12] But it's the differences that are key to our analysis here. Directed by T. Michael, *Venus Flytrap* starts with three street punks—leader Turk, his girlfriend B.B. and a sycophantic tagalong they call the Wimp—holding up a record store. During the robbery, two preppy rich kids named Danny and Ginger walk in and Turk watches one of them steal a cassette tape. Threatening to call the cops on the shoplifter, Turk browbeats them into letting his crew come along to a party at the home of their friends Rod and Arlene. Once they arrive, mind games commence similar to Deodato's film: a rigged game of strip darts; Russian roulette without a bullet; understated ridicule by the yuppies at the punks' expense. As things escalate, Turk tries to force Wimp to rape Ginger, but he refuses. Arlene skinny-dips in the pool to tease Turk, who follows her to her bedroom and rapes her. Meanwhile, Rod takes B.B. to the hot tub and Ginger mounts Wimp in the den. At this point, we cut to Danny in a hidden room, watching all these events on video monitors through the feed from cameras positioned around the house.

After this reveal, the yuppies turn the tables: Ginger stabs Wimp with a pair of scissors; Arlene bludgeons Turk; Rod drowns B.B. in the hot tub as she gives him a blow job and then has sex with her corpse. In the end, when all the punks are dead, we learn that the four preps do this all the time: They lure "degenerates" to their home, letting them think they have the upper hand, then seduce and murder them, videotaping everything for posterity in what they call "the game." As the credits roll, we watch them approach their next victims.[13]

While similar in superficial ways, *House on the Edge of the Park* and *Venus Flytrap* emerge from very different worldviews.[14] Although it depicts them as the aggressors, at no point does *House on the Edge of the Park* attempt to make the yuppies the bad guys or shift audience sympathy in favor of the punks. Alex's actions are so heinous that he crosses what tvtropes.org calls the "Moral Event Horizon" numerous times.[15] There is simply no redeeming him. *House on the Edge of the Park* begins in a city terrorized by blue-collar psychopaths, where the rich are innocent victims. It ends on the same note. The only difference is that the innocent rich victims have managed to claw their way to some well-deserved revenge. They even show mercy toward Ricky by letting him live after Gloria intercedes on his behalf.

Venus Flytrap also villainizes the punks, but only to a point. Turk is indeed a menace who arguably deserves his fate, but B.B. and the Wimp, for the most part, are deemed guilty by association only. B.B. drives the point home with her repeated insistence that she, Wimp and Turk should not be tarred with the same brush. Ultimately, B.B. and Wimp are victimized not because of what they have done, but because of the group they belong to. Like Deodato's film, *Venus Flytrap* suggests a community besieged by violent street punks. Turk says it himself in the opening scene when the record store clerk finds the 911 phone line busy: "This is a bad city!" Of course, an ironic echo comes later when Turk himself tries an emergency call but cannot get through. *Venus Flytrap* is full of this kind of generalization: While beating up Turk, Rod gives a speech about how "degenerates" need to learn respect for property, society and "your betters." When Ginger wonders what would happen if the cops got ahold of their videotapes, Arlene replies, "They'd probably give us a medal for helping them clean up the city."

These last two statements by the yuppies raise the question of motive. The rich group's motive in *House on the Edge of the Park* is clear and comprehensible. By contrast, *Venus Flytrap* leaves this matter ambiguous. To be certain, the yuppies are partly motivated by sexual gratification. Rod is a necrophile, Danny is a voyeur, and the women want to be raped, behave like teases or both. (Please note that minus questions of consent, I am not equating the other three forms of kink to necrophilia, but the film arguably does suggest this.)

There is also an indication that *Venus Flytrap*'s villains might have a consumerist motivation. In the final scene, Arlene is miffed about bloodstains on her rug, Rod is concerned about damage to his coffee table, and Danny is distraught over the breaking of his cameras. This suggests an obsession with material possessions that is consistent with a common critique of Reaganite yuppies. "Affluenza" is a term often used to mean a relentless desire on the part of the rich to accrue ever more money, possessions and power.[16] The more you have, the more you want. It's possible that Rod and his friends are collecting murder victims like baseball cards, with no real object other than "more."

The film welcomes all of these readings, but the best one might be something more nebulous: ennui. *Venus Flytrap* seems to exist in a world where rich kids float through life directionless, seeking some vague thrill and not too concerned with whom they have to hurt to get it. After all, in explaining to Turk why he does not use drugs, Danny remarks, "There's too many *real* kicks in life."

In 2013, a rich Texas teenager, Ethan Couch, received a relatively lenient penalty for a drunk driving escapade that killed four pedestrians. Some speculated that the light sentence was won by the defense's claim that Couch suffered from "affluenza," but the term had a different meaning from the one I explained above. The defense argued that the privilege of growing up wealthy had impeded the boy's judgment.[17] This language recalls the so-called "diseases of affluence" that drove scores of lethargic professionals into swimming pools to improve their physical fitness during the

Bad guy Alex (David Hess) gets his comeuppance at the hands of his yuppie would-be victims at the end of *House on the Edge of the Park* (1980).

progressive era we discussed in an earlier chapter.[18] Pseudoscientific though it may be, there is a kernel of truth in the notion that wealth and privilege can cause lapses of morality. While *Venus Flytrap* points this out, it stops well short of using it as an excuse like Ethan Couch's lawyers tried to.

The swimming pools' relative positions echo the shades of difference between Deodato's film and Michael's. In keeping with the more overt sexual dimension of *Venus Flytrap*, the pool is a place of seduction. Arlene skinny-dips to tease Turk, whom she cajoles into doing an awkward striptease similar to the one performed by Ricky in *House on the Edge of the Park*. *Venus Flytrap*'s characters express envy of the pool and hot tub, but it is mostly grounded in appreciation. "If I had one of these," B.B. says of the hot tub, "I'd be in it all the time." On the other hand, Alex's envy of the house and pool is rooted in resentment. After throwing Howard in the pool, he deliberately defiles the water by urinating in it. If he can't have a nice clean pool, his actions seem to say, he doesn't want anyone to have one.

Despite Alex's carnal aggression, he does not treat the pool as a sexy place. This signals that Alex's sexual violence is more about power and domination than sex, and casts a different light on his actions toward Howard. In *Venus Flytrap*, Wimp's reluctance to rape Ginger leads the other characters to mock him as gay, and he spends the next few scenes trying to convince them otherwise. Later in the film, Rod licks his finger excitedly while he tells Turk, "There is one thing I like more than getting beat up, and it's beating up bad boys like you." *House on the Edge of the Park*'s homoeroticism is more subtle. When Howard challenges Alex's dominance, Alex wets him in the pool before taking out his own genitals. He later says admiringly of Howard, "He's the only one with balls in the whole goddamn place," while asking

Ricky to take the belt off his pants to tie Howard up with. When Ricky refuses to rape Gloria, Alex does not call him gay, but rather shames him for challenging his authority. Alex, it seems, plays his power games with male and female parts alike.

The pool is also where Alex meets his end, and the sequence mirrors what has gone before. Tom, Lisa and Howard shoot Alex in the reverse order in which he victimized them. Tom starts by shooting Alex in the groin, symbolically taking away both his manhood and his weapon, which causes him to fall into the pool. The subsequent bullets injure him further as he feebly tries to swim away. Finally, Howard performs a parody of the torture Alex inflicted on him earlier, and then puts him out of his misery. His dead body remains in the pool, an image of finality in the place where all the night's horrors intersect.

Whether it's the poor terrorizing the rich, the rich abusing the poor, or a cycle of violence where the two reinforce each other, the backyard swimming pool is a perfect locale for portraying the have-nots' resentment of the haves. Most of the films in this chapter climax in physical confrontations inside the home, and end with the villain falling from a height. Fittingly for films portraying struggles between different versions of domestic bliss, these endings transform the family home itself into a battleground. When the intruder falls—down the stairs, out the window, off the roof, into the pool—they are symbolically being toppled from the heights they achieved through their conniving.

Interloper and home invasion films revolve around the *idea* of a home, but there is another horror subgenre that centers the home as a tradable commodity. If you've ever thought about putting in a pool to increase your house's resale value, the next chapter is for you.

Chapter 16

Underwater Mortgage

Housing and Class Struggle

> No lobby, no swimming pool, no need in buying no swimwear [...]
> They say America fights fair, but they won't demolish your timeshare.
> —Open Mike Eagle, "My Auntie's Building"

Home prices in the United States have risen steadily for as long as anyone alive can remember. Between 1970 and 2020, the median home price rose from $23,400 to $336,000, an increase of more than 1400 percent.[1] This is over 2.5 times the U.S. dollar's rate of inflation over that same period. The rise in home prices has outpaced inflation since 1972.[2] Based on the rule of thumb that the cost of your home should not exceed three times your yearly income, the last time a median-income family could afford a median house was sometime in the early 1970s.[3] According to one 2023 analysis, the average down payment on a home was more than 71 percent of mean local income.[4] A 2024 survey found that 61 percent of respondents doubted that they would ever be able to afford a home,[5] and a Redfin study from the previous year deemed only 16 percent of houses on the market to be affordable for the typical American family.[6] Despite home ownership still being touted as an essential part of the American dream, the last half-century has seen a consistent narrowing of the population who can feasibly attain it.

With housing anxiety so pervasive in the American psyche, and with such an apparent gulf between what we are told we can achieve and what is actually probable, for many people the backyard swimming pool has taken on a darker connotation. Rather than aspiration, it can inspire resentment: a discretionary indulgence, a symbol of waste and extravagance for those insensitive to how much the average person must struggle simply to get by. Many of the films in this chapter feature characters driven to violence by the housing inequality of the hypercapitalist United States and the swimming pools it promises, but doesn't always deliver. As we'll see, the identity of the bad guy is never as clear as it looks on the surface.

Though the haunted house is one of the oldest tropes in horror, the thematic subgenre of real estate horror—films that focus specifically on the buying and selling of houses—came into its own in the last few decades of the 20th century. A good example is director Jag Mundhra's *Open House* (1987), which portrays a spate of murders being committed against real estate agents inside the houses they are trying to sell. A man calling himself Harry begins phoning radio psychologist David with rants about the murders, leading David and others to suspect he is the perpetrator. David's girlfriend Lisa, who runs a real estate brokerage, has a slimy business rival named Barney. One night Barney visits the house of a prospective client who agrees to give him the listing in exchange for a sexual dalliance. Afterward, the murderer decapitates Barney with an axe and tosses his severed head into the pool where the homeowner is swimming nude. Upon discovering Barney's remains, she too is murdered. Harry later kidnaps Lisa and takes her to a house she is listing. David and the police track them down. During a standoff, Harry explains that he is homeless and was squatting in an abandoned house until a property company sold it, robbing him of what he had come to think of as his home. The real estate industry, he says, has driven home prices so high as to be inaccessible to average people, which has turned him into a murderer. Harry then dies in a confrontation with the police.[7]

Even though real estate agents are the good guys in *Open House*, the film and its characters spare them no criticism. This criticism is often explicitly gendered, since practically all the real estate agents we see in the movie are women. Early in the film, one cop says to another, "Is there any way we can keep these real estate bimbos out of their empty houses?" His colleague responds, "They'd sell their mothers for a commission." Later in the film, during one of his calls to the radio station, Harry frames his crimes in terms that bluntly evoke sexual assault: "All these uppity little real estate bitches are just asking for it."

The journey that real estate sales took to becoming a pink-collar field was a swift one. The National Association of Realtors started in 1908 with exactly zero female members, and it stayed that way more or less through the 1940s.[8] Women got a foothold in the industry thanks to the World War II–era rush of women in the workplace and the postwar housing boom discussed earlier in this book.[9] Still, in 1975, women accounted for less than 40 percent of full-time real estate agents. By 1987, the year of *Open House*'s release, that portion had ballooned to two-thirds,[10] where it remains to this day.[11] Clearly the 1980s saw an explosion of women in real estate, and we can make some inferences as to why. Cost of living and inflation surges early in the decade[12] forced many single-income households to become two- (or more) income households. Between 1979 and 1986, the share of married women holding jobs increased by almost 11 percent.[13] Real estate was a professional, well-paying job with a relatively low barrier to entry; but more importantly, it offered schedule flexibility that could accommodate childcare and other household responsibilities.[14] Less tangibly, selling houses had long been one of the jobs that were socially acceptable for women to hold, due to their "moral and nurturing flair as well as their knowledge of all things domestic," in the words of journalist Grace Stetson.[15] So while men were willing to see real estate as women's work, many still felt an underlying unease about women being responsible for the buying and selling of that fundamental token of identity, the family home. This unease can be heard in some of *Open House*'s dialogue as quoted above, which plays into the stereotype of the venal, amoral businesswoman—far from the nurturing female ideal, but rather the kind who would "sell their mothers for a commission."

In *Open House*, the only male real estate agent we spend much time with is the truly loathsome Barney Resnick, a character who is openly misogynistic, sexually harassing, and not above sabotaging properties to undercut his competitors. In short, he is everything the film's characters accuse female agents of being. Partway through the film, a homeowner tells Barney that she will allow him to list her home in exchange for kinky sex—a chauvinist's dream come true. The dream ends when the Open House Killer severs Barney's head while the homeowner takes a post-coital dip in her pool, which is fed by a decorative waterfall. When the killer deposits Barney's head in the waterfall, his blood begins to drip into the pool. This intrusion of death into the pristine, controlled environment of the pool, this unclean discoloration, reminds us of similar intrusions in *Confessions* and *Swimfan*. The home's sanctity has been violated. Once again, the pool transforms from a site of sexuality into a grave.

"Pretty expensive houses they died in," Harry tells David on the telephone. "Plenty of people out there wish they just had something to eat." This is one of several speeches in which the killer explains his resentful worldview. Is it fair that these people—especially women—toy with the buying and selling of luxurious homes while so many others struggle? Harry, a homeless person, is like Mary in *8MM*, Glumley in *The Apartment Complex*, Dorothy in *The House on Sorority Row*, Violet in *Poison Ivy III*: essentially invisible to the people that matter, and notable only for what he represents rather than his personhood. In the climax when Harry asks David whether he is "blind to the homeless," David dodges the question, but the viewer knows the answer. The only acknowledgment of homelessness on David's radio show is by a caller who rants, "I just want to exterminate them." Like the yuppies of *Venus Flytrap*, the film posits a monolithic "homeless" deserving of extermination without taking the individuals' humanity into account. To some extent, turnabout is fair play when it comes to depersonalization, so when David asks what Lisa has done to him, Harry understandably replies, "It's what they all done ... they made homes too damn expensive."

Without condoning his murderous response to it, we can still feel for Harry. He had been squatting in an empty house for a whole year before it was sold. On the verge of tears, Harry says simply, "It was my home." While the industry is not responsible for his rampage, it's possible that his homicidal potential would have never been triggered if he were not priced out of the market. What follows is a misguided but desperate cry for fairness. Until they are accessible to everybody, Harry's crusade says, your swimming pools will run red with blood.

Rob Zombie's *Halloween* (2007) is the first *Halloween* franchise film to frame the Michael Myers story in explicit class-struggle terms. This remake of the 1978 film devotes a lengthy prologue's worth of backstory to the young Michael Myers

Dr. Loomis (Malcolm McDowell, with gun) rescues Laurie (Scout Taylor-Compton) from the approaching Michael (Tyler Mane) in the Myers house's pool on a bloody *Halloween* (2007).

and the circumstances leading up to his Halloween night murders. In the prologue, ten-year-old Michael lives in poverty with his mother Deborah, his teenage sister Judith, baby sister Angel and Deborah's abusive boyfriend Ronnie. Deborah, who works as a stripper, is the family's sole breadwinner. When a bully at school torments him over his mother's line of work, Michael, who tortures small animals in secret, beats the bully to death in the woods. On Halloween, after Deborah goes to work, Judith reneges on her promise to take Michael trick-or-treating in favor of spending the evening with her boyfriend Steve. Michael kills Ronnie, Steve and Judith but spares baby Angel, sitting with her on the stoop to await their mother's return. Michael spends the next 17 years in a mental institution, under the care of psychologist Samuel Loomis, during which time Deborah takes her own life. The now-adult Michael, silent for 15 years, escapes the institution and returns to Haddonfield on Halloween night.

Meanwhile, real estate broker Mason Strode and his wife Cynthia have adopted Angel Myers and given her the name Laurie. Now 17 and unaware of her birth family, Laurie is preparing to spend Halloween babysitting, while Mason readies the abandoned Myers house for potential buyers. Michael murders Mason and Cynthia in their home, as well as Laurie's friend Lynda, her boyfriend and others. Dr. Loomis, having heard of Michael's escape, arrives in Haddonfield and buys a handgun. Michael abducts Laurie and takes her to the Myers house, where he shows her a picture of the two of them as kids. Not understanding, Laurie stabs him and runs away, only to fall into the Myers house's empty backyard swimming pool. She tries in vain to climb out as Michael approaches her. Dr. Loomis shows up and shoots Michael three times, apparently killing him. Michael soon reappears to grab Laurie and take her back into the house. They fall together off an upstairs balcony, and Laurie finally shoots Michael in the head.[16]

When Angel Myers becomes Laurie Strode, more changes than just her name.

To emphasize Laurie's class transition, the Strode house is portrayed as exaggeratedly wholesome, while the Myers home is exaggeratedly dysfunctional. Deborah Myers is raising three children on an exotic dancer's income, as well as supporting Ronnie, who cannot work due to a disability. Michael is ostracized at school because of the stigma of his mother's profession. By contrast, Mason Strode is a respected white-collar professional. Everybody in the Myers house, young and old, screams obscenities at one another, whereas Cynthia Strode cannot bear to hear Laurie talk about sex, even jokingly. Ronnie sexually harasses Judith and taunts Michael with homophobic insults; Mason implores Laurie to be safe on Halloween. Deborah leaves the kids on Halloween to work; the Strode family greets trick-or-treaters together and embraces on the front porch as night falls. Deborah's kitchen is messy; Cynthia's is homemaker-magazine worthy. Despite all of this, it is the Myers house that has a backyard pool. Perhaps the family was in better financial shape before Deborah became a single mother. Judith mentions that her father is dead; if we assume that Judith and Angel have the same dad, he must have died quite recently. It's possible that we are seeing a family in the midst of downward social mobility.

Halloween's essentialist view of adoption is reminiscent of *Society*. The protagonists of both films are adopted into wealthier households than their birth families, but the reality of their origins makes them vulnerable. Bill in *Society* is seen as food by his family thanks to his "low birth"; in *Halloween*, Michael is the ghost from the past who shows up to remind Laurie where she came from. In the hospital, young Michael tells his mother that he wants to remain masked because "it hides my ugliness." Laurie's new, more privileged life is a kind of mask, hiding the ugliness of her family of origin. Mason has gentrified Laurie and, as a real estate broker, he is in the process of gentrifying the Myers house as well. But one thing he forgot to do was clean up the pool.

Michael kidnaps Laurie with the intention of reuniting in their childhood home. He even brings along a photograph to prove they are brother and sister. Laurie, resisting the message, tries to flee the place she came from and ends up trapped in the empty pool. The dry pool filled with dead leaves, like the holiday of Halloween itself, suggests the end of summer, and with it, the end of childhood innocence. The absence of water recalls the void left by people Laurie has lost: a friend, a sister, two sets of parents. She scrambles to escape the pool, but the lip is too high and the side too steep. Just like *Night Swim*, *Halloween* reminds us how things can be going great until we find ourselves, in the wake of a sudden tragedy or the loss of a support structure, in a hole that seems impossible to climb out of. Before you know it, the backyard pool, aspirational totem of upward mobility, turns into a trap.

Laurie Strode is not the only 21st-century horror remake teen protagonist to have a parent who works in real estate. Charley Brewster, the lead in Craig Gillespie's *Fright Night* (2011), lives in the Las Vegas suburbs with his divorced mother Jane, a real estate agent. Charley's childhood friend Ed thinks Charley's new neighbor Jerry is a vampire, responsible for several of their classmates' disappearances. Charley,

At a vacant house with a full swimming pool, Jerry (Colin Farrell) corners and vampirizes the willing Ed (Christopher Mintz-Plasse) in 2011's *Fright Night* remake.

who is embarrassed by the geeky Ed and would prefer to spend time with his new girlfriend Amy, blows him off, so Ed continues the investigation alone. That night, Jerry intercepts Ed on his way home and reveals that he is aware of Ed's interest in him. Jerry chases Ed through an abandoned house and into its backyard pool, where he corners Ed and vampirizes him. After he realizes Ed is missing, Charley gradually uncovers the truth. Sneaking into Jerry's house, he finds prison cells where Jerry keeps victims while slowly feeding on them. Charley seeks help from Peter Vincent, a Vegas performer with expertise in the occult, but is turned away. Jerry shows up at Charley's house and blows it up by igniting the gas line. Charley, Amy and Jane flee together in Jane's car, and Jerry gives chase through the desert, almost killing them before Jane stakes him with a real estate sign. Peter contacts Charley, having changed his mind and wanting to help, but Ed, now a vampire, attacks Peter's penthouse when they arrive. Amy and Charley flee into a nightclub, where Amy is bitten and abducted by Jerry. Peter and Charley return to Jerry's house to confront the vampires, whom they defeat by shooting holes in the walls and floor to let in the sunlight. In an epilogue, Jane is shown to be in the market for a new house.[17]

Teenage social anxieties and suburban housing alienation collide in *Fright Night* with literally explosive results. Charley's neighborhood, which Jane is partially responsible for populating, is a transient one. People move away often enough that sudden disappearances are unremarkable. Many of the residents work nights on the Vegas strip, so Jerry can sleep all day and black out his windows without arousing much scrutiny. But more than anything else, what makes this suburb perfect hunting ground for a vampire is its soullessness. It's a flat square of mass-produced cardboard dropped into the middle of the desert. Hardly anyone hails from there, and hardly anyone stays long enough to form a relationship with the land. No one is likely to bat an eye at a remorseless vampire walking among them.

The abandoned houses that dot the landscape echo Jerry's moral emptiness, and at the same time communicate the sadness of a slowly dying neighborhood. The film makes use of lore that says a vampire cannot enter a dwelling unless invited in. Ed flees from Jerry into a vacant house and thinks he is safe. Jerry scoffs, saying the rule does not apply to abandoned homes. Later, Jerry destroys Charley's house, taunting, "Don't need an invitation if there's no house." *Fright Night* thus toys with the definition of "home," suggesting that it requires both permanent occupancy and a sound physical structure. In this suburb, neither is guaranteed.

Early in the film, Jane makes a comment about how cheaply built the houses in the community are. After all, in a bedroom community where people tend not to stay long, the dwellings don't need to be high-quality. They need to be functional, abundant and affordable. Real estate, like the show biz–associated service field many of the residents work in, is a support industry that benefits from the churn of people entering and leaving the region. In this way, the dwellings Jane brokers are like the prison cells in Jerry's house. Move people into them, profit for a while from their excess labor, and then flip them for the next occupant. Ironically, these capitalist realities help the characters defeat the vampires twice in the film: first, when Jane stabs Jerry with a real-estate sign, a sharp wooden stake she happens to have in the car with her; second, in Jerry's house, when the cheap building materials make it easy for the heroes to shoot holes in the walls and floor, creating shafts of sunlight that weaken the monsters. The profit-maximized housing industry may have worked in Jerry's favor for a while, but it ultimately proves inhospitable even to a vampire. As the film ends, Jane is looking for a new house, perhaps signaling that she finally wants to escape the exurban churn.

Despite his history of making backyard superhero movies with Evil Ed, Charley is eager to shed his nerdy image so he will have better luck with girls. Ed, like Frank in *The Pool* (2001), is a proto-incel. He holds some deeply misogynist views, which are not well concealed before his vampire transformation, and loudly shouted thereafter. He is resentful of Charley's desire to spend time with Amy, but that is no excuse for saying things like, "Girl's made you lazy in the head. Pussy'll do that." Amy, he says, is a "bimbo" whose only asset is being "doable." Ed feigns indifference to his place in the high school hierarchy, but in reality he is more concerned with it than anyone. He is frustrated with Charley, not for caring about his image, but rather for his success in altering it. Amy, on the other hand, is indifferent to these matters: "I knew you were a dweeb," she reassures Charley.

Cornering him in the abandoned house's pool, Jerry uses Ed's complex feelings about his outsider status against him. "You say you're glad you're different," says Jerry as he slowly approaches Ed in the pool. "How can you be, in a place like this?" Since Ed has found it hard to play by the suburban rules that encourage conformity and punish difference, Jerry offers him a "gift": the ability to live outside them.

Don't get them wet: At the YMCA pool, Billy (Zach Galligan) sees the start of a *Gremlins* (1984) population boom.

The tactic works: Alienated by his best friend and feeling he has nothing to lose, Ed finally submits to the vampire's kiss. Ed's feelings of abandonment by his community, like a vacant house in the suburbs, and unbelonging, like a swimming pool in the desert, lead him to decide in a moment of despair to give up the fight.

Gremlins (1984), directed by *Piranha*'s Joe Dante, features a small subplot where a Scrooge-like landlord threatens to evict a family at Christmastime. Though brief, it gestures toward the film's dominant theme: a xenophobic fear of a larger kind of eviction, with a dollop of '80s anxiety about economic globalism. In this analysis, I am indebted to John Kenneth Muir's reading of the film in *Horror Films of the 1980s*.

In *Gremlins*, traveling salesman Randy Peltzer is shopping in an unnamed city's Chinatown when he sees a small furry creature called a mogwai. Against his better judgment, the shop's owner agrees to sell the mogwai, named Gizmo, to Randy as a gift for his son Billy. Randy takes Gizmo back to his small town of Kingston Falls at Christmastime. One by one, the three rules of mogwai care—keep them out of bright light (which hurts them); don't get them wet (which causes them to reproduce asexually); don't feed them after midnight (which turns them into malevolent reptilians)—are violated. The critters find their way to a YMCA swimming pool where they reproduce en masse, resulting in a plague of pint-sized terrors that wreak havoc on the small community.[18]

Muir points out the economic anxiety that lies at *Gremlins*' heart. He calls Kingston Falls a "wealth- and property-obsessed" community" lorded over by "the creepy self-indulgent rich," a place where "absolutely everything is a commodity."[19] Add the wealthy Mrs. Deagle's callous attitude toward a family facing eviction, a local xenophobic crank suspicious of foreign-made goods, and set it against the backdrop of hyper-consumerist Christmas in a Norman Rockwell–quaint American town, and you have all the ingredients for a satire of go-go Reagan-era capitalism.

"You gotta watch out for them foreigners," says Mr. Futterman, "'cause they plant gremlins in their machinery." He evokes stories of mischievous creatures who were said to sabotage airplanes in World War II, though the word "gremlin" apparently has its origins in the superstitions of British RAF pilots during the first World War, as a way to elide the oversights of operators and mechanics.[20] "They're still shipping them over here," Futterman says, connecting global commerce to armed conflict. Futterman's implied "they" are the Japanese, against whose booming 1980s manufacturing economy the U.S. was widely thought to be losing.[21] The unspecified east–Asian nationality of Gizmo's original caretakers evokes America's erstwhile World War II enemies and then-current commercial rivals. A Japanese businessman in another '80s classic, *Die Hard* (1986), offers the quip, "Pearl Harbor didn't work out, so we got you with tape decks."[22] Where it pertains to the global economy, then, *Gremlins* is making what Muir calls "the protectionist argument, that one can only trust American technology."[23]

When the gremlins enter the swimming pool, the film invokes another 1980s American fear: being overwhelmed by immigrants. In 1983, Reagan's administration formed its Mass Immigration Emergency Plan, which provided for the detention of 10,000 migrants at any given time.[24] It was a response to the perceived crisis caused by the 1980 Mariel boatlift when roughly 150,000 Cuban and Haitian refugees arrived on U.S. shores. The press, particularly in Florida, connected the migrant influx with a rise in crime and depression in local wages,[25] which "converged with Reagan's dog-whistle signaling on race, deviance, and crime," in the words of historian Kristina Shull.[26] The Mass Immigration Emergency Plan also led to the first federally contracted private prisons, establishing the for-profit detention industry that supercharged the mass incarceration era.[27]

Although it charges membership fees, the YMCA, where *Gremlins*' antagonists reproduce, is run by a charitable non-profit and generally fills the role of a public space. After multiplying in the pool, the gremlins threaten to overwhelm the town with sheer numbers. This connects them to a longstanding stereotype about immigrant fertility—particularly that of Latin Americans like the Mariel Cubans. Anthropologist Leo R. Chavez writes that the idea of Latina fertility "produces a limited range of meanings, often focusing on their supposedly excessive reproduction, seemingly abundant or limitless fertility, and hypersexuality, all of which are seen as 'out of control' in relation to the supposed social norm." Part of the perceived threat, says Chavez: "Latino babies transgress the border between immigrants and citizens." When we keep in mind our concept of the swimming pool as a symbolic border and space of liminality, it's even more interesting when Chavez notes that these transgressions are often described using water metaphors: "leaky borders" and "the permeable category of citizenship."[28]

The gremlins, like the most bigoted stereotypes of non-white immigrants, are somewhat more than animal but somewhat less than human. Their physiology is alien, but they walk on two legs, speak, use tools and, most importantly, consume resources. Chavez quotes California anti-immigration activist Bette Hammond: "They come here, they have their babies, and after that they become citizens and all those children use social services."[29] When this collided with Reagan's well-known inveighing against "welfare queens," i.e., poor women of color whose reproductiveness drains public resources,[30] it's easy to see the political implications of this dehumanized public swimming pool peril. Taken as a whole, the gremlins—traded as commodities, arriving from overseas and using public resources to reproduce out of control and threaten a town's social fabric—embody 1980s conservative fears of a multi-pronged foreign attack on the American way of life.

As *Gremlins* proves, class warfare is not limited to the private, residential pool. Certain other kinds of pools, while technically more democratic, can still be exclusionary, and make those they exclude even less visible. The disadvantaged people in this chapter at least have the opportunity to make their frustration known. Those in the next chapter are in danger of being even more thoroughly erased.

CHAPTER 17

Pool, A/C, Cable TV

Travel for the Leisure Class

> Down the windy halls of friendship to the rose clipped by the bullwhip, the motel of lost companions waits with heated pool and bar.
> —Neil Young, "Thrasher"

> If it doesn't have a pool, then we're going someplace else.
> —Kate Fuller, *From Dusk Till Dawn*[1]

The process of writing this book has called upon me to do a great deal of analytical thinking about swimming pools. So I guess I should not have been surprised when my Google results for "Why do motels have swimming pools?" seemed to indicate that I was one of just a handful of people who have asked this question. Most of the results were websites for professionals in the hospitality industry, pitching the business benefits of building or upgrading pools. One person asked the question on the crowdsourcing answer platform Quora with a psychological hypothesis, and all of the responses boiled down to this: Motels and hotels have pools because people want them.[2] To me, this is not an answer, but rather the product of circular reasoning. People want motel pools because they are used to them; motels have them because people want them. Analysis abhors a tautology, so as the one asking the question, I guess it's incumbent on me to try to answer it.

To begin with, a swimming pool is not a destination. Part of a pool's appeal is that one can be built almost anywhere. By simply digging a hole, you can create a place to cool off and play in the water without having to be near a natural water source. Is your local climate too cold for comfortable swimming? Good news: For a bit more money, you can build a heated indoor pool. With some exceptions for truly extraordinary pools, the presence of a swimming pool in a certain place is not a reason to travel there.

Most of today's hotels exist because of vacation culture. Historian Cindy S. Aron writes, "Few people traveled for pleasure in eighteenth-century America. The dearth of good roads, bridges, maps, or places to stay en route made travel slow, onerous, and sometimes dangerous." During this period, there were a few resorts at the seashore or around natural springs—collectively known as watering places—but their use was reserved for the ultra-wealthy.[3] Until 1829 when Tremont House was built in Boston, there was nowhere in America outside of a private residence where a traveler could sleep in a room that had a lock on the door.[4] But by the 1890s, travel lodging was widespread enough for a *Century Magazine* article to proclaim, "Summer hotels are everywhere."[5] The motel, with its ubiquitous swimming pool, is an even more recent fixture, emerging with the growth of large highway systems in the early 20th century.[6]

Vacation, for a lot of Americans, means summer, but the concept is not as old as many think. Aron argues that vacation as we know it in the U.S. was "invented" by the emerging middle class in the decades following the Civil War.[7]

There are a few common misconceptions about summer vacation. One is that the tradition was created by the school calendar, when in fact it was the other way around. It's also a myth that summer break from school was started to give kids time to work on family farms. The most labor-intensive seasons for farming are the spring and autumn.[8] Besides, speaking from my own experience as a teacher in an under-resourced rural village, kids who are badly needed in the fields are needed year-round, and are more likely to forgo school entirely than to skip summers.

Actually, summer vacation began in urban areas and spread to rural ones.[9] Although the widespread availability of air conditioning has made them more comfortable, cities have always been maddeningly hot places in the summertime—so-called "heat islands" compared to the surrounding countryside, thanks to hot surfaces like pavement and roofing, less greenery, more machinery, and greater population density.[10] Leaving cities during the summer for cooler regions was a centuries-old upper-crust practice in Europe; it expanded to the American middle class in the 19th century thanks to two developments: railroads, and so-called "brain work."[11] The latter was an early term for the growing ranks of midlevel workers—bookkeepers, clerks, etc.—who did not engage in manual labor. Starting in the 1840s, public concerns about the medical consequences of overwork led corporations to begin offering paid time off for brain workers.[12] This, combined with the incorporation of school summer break in rural areas to standardize school calendars and avoid the insalubrious effects of overheated classrooms, made it so that by the late 19th century, lots of Americans had free time during the summer.[13] With railroads making travel accessible, and hotels built for accommodation, the stage was set for the mass adoption of vacation culture.

So we are closing in on an answer to why hotels have pools. If, in middle-class American shorthand, hotels mean vacation, vacation means summer, and summer means pools, then the presence of a pool in a hotel or motel is essentially symbolic. Architecture critic John Margolies agreed with me, writing in his history of the American motel, *Home Away from Home*, that motel pools' real function was symbolic: "What was important about the pools, patios, and surrounding landscaping is that they represented a taming and refinement of the landscape."[14] Even if it's not summer and you're not on vacation, and even if you have no intention of using it, a pool is always a selling point—enough for every motel to scream it from the marquee.

There is, of course, a darker side to the American vacation, and that's where horror films come in. There is a vulnerability to being in an unfamiliar place, perhaps even one where you don't speak the language. You sleep in a strange bed. Routines are upended. When on vacation, those who work in the service industry may be in the unfamiliar position of being waited on themselves. There is a topsy-turvy liminality to the "home away from home" concept, a tension between ease and disruption that can throw us off balance. The hospitality industry tries to counteract this by making their guests feel they know what to expect. Room layouts are more or less standardized across the industry, as are procedures and amenities, like pools. This is another symbolic function that hotel swimming pools serve: If the place has a pool, you know you're in at least somewhat familiar territory.

Year-round residents of tourist destinations do not always share the leisure of the vacationing class. Asbury Park, New Jersey, which topped Thrillist[15] and Newsweek's[16] recent lists of best U.S. beach towns, had a 2022 poverty rate of 19.7 percent,[17] over eight percent higher than the national one.[18] Summer vacation spots where the tourism industry drives the economy often see hardship in the off-season. Additionally, a 2018 study found that tourism is responsible for eight percent of global carbon emissions—a huge portion for optional leisure activities.[19] The horror films in this chapter, and their pools, shine a subaqueous light on these forgotten and overlooked consequences of our summer vacations.

The first stop on our tour lands us in Gatlin Lake, a secluded woodland campground turned battleground and the setting for *The Strangers: Prey at Night* (2018), second entry in the *Strangers* franchise, directed by *47 Meters Down*'s Johannes Roberts. Cindy, niece to the facility's owners, is on a road trip with her husband Mike and their teenage children Luke and Kinsey. En route to dropping Kinsey off at boarding school, they stop at Gatlin Lake overnight. Since it is the off-season, they are the campground's only guests. Shortly after arriving, they discover the slain bodies of Cindy's aunt and uncle, and find themselves besieged by a trio of masked murderers. The killers terrorize the family, slaughtering both parents; Luke is able to make it to the reception building to call for help. The killers chase him into the swimming pool area. Luke fights back, killing one of them poolside, but another attacker knocks him into the water and stabs him nearly to death in a struggle. Kinsey, despite a stab wound to her leg, manages to defeat the other two killers and get herself and her brother to safety.[20]

When is a family vacation not a family vacation? The parents' decision to send Kinsey to boarding school due to some bad behavior has created tension in the family: Kinsey feels she is being abandoned and given up on, and the parents have to make sacrifices to pay for it. Still, they are trying to make the best of it by turning the road trip into a family getaway. Mike in particular seems attached to the American vacation ideal. He tries to get the kids off their phones to play cards with him,

In *The Strangers: Prey at Night* (2018), Luke (Lewis Pullman) finds the pool at an off-season campground to be a very unfriendly place when a masked killer (Damien Maffei) is around.

but they are not receptive. This tension reminds us how strained attempts at canned togetherness can often be.

Befitting a family on a not-really-vacation, they are also not-really-tourists. As relatives of the campground's owners, they are in a middle position: not paying guests, but still unfamiliar with the environment. They get to see a side of the campground that most guests don't: the strangeness of a tourist place in the off-season. Upon entering the empty campground, Cindy remarks that everybody must leave after Labor Day. Like other examples of the eerie we've seen, from the empty pool symbol to the Rey household's quiet nighttime patio in *Paranormal Activity 2*, Gatlin Lake in the off-season fits Marc Fisher's sketch of the creepy sensation. "There is nothing present when there should be something."[21] But the horror film setting we've looked at so far that most closely resembles Gatlin Lake is the apartment complex of Shadow Woods from *Blood Rage*. Both are deliberately built in secluded forests. Both are easy to get lost in because of the environment's homogeneity. *The Strangers: Prey at Night*, like the franchise as a whole, draws on a long horror tradition of exploiting urban dwellers' fear of rural spaces. Establishing shots of this family's home and neighborhood show that they are absolutely city people. At one point, in Gatlin Lake, Kinsey and Luke are trying to flee back to their parents when they seem to get turned around. "Everything looks the same!" Kinsey despairs. The film stages multiple set pieces in identical-looking trailers. This emphasizes not only the environment's spookiness and the hospitality industry's tendency toward standardization, but also the family's disadvantage in not knowing the lay of the land. It's never entirely clear which are the "strangers" of the title—the nameless, masked killers, or the out-of-towners they menace.

Kinsey asks Luke, "What do you think Uncle Marv and Aunt Sheryl do here all alone in the winter?" It's a question that might provide a key to the famously obscure motives of *The Strangers* franchise's killers. Like *Venus Flytrap*, none of the *Strangers* movies give the viewer a satisfying answer as to why they murder. In each film, the victims ask why, and the killers give blasé responses like "Because you were home."[22] This film's version of the answer to the "Why?" question is, "Why not?" This may be a symptom of the above-noted urban fears, but it points out a real issue. In many rural areas, economic decline and the loss of local jobs and culture has left large populations with nothing to do. Such boredom is speculated to be a partial driver of the opioid epidemic.[23] Murder is, of course, an exaggerated response to a lack of local amenities, but everything else that happens in the film is predicated on tourist areas being lonely places for much of the year, so it's not outrageous to think the killers' motive might be too.

The pool sequence is grandly orchestrated, with vivid color, music and extravagant camerawork. After Luke enters the darkened pool deck, the killer turns on the lights to reveal that the swimming pool is surrounded by neon palm trees. This is another nod to the myth of the American vacation: a tacky embellishment on a mid-century ideal of the tropics, a garish oasis plopped into middle America. When Luke gets stabbed in the pool, a long overhead shot shows his blood spreading into the water. Like other bloody pools we've seen, it indicates an intrusion. In this case, it is a pollution of the picture-postcard American vacation, corrupted by family strife, by poverty and by ennui. The camera dips below the water multiple times during this sequence, muffling the epic pop soundtrack, deadening the glamor, and reminding us of another perspective on this tourist locale. The underside, it turns out, is full of blood.

Our next stop takes us to Comley Suites, a defunct hotel recently inherited by Ruthie, the main character of Stewart Thorndike's *Bad Things* (2023). Ruthie arrives for a brief wintertime stay with three companions: her girlfriend Cal, their friend Maddie, and Maddie's casual lover Fran, whom Ruthie has previously cheated on Cal with. While the quartet is enjoying the heated indoor pool, they are greeted by hotel handyman Brian. Ruthie insists that her estranged mother, who has been living in the hotel, has left town, despite her car still being there. She also says that her mother had arranged a meeting with a buyer for the next day. This news disappoints Cal, who wants Ruthie to reopen the hotel so they can run it together, and has been sending Ruthie videos by a hospitality guru and motivational speaker named Ms. Auerbach. After cheating again with Ruthie, Fran starts seeing ghostly visions, but the others think she is lying and put her on a train. Back at the hotel, Brian is murdered and Maddie is attacked by an unseen assailant. Ruthie claims the killer is Fran, but Maddie and Cal think it is Ruthie herself, who has begun having hallucinations, including a buyer meeting that Ms. Auerbach shows up at. Fran returns to the hotel and Cal, thinking her presence means Ruthie was telling the truth, knocks her over the head. Ruthie then pushes Fran out of a window and she ends up in the frozen outdoor pool, dead from the fall. When Maddie finds the corpse of Ruthie's mother, who is also Ms. Auerbach, they and Cal realize that Ruthie has murdered her. The unhinged Ruthie kills Cal and Maddie with a chainsaw after a parking lot chase.[24]

Fran's (Annabelle Dexter-Jones) deadly fall into the frozen swimming pool is only one of the *Bad Things* (2023) that happen at the vacant Comley Suites.

Like *The Strangers: Prey at Night*'s Cindy, Ruthie has a family connection to the hospitality world but is not part of it herself. However, having grown up with the hotel, she is familiar with it and its inner workings. This is apt, since the Comley Suites are symbolic of Ruthie herself—what she shows the world and what she hides. There is a part of the hotel Ruthie warns everyone to leave alone, and when Maddie explores this mysterious area they learn the awful truth about her. Through Ruthie's middle position—not quite a hotelier but not quite a guest—the film explores themes of doubling. There are two Ruthies—the killer and the innocent—two Frans—also the killer and the innocent—and two Ms. Auerbachs—the ne'er-do-well mother and the powerful influencer. Either Ruthie has been mentally substituting her mother's face for Ms. Auerbach's when she watches the videos, or Ms. Auerbach does not exist at all, and the videos are complete hallucinations. The latter possibility casts new light on Auerbach's speech about the hospitality industry: "Think of a hotel as not just a space, but an experience. In hospitality we curate a world that allows one to escape their life."

Once again, we get the eeriness of a lodging place devoid of people. In one of the film's many nods to *The Shining*, characters have visions of former guests and remnants of the traumas they suffered there. One of those remnants is Ruthie herself, whose childhood pain, and what caused her to become estranged from her mother, are centered in the hotel. Like *The Shining*, the film leaves it ambiguous whether the apparitions are ghosts *per se*, or left-behind psychic residue that gives the new guests visions of past terrors on an endless loop. Ms. Auerbach's speech would seem to suggest the latter: As the hotel owner, Ruthie has created the Comley Suites in her own image. It's Ruthie's world, the others are just living in it.

Chapter 17. Pool, A/C, Cable TV

The facility has two pools: a heated indoor one and an empty, frozen outdoor one. These two pools represent the two Ruthies: as she believes herself to be internally—warm and inviting—and as she is on the outside—cold and dangerous. In the indoor pool scene, we follow Ruthie's erotic gaze as she watches Fran enter and play in the water. Fran meets her death in the other pool, after Ruthie pushes her out a window. It's this push and pull of desire and violence that defines Ruthie's duality. But as usual with shifting identities, the boundaries are slippery. In the heated pool, the foursome talks about the hotel's ghost stories. Even as the friends relax, on some level they know they are sitting in a grave—the mass grave of the people erased and left behind when a hotel goes dark.

Another off-season hotel with family ties awaits us at our next port of call: Tower Bay, the Bahamas resort that provides the setting for *I Still Know What You Did Last Summer* (1998). In Danny Cannon's sequel to the previous year's *I Know What You Did Last Summer*, Final Girl Julie is now enrolled in college and still dating Ray, the other survivor from the previous film, who remains in their hometown working as a fisherman. Julie and her college roommate Karla answer a radio giveaway trivia question and win a trip for four to the Bahamas. Karla brings her boyfriend Tyrell; when Ray turns down the invitation, the group brings their friend Will instead. The quartet arrives at the resort to find all the guests leaving. The tourist season has just ended, and the island is about to be buffeted by storms. The four friends are the lone guests at the sumptuous resort, staffed by an off-season skeleton crew. The stage is set for the return of Ben Willis, the hook-wielding killer from the first film. Ben, who slices his way through most of the staff as well as Tyrell, used to work at the Tower Bay hotel before disappearing with his son and daughter many years ago after his wife was murdered. It's then revealed that Will is Ben's son, and was the one who set up the fake radio contest to lure Julie to the hotel to die. At the last moment, Julie is rescued by Ray, who realized Ben was alive after being attacked back home, and has spent most of the movie trying to get to the island.[25]

Though the swimming pool is not prominent, *I Still Know What You Did Last Summer* features the same themes we've been exploring: the vacation as a fraud, more image than reality; eerie off-season tourist locales as places of death and destruction; the erasure of hospitality staff. Will is able to fly under the radar because Julie and her friends assume he is a middle-class college student like them; they cannot picture him as the son of an itinerant seafaring laborer like Ben. It is only the blue-collar fisherman Ray who is able to see through the facade and understand from the start that something is wrong.

Although Julie is Ben's main target, he makes sure to eliminate all the hotel staff members before he gets to her. In the film's lens, these aren't quite people—they are red herrings to confuse the viewer about the identity of the killer when they are alive, and later a victim pool to pad the film's body count. In one scene, the pothead pool boy Titus swims up and interrupts a romantic moment between Karla and Tyrell in the pool-adjacent hot tub. After unsuccessfully trying to sell them weed for the second time, Titus swims away. Before the love scene can recommence, Will shows up to join them in the hot tub. It's a comic relief scene that gets its humor from the cockblocked Tyrell's frustration, but it also reminds us of the pool as a commons—a gathering place where classes mingle, where different people come with different things on their minds. But only for Titus does it become a place of death, when Ben murders him later in his poolside cabana. The college kids are on vacation, but Titus and the other staff members are at work, victims of circumstance in the wrong place at the wrong time. Julie faces down two murderers out for vengeance, and she survives. Lest we forget, Julie is being targeted for running over Ben, leaving him for dead, and covering up the crime. All Titus did was work a thankless job and sell a little weed on the side. His labor helps to keeps the place running, but he ends up collateral damage—killed by his job.

Before we sail for parts unknown, we will head back to the mainland for one more brief stop stateside in Dick Richards' *Death Valley* (1982). Young Billy travels from New York City to the West Coast to see his divorced mother Sally, who together with her new boyfriend Mike are taking him on a road trip to Arizona. Passing through Death Valley, they stop at an abandoned gold mine, where Billy wanders into an RV and almost stumbles upon the bodies of three people who have just been murdered there. He pockets a necklace at the scene, which he later gives to the sheriff after he sees the same RV pulled out of a roadside ditch. The sheriff recognizes the medallion and visits a waiter named Hal, who lives nearby with his brother Stu. From their dialogue, we learn that the murders have been going on for years, and seem to center around the gold mine that Hal and Stu's father used to work. The encounter ends with the sheriff dying at the hands of the unseen Stu.

When Sally and Mike leave Billy at the hotel for a date night, Hal accosts Billy and pursues him through the hotel grounds. He tracks the boy to the pool area, stopping to splash some water on his face, and moves on. Billy exits his hiding place behind some deck furniture, but Hal hears him and gives chase. Billy next hides in a car that turns out to be Hal's when he gets in and drives home. Meanwhile, Sally and Mike have returned to find Billy missing and go to Hal's house to get him back. Mike is able to kill Hal in a struggle, but is then confronted by Hal's identical twin Stu, who chases them through an empty tourist attraction. Mike finally runs him down in his car.[26]

Keenly interested in American myth-making, *Death Valley* links the fantasy family vacation to the folk mythology of the Old West, pointing out the inconsistencies of both. This road trip, like the one in *The Strangers: Prey at Night*, is tense from the beginning because Billy is upset over his family's breakup. Mike, eager to win Billy's favor, takes him to a tourist attraction in a reconstructed frontier town. Actors portraying sheriffs and outlaws roam the attraction, staging gunfights and incorporating the guest children into their recreations. When Billy enters the museum, he is stalked by the killer and threatened with a real gun. Billy, thinking it is part of the attraction's immersive fiction, defends himself with his toy cap pistol.

Mike (Paul Le Mat, left) and Billy (Peter Billingsley) try to reconcile their differing visions of family happiness while on vacation in *Death Valley* (1982).

He only escapes thanks to another tourist couple who blunder in, thinking the killer is one of the actors, and ask for a picture.

The dialogue makes repeated reference to Billy the Kid. The name resonates, of course, because Billy, our protagonist, is just a kid, with all the bravado and limitations that come with being one. But the invocation of that figure is doubly significant, since Billy the Kid, by any standard, was a deplorable person: a thief, cattle rustler and murderer responsible for at least eight deaths. History has somehow turned him into a folk hero. In the film, Mike gives Billy a toy six-gun as a present, and she and Sally grin as staged scenes of violence and death are played out before them. Billy even says, "I'm gonna go in there like Billy the Kid and plug anyone that gets in my way," which earns a wry smile from his mother. But then they are confronted with a real-life, modern-day outlaw, who even has an Old West–style murder motive: to keep people away from his gold. In its critique of the American lionization of violent criminals, *Death Valley* understands the gulf between folklore and reality.

Another gulf the film understands is the one between tourists and the people whose jobs it is to serve them. Hal, a waiter in the hotel restaurant, seems to be fixated on how much things cost. He clips coupons at the kitchen table while telling the sheriff how lucky he is to be on the county payroll and not need to pinch pennies. He bemoans the cost of his recent home renovation, rhapsodizes about the price of gold, and seems to relish the idea of how rich he and Stu will be once they finally find gold in the old mine their family has been working for six decades. When Billy barricades himself in a hotel bathroom, Hal explains that the door is a cheap one and he could easily break it down. However, possibly remembering his renovation expenses, he

In *Death Valley* (1982), killer Hal (Stephen McHattie) stops to cool off at a makeshift watering hole while tracking his quarry.

opts to pry the trim from around the door so that it can be put back on. Even when threatening murder, Hal recoils at the idea of wasting money.

It is easy to understand the resentment Hal and Stu feel toward the people with enough disposable income to stay at the hotel, lounge around the pool, and visit all the tourist traps, who don't have to worry about scrounging to make ends meet—or the caravanning kids who get too close to their gold mine. The climactic chase through an eerily empty tourist attraction sums up our theme. The vacationers are trapped in a part of the tourism world they don't normally see: the way things look after they all go home, to the people they leave behind.

Death Valley, like *I Still Know What You Did Last Summer* and *Bad Things*, takes care to show us the pool as a place of leisure before it becomes a place of fright. But as in those other films, the scene comes with its own kind of tension. While their fellow vacationers splash and play in the bright sun, Mike explains to Billy that he wants them to be a family. With the pool in the background, symbol of someone's American dream, Mike and Billy both work through their disillusionment with the ideal of family perfection. Later, Billy cowers in night shadows beside that same pool as he undergoes the shattering of another American fantasy: that of the dashing, romanticized outlaw. As Hal splashes pool water on his face like a dusty cowboy by a stream, Billy the kid realizes that violence in the American west, no matter the era, is a brutal business.

Friends, we have arrived at our final destination: a fancy seaside resort in the fictional nation of Li Tolqa, in the world of Brandon Cronenberg's *Infinity Pool* (2023). James Foster, a struggling novelist, and his wife Em, whose family money provided the swanky accommodations, are vacationing there in a bid to save their marriage. After they spend a day in the countryside with fellow rich guests Gabi and Alban, James drives drunk and hits a local man with a borrowed car, killing him. The next day, James is introduced to Li Tolqa's peculiar criminal justice system when he is arrested, convicted and sentenced to death for the crime. However, as a foreigner, he can opt to pay a large fee to have a clone executed in his place. After watching his duplicate killed, James finds that his passport is missing, trapping him at the resort. Gabi and Alban reveal themselves as part of a group of rich tourists who have made a game out of traveling to Li Tolqa, murdering people, and paying to watch their clones executed, over and over again. James briefly joins the group, but after becoming disgusted by their behavior he attempts to flee, revealing that he had hidden his passport himself as an excuse to stay behind without Em. The group captures him, explains that they had targeted him for their amusement, and forces him to kill his own clone. Their game over, the tourist group leaves, but James decides to stay at the resort. The final shot shows him sitting alone and traumatized next to the hotel's infinity pool in the pouring rain.[27]

Though the infinity pool only appears once in the film, its presence in the final shot underscores the triple meaning of *Infinity Pool*'s title. First, the infinity pool is an expensive type of swimming pool that has come to symbolize wealth and indulgence even more than the standard pool. Second, the tourists will never be held accountable for their actions, because as long as they have the money, there is an infinite pool of disposable clones to doom in their place. They murder and exploit the locals, knowing they will pay no penalty other than a financial one. In a position of being able to buy their way out of trouble, the tourist group feels no need to conceal their contempt for the working class. They set their sights on James because he is not truly one of them. He is a struggling artist who married into money, making him no different from the locals whose lives they play with. Near the end, when he looks into the eyes of his clone and sees how vulnerable he is (a person, not a dog as Gabi calls him) and refuses to kill, James shows a glimmer of class solidarity. In a reverse Narcissus, he peers into the infinite pool and sees what looks like his reflection, but knows it to be another person, deserving of respect.

The title's third meaning is related to the second and, along with the final scene's rainfall, points to an ecological reading of the film. At the end, we are shown a literal climate change, from the sunny skies of the preceding days to gray rain. For much of human history, we have behaved as if there is an infinite pool of natural resources. In modern times, knowing that human activity is harming the planet, turning a blind eye takes a conscious decision. *Infinity Pool*'s ugly rich tourists know there is a causal link between the excess they revel in and the degraded glimpses we get of local life, the broken-down shacks barricaded from the tourist highway by a fence of barbed wire. But the tourists don't care, because they do not have to stay there. They visit, have their fun, and move on. Such is the privilege of the vacationer—of *Fever Dream*'s Amanda, of *I Still Know What You Did Last Summer*'s Julie, of *Death Valley*'s Mike and Sally. The locals, like the rest of us, might struggle against it, but as long as the ultra-elites see no reason to change, our efforts are as futile as rainfall into a swimming pool.

Compared to the spookily empty Gatlin Lake, the dilapidated Comley Suites, the storm-wracked Tower Bay and the middle-class shabbiness of the Death Valley motel, the resort in Li Tolqa seems like a lovely place to visit—just so long as you give your fellow guests a wide berth. Talk to the man by the pool to understand why. After reading this chapter, though, you might wish to avoid vacation resorts altogether, in which case I am sorry, but I have to leave you here.

Postscript

> One thing at least is certain: Water and madness have long been linked in the dreams of European man.
> —Michel Foucault, *Madness and Civilization*

> And yet the swimming pools are full of children
>   laughing in that deafening sun.
> —John Tranter, "Fine Arts"

When I was 11 going on 12, I had a nightmare: I was being raised in a fenced-in compound with a large swimming pool at its center. The community consisted entirely of boys my age and their mothers. A daily regimen of swimming was required. We were subject to punishment if we did not do so, but the rule seldom needed enforcing because we all enjoyed the pool. All we did was swim and lie around in the sunshine, which was eternally hot and direct, with very little shade to be found on the huge pool deck that was my home. As time went by, I began to notice some peculiarities. For one thing, many of the other boys looked uncannily like me. I also noticed our shoulder-length hair had begun to change color from straw blond to pale green. Finally I stumbled upon the secret of the conspiracy of mothers and watched a boy my age undergo the final procedure to turn him into a tree; an injection was administered and his feet grew into the ground, his cry cut off as his mouth froze into a silently screaming knothole, his hair a crown of tender young leaves. As my own hair grew longer, greener and more fibrous, I knew my time was near. I planned an escape, after which I would come back and free my brothers. But I was captured and taken to the transformation chamber. My last words were a murmured apology to the other boys as I felt the needle pierce my skin.

I wrote the dream into a short story called "Chlorine Will Turn Your Hair Green." It was an understandable dream for a precocious boy on the cusp of puberty, with mommy issues and a morbid imagination. But I made the mistake of showing it to my mother—my ill, emotionally unreliable mother who would attempt suicide that same year. She told me the story was bleak and nasty and that she hated it. I learned three things that day: (a) never tell a child that you hate something they created; (b) never tell someone about a nightmare you had unless you're certain it wasn't subconsciously about them; and (c) there is something about a swimming pool that beckons me to throw all my fears into it.

I will leave the interpretation of that dream up to you. To be certain, it hits plenty of this book's themes: secrets, gender, atavism, metamorphosis, segregation, the blurred line between the human and natural worlds. But here I want to focus on the transformation into a tree, the idea of becoming rooted to a spot. A swimming pool, after all, is a space devoted to a specific function. Each of this book's three parts looks at the pool as a different kind of site. It is interesting to note how many of these films are named after their locations: *House, 47 Meters Down, Mortuary, Sunset Blvd., The Apartment Complex, 1BR, The House on Sorority Row, The Glass House, Open House, House on the Edge of the Park, Death Valley* and, of course, *The Pool* (both of them). Works in the horror genre have demonstrated a fascination with the idea that places have histories, personalities—perhaps souls—separate from but influenced by the humans who inhabit them. Swimming pools, with all they symbolize in modern life, are blue shards of spacetime charged with special energy—whether it's a public pool, where social lines are crossed, gazes are exchanged and sexual desires sublimated, or a residential pool, a little square of the natural world transported to a human dwelling place.

Horror cinema can show us where we've been and where we are, but it also has a habit of telling us where we're going. *The Stepford Wives* (1975) forecasted the late-1970s failure of the Equal Rights Amendment and the ground lost by the women's movement under Reagan-era conservatism. *The Rage: Carrie 2* (1999) sounded an early alarm about the revenge porn crisis that would infest the 2010s and inspire films like *Assassination Nation*. With almost no changes, *The Pool* (2001) could have been remade 20 years later about an online radicalized incel and it would have felt fresh and vital. All the conditions that drove the underprivileged killers of *Death Valley* (1982) and *Open House* (1987) to murder aren't quite the same as back then—they're worse. Forty years after *Shock Waves* (1977), Nazis rose *again* from what we thought was a watery grave.

So what is the future of the swimming pool horror film? As climate change becomes harder to ignore, I think we'll see more films that link pools with ecological concerns. *Fever Dream* and *Infinity Pool* have made a nice start, but if "cli-fi" science fiction teaches us anything, it's that there are many such stories to be told. Humanity's future will be defined by water: too much water when we don't want it, in the form of increasingly savage storms, and lack of water when we do want it, in the form of droughts. Swimming pools have been touted as both an accelerator of climate catastrophe and a means for surviving it. A 2023 study in Cape Town, South Africa, found that the wealthiest 14 percent of the population used 51 percent of the water, a large part of which went into swimming pools. On the other hand, pools are a vital resource for keeping people cool in ever-hotter summers. Neighborhood pool parties seem to offer a way to cool down the masses without as much water waste as a backyard pool reserved for just one family.

But an even better solution is to build more public pools.[1] The legacy of racist public pool neglect and bourgeois backyard pool construction lives on. The CDC estimates that there are more than ten million private pools in the nation, compared to just over 300,000 public ones. As Mara Gay put it in a *New York Times* editorial, "We should treat public pools like public libraries, public parks, and public schools. They are a vital piece of social infrastructure."[2] As so many films in this book have shown, the pool can be our doom or our salvation—depending on whether we look at it from above or from beneath.

In my adult life I have only lived in one place that had a swimming pool: a roach-infested apartment building in Falls Church, Virginia. I spent two years there in my early 20s, and never once used the pool. I was socially isolated in that season of my life, and I did not want to see or talk to people. I did not want others to wonder why I was there alone. I did not feel good about my body and did not want to be seen in a swimsuit. Like the tree-hugging mothers in my childhood dream, all three of this book's overarching tensions had ahold of me again—but this time they were keeping me out of the pool rather than pushing me into it. On the other hand, that roach apartment was where I first watched *Piranha, Shivers, Rabid, Tombs of the Blind Dead, The Prowler, House on the Edge of the Park* and many others, so those two years weren't a total waste. But if I could talk to my 21-year-old self, I'd tell him to pay attention to what those films were saying about community.

Part of the ceremony of entering a pool is the undressing ritual. Horror cinema dares us to take off more than just our clothes. Whether it's the lies we drape ourselves in, the sexual hang-ups we wear around our midsections, or the armor we use to shut the world out, the horror film swimming pool, yawning in the ground, invites us to disrobe and give ourselves to its generous blue embrace. To gaze at the mirrored surface and try to see our true faces. To dive to the bottom, turn our gaze skyward, and see what the world looks like from the other side. Day or night, the bottom is only a few feet away, even when they turn out the lights. Also lurking down there somewhere, we can be sure, is the end. Maybe we'll meet it this time, and maybe we won't. Either way, I'd like to be able to say I went swimming when I had the chance.

Filmography

Films are listed here, and referenced in the text, under the title by which I first encountered them. Original-language titles and common alternate titles are given in parentheses where applicable.

All the Boys Love Mandy Lane (2006), director: Jonathan Levine; USA
Alligator (1980), director: Lewis Teague; USA
The Apartment Complex (1999), director: Tobe Hooper; USA
Asmodexia (2014), director: Marc Carrete; Spain
Assassination Nation (2018), director: Sam Levinson; USA
Bad Things (2023), director: Stewart Thorndike; USA
"The Bewitchin' Pool" (*The Twilight Zone* S5.E36), 1964, director: Joseph M. Newman; USA
Blood Rage (1987), director: John Grissmer; USA
Burnt Offerings (1976), director: Dan Curtis; USA
The Cannibal Man (*La semana del asesino*) (1972), director: Eloy de la Iglesia; Spain
Carrie (2013), director: Kimberly Peirce; USA
Cat People (1942), director: Jacques Tourneur; USA
Cat People (1982), director: Paul Schrader; USA
C.H.U.D. II: Bud the Chud (1989), director: David Irving; USA
Colossal (2016), director: Nacho Vigalondo; USA
Confessions (告白) (2010), director: Tetsuya Nakashima; Japan
The Craft (1996), director: Andrew Fleming; USA
Crawl (2019), director: Alexandre Aja; USA
A Cure for Wellness (2016), director: Gore Verbinski; USA
Death Valley (1982), director: Dick Richards; USA
Diabolique (1996), director: Jeremiah S. Chechik; USA
Les Diaboliques (1955), director: Henri-Georges Clouzot; France
Don't Breathe 2 (2021), director: Rodo Sayagues; USA
Don't Worry Darling (2022), director: Olivia Wilde; USA
Dumplings (餃子) (2004), director: Fruit Chan; Hong Kong
Eegah! (1962), director: Arch Hall Sr.; USA
8MM (1999), director: Joel Schumacher; USA
The Faculty (1998), director: Robert Rodriguez; USA
Fear (1996), director: James Foley; USA
Fever Dream (*Distancia de rescate*) (2021), director: Claudia Llosa; Peru
47 Meters Down (2017), director: Johannes Roberts; USA
The Fourth Victim (*La última señora Anderson*) (1971), director: Eugenio Martín; Spain
Fright Night (2011), director: Craig Gillespie; USA
Glass (2019), director: M. Night Shyamalan; USA

The Glass House (2001), director: Daniel Sackheim; USA
Gremlins (1984), director: Joe Dante; USA
Halloween (2007), director: Rob Zombie; USA
Halloween Ends (2022), director: David Gordon Green; USA
Hellbender (2021), directors: John Adams, Zelda Adams and Toby Poser; USA
House (1985), director: Steve Miner; USA
The House on Sorority Row (1983), director: Mark Rosman; USA
The House on the Edge of the Park (*La casa sperduta nel parco*) (1980), director: Ruggero Deodato; Italy
The Hunger (1983), director: Tony Scott; USA
I Still Know What You Did Last Summer (1998), director: Danny Cannon; USA
In My Skin (*Dans ma peau*) (2002), director: Marina de Van; France
Infinity Pool (2023), director: Brandon Cronenberg; Canada
It Follows (2014), director: David Robert Mitchell; USA
Jennifer's Body (2009), director: Karyn Kusama; USA
John and the Hole (2021), director: Pascual Sisto; USA
The Kiss (1988), director: Pen Desham; Canada
Lady in the Water (2006), director: M. Night Shyamalan; USA
Let Me In (2010), director: Matt Reeves; USA
Let the Right One In (*Låt den rätte komma in*) (2008), director: Tomas Alfredson; Sweden
La Llorona (2019), director: Jayro Bustamante; Guatemala
MaXXXine (2024), director: Ti West; USA
Mermaid Legend (人魚伝説) (1984), director: Toshiharu Ikeda; Japan
M.F.A. (2017), director: Natalia Leite; USA
Mortuary (1983), director: Howard Avedis; USA
Naked You Die (*Nude ... si muore*) (1968), director: Antonio Margheriti; Italy
The Neon Demon (2016), director: Nicolas Winding-Refn; USA
Night Swim (2024), director: Bryce McGuire; USA
A Nightmare on Elm Street (2010), director: Samuel Bayer; USA
A Nightmare on Elm Street: The Dream Child (1989), director: Stephen Hopkins; USA
A Nightmare on Elm Street 2: Freddy's Revenge (1985), director: Jack Sholder; USA
1BR (2019), director: David Marmor; USA
Open House (1987), director: Jag Mundhra; USA
Paranormal Activity 2 (2010), director: Tod Williams; USA
Piranha (1978), director: Joe Dante; USA
Piranha 3DD (2012), director: John Gulager; USA
Poison Ivy: The New Seduction (1997), director: Kurt Voss; USA
Poltergeist (1982), director: Tobe Hooper; USA
Poltergeist III (1988), director: Gary Sherman; USA
The Pool (*Swimming Pool—Der Tod feiert mit*) (2001), director: Boris von Sychowski; Germany
The Pool (2018), director: Ping Lumpraploeng; Thailand
The Prowler (1981), director: Joseph Zito; USA
Rabid (1977), director: David Cronenberg; Canada
Rabid (2019), directors: Jen and Sylvia Soska; Canada
The Rage: Carrie 2 (1999), director: Katt Shea; USA
Revenge (2017), director: Coralie Fargeat; France
The Rocky Horror Picture Show (1975), director: Jim Sharman; UK
Shivers (1975), director: David Cronenberg; Canada

Shock Waves (1977), director: Ken Wiederhorn; USA
The Slumber Party Massacre (1982), director: Amy Holden Jones; USA
Slumber Party Massacre II (1987), director: Deborah Brock; USA
Society (1989), director: Brian Yuzna; USA
Starry Eyes (2014), directors: Kevin Kölsch and Dennis Widmyer; USA
The Stepfather (2009), director: Nelson McCormick; USA
The Stepford Children (1987), director: Alan J. Levi; USA
The Stepford Wives (1975), director: Bryan Forbes; USA
The Strangers: Prey at Night (2018), director: Johannes Roberts; USA
Sunset Blvd. (1950), director: Billy Wilder; USA
Suspiria (1977), director: Dario Argento; Italy
Swimfan (2002), director: John Polson; USA
"The Tale of the Dead Man's Float" (*Are You Afraid of the Dark?* S5.E1), 1995, director: D.J. MacHale; Canada
Taste of Fear (*Scream of Fear*) (1961), director: Seth Holt; UK
TerrorVision (1986), director: Ted Nicolaou; USA
Thelma (2017), director: Joachim Trier; Norway
Tombs of the Blind Dead (*La noche del terror ciego*) (1972), director: Amando de Ossorio; Spain
Traffik (2019), director: Deon Taylor; USA
Trick or Treat (1986), director: Charles Martin Smith; USA
Unbreakable (2000), director: M. Night Shyamalan; USA
The Velvet Vampire (1971), director: Stephanie Rothman; USA
Venus Flytrap (1987), director: T. Michael; USA
The Woman (2011), director: Lucky McKee; USA

Chapter Notes

Preface

1. "Partnership for a Drug-Free America—Diving Board," PSA/PIF Wiki, accessed January 17, 2024, https://pif.fandom.com/wiki/Partnership_for_a_Drug-Free_America_-_Swimming.
2. Newsweek Staff, "Public Glory, Secret Agony," *Newsweek*, March 5, 1995, https://www.newsweek.com/public-glory-secret-agony-180724.
3. Thomas M. Lachocki, "More Swimmers Will Result in a Healthier Society, Fewer Drownings and Reduced Healthcare Costs," *WCandP Online*, August 5, 2012, https://wcponline.com/2012/08/05/swimmers-will-result-healthier-society-fewer-drownings-reduced-healthcare-costs/.
4. Michael George and Sara Moniuszko, "Nearly 400 children die yearly from drowning in pools and spas, report finds. Here's how to keep your kids safe," *CBS News*, June 8, 2023, https://www.cbsnews.com/news/keep-kids-safe-drowning-pools-spas/.
5. "Are Diving Boards Dangerous? A Look At The Safety Of Diving Boards," InstaSwim USA, May 14, 2023, https://instaswimusa.com/are-diving-boards-dangerous-a-look-at-the-safety-of-diving-boards/.
6. "Fatality Facts 2022: Bicyclists," IIHS.org, June 2024, https://www.iihs.org/topics/fatality-statistics/detail/bicyclists.
7. Commentator Rob Zombie, "Commentary by Writer/Director Rob Zombie," Disc 1, *Halloween*, 2-Disc Unrated Collector's Edition, directed by Rob Zombie (Dimension Home Entertainment, 2008), Bluray.
8. Barbara Creed, *The Monstrous-Feminine*, Second edition (Routledge, 2024), Part I, chap. 1, Kindle.

Part I

Introduction to Part I

1. *Are You Afraid of the Dark?*, season 5, episode 1, "The Tale of the Dead Man's Float," directed by D.J. MacHale, aired October 7, 1995, on Nickelodeon, https://www.amazon.com/gp/video/detail/amzn1.dv.gti.96bf10f6-f271-4473-9cc0-0ece8b69685b.
2. *A Nightmare on Elm Street*, directed by Samuel Bayer (New Line Cinema, 2010), DVD.
3. Dick Hebdige, "Swimming … Floating … Sinking … Drowning," in Daniell Cornell, ed., *Backyard Oasis: The Swimming Pool in Southern Californian Photography, 1945–82* (Palm Springs Art Museum: Prestel & Delmonico Books, 2012), 199.

Chapter 1

1. Lidia Yuknavitch, *The Chronology of Water: A Memoir* (Hawthorne Books, 2011), Part I, chap. 1, Kindle.
2. *House*, directed by Steve Miner (New World Pictures, 1985), DVD.
3. Stephen King, *Danse Macabre* (Berkley Books, 1983), 142–144.
4. *Night Swim*, directed by Bryce McGuire (Blumhouse, 2024).
5. Cindy S. Aron, *Working at Play: A History of Vacations in the United States* (Oxford University Press, 1999), 19.
6. Jeff Wiltse, *Contested Waters: A Social History of Swimming Pools in America* (University of North Carolina Press, 2007), 17.
7. Dan Witters, "50% in U.S. Fear Bankruptcy Due to Major Health Event," Gallup.com, September 1, 2020, https://news.gallup.com/poll/317948/fear-bankruptcy-due-major-health-event.aspx.
8. Noam Levey, "Sick and struggling to pay, 100 million people in the U.S. live with medical debt," *Shots: Health News from NPR*, June 16, 2022, https://www.npr.org/sections/health-shots/2022/06/16/1104679219/medical-bills-debt-investigation.
9. Stephen King, *Pet Sematary* (New York: Signet, 1984).
10. *Poltergeist*, directed by Tobe Hooper (Metro-Goldwyn-Mayer, 1982), DVD.
11. John Kenneth Muir, *Horror Films of the 1980s* (McFarland, 2007), 271.
12. *Poltergeist III*, directed by Gary Sherman (Metro-Goldwyn-Mayer, 1988), VHS.
13. Roger Ebert, "Ebert's Guide to Practical Filmgoing: A Glossary of Terms for the Cinema of the '80s," June 23, 1985, https://www.rogerebert.

com/roger-ebert/eberts-guide-to-practical-filmgoing-a-glossary-of-terms-for-the-cinema-of-the-80s.
14. Muir, *Horror Films of the 1980s*, 33–34.
15. *Burnt Offerings*, directed by Dan Curtis (United Artists, 1976), https://tubitv.com/movies/100001275/burnt-offerings.

Chapter 2

1. "Thalassophobia," accessed July 17, 2024, https://www.reddit.com/r/thalassophobia/.
2. "Responding to a Dead Animal in the Pool," CDC.gov, June 5, 2024, https://www.cdc.gov/healthy-swimming/response/responding-to-a-dead-animal-in-the-pool.html.
3. Alise Everton, "Animals in the Pool," *Pool Magazine*, October 29, 2021, https://www.poolmagazine.com/lifestyle/animals-in-the-pool/.
4. Claire Fahy, "Authorities Seize Alligator Being Held Illegally in Home Near Buffalo," *New York Times*, March 16, 2024, https://www.nytimes.com/2024/03/16/nyregion/albert-alligator-buffalo-ny.html.
5. Somini Sengupta, "Let's Talk Books," *The New York Times Climate Forward Newsletter*, December 9, 2002, https://www.nytimes.com/2022/12/09/climate/books-about-climate.html.
6. Kelley Bulkeley, "Dreaming of Water," *Psychology Today*, June 2, 2022, https://www.psychologytoday.com/us/blog/dreaming-in-the-digital-age/202206/dreaming-water.
7. Brigid Cherry, "Fan Totems: Affective Investments in the Sea Creatures of Horror and Science Fiction," in John Hackett and Seán Harrington, eds., *Beasts of the Deep: Sea Creatures and Popular Culture* (John Libbey, 2018), 114.
8. *Piranha*, directed by Joe Dante (New World Pictures, 1978), https://www.shudder.com/movies/watch/piranha/b31932987cca7d01.
9. Belinda Eve Stillwell, "The Subjective Experiences of Those Afraid in Water," *International Journal of Aquatic Research and Education* 5, no. 1 (February 2011): Article 7.
10. *Jaws*, directed by Steven Spielberg (Universal Pictures, 1975), VHS.
11. *Piranha 3DD*, directed by John Gulager (Dimension Films, 2012), DVD.
12. *Alligator*, directed by Lewis Teague (Alligator Inc, 1980), https://www.shudder.com/movies/watch/alligator/b33ab34cd6e1f723.
13. Barbara Mikkelson, "Can Alligators Live in Sewers?" Snopes.com, July 10, 1999, https://www.snopes.com/fact-check/alligators-sewers/.
14. "A Guide to Living With Alligators," Florida Fish and Wildlife Conservation Commission, February 2012, https://myfwc.com/media/1690/alligator-brochure.pdf.
15. Spielberg, dir., *Jaws*.
16. *The Pool*, directed by Ping Lumpraploeng (TMOMENT, 2018), https://www.shudder.com/movies/watch/the-pool/4548278292a3f70e.
17. Mark Fisher, *The Weird and the Eerie* (Repeater Books, 2016), 61.
18. Raymond Chandler, *The Long Goodbye* (Ballantine Books, 1984), chap. 16, Kindle.
19. Paul Guzzo, "Horror movie Crawl filmed in Tampa Bay, in waters where body was found," *Tampa Bay Times*, July 10, 2019, https://www.tampabay.com/arts-entertainment/horror-movie-crawl-filmed-in-tampa-bay-in-waters-where-body-was-found-20190710/.
20. *Crawl*, directed by Alexandra Aja (Raimi Productions, 2019), DVD.
21. Dagmar Dahl and Åsa I. Bäckström, "Meeting, Moving, Mastering—A Text Analysis of the Aesthetic Attractions of 'Wild Swimming,'" *International Journal of Aquatic Research and Education* 14, no. 1 (May 2023): Article 12.
22. *47 Meters Down*, directed by Johannes Roberts (The Fyzz Facility, 2017), Bluray.
23. *Snuff*, directed by Michael Findlay (Selected Pictures, 1976).
24. Dahl and Bäckström, "Meeting, Moving, Mastering."
25. *Shock Waves*, directed by Ken Wiederhorn (Zopix Company, 1977), https://www.amazon.com/gp/video/detail/0L8GTIN00RY3TE7NDS5V5AVII4/.
26. Bonnie Tsui, *Why We Swim* (Algonquin Books, 2020), 6.

Chapter 3

1. Thomas Bulfinch, *Bulfinch's Mythology* (Random House, 1993), 96.
2. "Narcissus (Greek mythology)," Encyclopedia Britannica, accessed July 27, 2024, https://www.britannica.com/topic/Narcissus-Greek-mythology.
3. Seán Harrington, "The Depths of Our Experience: Thalassophobia and the Oceanic Horror," in John Hackett and Seán Harrington, eds., *Beasts of the Deep: Sea Creatures and Popular Culture* (John Libbey, 2018), 30.
4. *Blood Rage*, directed by John Grissmer (Film Limited Partnership, 1987), DVD.
5. Natalia A. Polskaya and Mariya A. Melnikova, "Dissociation, Trauma and Self-Harm," *Konsul'tativnaia psikhologiia i psikhoterapiia* 28, no. 1 (2020): 25–48.
6. Nina M. Lutz, et al., "Why Is Non-suicidal Self-injury More Common in Women? Mediation and Moderation Analyses of Psychological Distress, Emotion Dysregulation, and Impulsivity," *Archives of Suicide Research* 27, no. 3 (June 13, 2022): 905–21.
7. Andrea Nelson and Jennifer J. Muehlenkamp, "Body Attitudes and Objectification in Non-Suicidal Self-Injury: Comparing Males and Females," *Archives of Suicide Research* 16, no. 1 (January 2012): 1–12.

8. *In My Skin*, directed by Marina de Van (Lazennec et Associés, 2002), DVD.
9. *Gaslight*, directed by George Cukor (Metro-Goldwyn-Mayer, 1944), DVD.
10. *Taste of Fear*, directed by Seth Holt (Hammer Film Productions, 1961), https://tubitv.com/movies/100009670/scream-of-fear.
11. Angela M. Smith, *Hideous Progeny: Disability, Eugenics, and Classic Horror Cinema* (Columbia University Press, 2011), 3.
12. John Kenneth Muir, "Is He Unbreakable? The Shyamalan Series Begins," *John Kenneth Muir's Reflections on Cult Movies and Classic TV* (blog), August 27, 2015, https://reflectionsonfilmandtelevision.blogspot.com/2015/08/is-he-unbreakable-shyamalan-series.html.
13. *Lady in the Water*, directed by M. Night Shyamalan (Legendary Pictures, 2006), DVD.
14. *Unbreakable*, directed by M. Night Shyamalan (Touchstone Pictures, 2000), VHS.
15. *Split*, directed by M. Night Shyamalan (Universal Pictures, 2016), https://www.hulu.com/movie/36a228fb-7c40-4499-af85-c99906bf4bd4.
16. *Glass*, directed by M. Night Shyamalan (Universal Pictures, 2019), https://www.netflix.com/title/81011819.

Part II

Introduction to Part II

1. Sharon Olds, "California Swimming Pool," *Los Angeles Times*, March 15, 1987, https://www.latimes.com/archives/la-xpm-1987-03-15-bk-10671-story.html.
2. Jeff Wiltse, *Contested Waters: A Social History of Swimming Pools in America* (University of North Carolina Press, 2007), 113–14.
3. Viola Parente-Čapková, "Narcissuses, Medusas, Ophelias … Water Imagery and Femininity in the Texts By Two Decadent Women Writers," *Wagadu: A Journal of Transnational Women's & Gender Studies* 3 (Spring 2006): 189.
4. Sigmund Freud, *The Interpretation of Dreams*, translated by James Strachey (Basic Books, 2010), 410–12.
5. Barbara Creed, *The Monstrous-Feminine*, Second edition (Routledge, 2024), Part I, chap. 4, Kindle.
6. *The Pool*, directed by Ping Lumpraploeng (TMOMENT, 2018), https://www.shudder.com/movies/watch/the-pool/4548278292a3f70e.
7. *Asmodexia*, directed by Marc Carreté (XYZ Films, 2014), DVD.
8. Thomas A.P. van Leeuwen, *The Springboard in the Pond: An Intimate History of the Swimming Pool* (The MIT Press, 1998), 2.

Chapter 4

1. Sarah St. Lifer, "Rebel Wilson Talks Mermaids, Crystal Meth, & More … in 60 Seconds," Refinery29, October 2, 2012, https://www.refinery29.com/en-us/rebel-wilson.
2. Barbara Creed, *The Monstrous-Feminine*, Second edition (Routledge, 2024), Part III, Introduction, Kindle.
3. Angela M. Smith, *Hideous Progeny: Disability, Eugenics, and Classic Horror Cinema* (Columbia University Press, 2011), 50.
4. Lidia Yuknavitch, "I Will Always Inhabit the Water," Literary Hub, April 12, 2017, https://lithub.com/lidia-yuknavitch-i-will-always-inhabit-the-water/.
5. Maria Mellins, "Mermaid Spotting: The Rise of Mermaiding in Popular Culture," in John Hackett and Seán Harrington, eds., *Beasts of the Deep: Sea Creatures and Popular Culture* (John Libbey, 2018), 134.
6. Creed, *The Monstrous-Feminine*, Part III, Introduction.
7. Harappa.com, "'Great Bath' Mohenjo-Daro," n.d., accessed July 27, 2024, https://www.harappa.com/indus/8.html.
8. *Cat People*, directed by Jacques Tourneur (RKO Radio Pictures, 1942), Bluray.
9. Alex Naylor, "'The Anatomy of Atavism': American Urban Modernity, Gothic Trauma and Haunted Spaces in *Cat People*," in Christopher Brown and Pam Hirsch, eds., *The Cinema of the Swimming Pool* (International Academic Publishers, 2014), 51.
10. Ibid., 53.
11. *Cat People*, directed by Paul Schrader (Universal Pictures, 1982), VHS.
12. *The Kiss*, directed by Pen Desham (TriStar Pictures, 1988), DVD.
13. Creed, *The Monstrous-Feminine*, Part I, Introduction, Kindle.
14. *Colossal*, directed by Nacho Vigalondo (Voltage Pictures, 2016), https://tubitv.com/movies/100015806/colossal.
15. Jeff Wiltse, *Contested Waters: A Social History of Swimming Pools in America* (University of North Carolina Press, 2007), 34–36.
16. John W.M. Bunker, "The Hygiene of the Swimming Pool," *American Journal of Public Hygiene* 20, no. 4 (November 1910): 810–12.
17. Newsweek Staff, 1995, "Public Glory, Secret Agony." *Newsweek*, March 5, 1995, https://www.newsweek.com/public-glory-secret-agony-180724.
18. "What to Do When There is Blood or Vomit in the Pool," CDC.gov, May 7, 2024, https://www.cdc.gov/healthy-swimming/response/responding-to-blood-and-vomit-in-the-pool.html.
19. Sharon Begley, "The Risk Pool: The Dangers are Off the Field," *Newsweek*, March 5, 1995, https://www.newsweek.com/risk-poolthe-dangers-are-field-180768.
20. Newsweek Staff, "Public Glory, Secret Agony."
21. Reuters Fact Check, "Fact Check: HIV cannot have been transmitted by water in Texas swimming pool," Reuters.com, May 7, 2024, https://www.reuters.com/fact-check/hiv-cannot-have-been-transmitted-by-water-texas-swimming-pool-2024-05-07/.

22. Chris Wiant, "A Snapshot of Swimmer Hygiene Behavior," *International Journal of Aquatic Research and Education* 5, no. 3 (August 2011): Article 3.

23. Judy S. LaKind, et al., "The Good, the Bad, and the Volatile: Can We Have Both Healthy Pools and Healthy People?" *Environmental Science & Technology* 44, no. 9 (May 1, 2010), 3205–210.

24. *Shivers*, directed by David Cronenberg (Cinépix Film Properties, 1975), DVD.

25. Denise Grady, "A Lasting Gift to Medicine That Wasn't Really a Gift," *The New York Times*, February 1, 2010, https://www.nytimes.com/2010/02/02/health/02seco.html.

26. Sarah Spettel and Mark Donald White, "The Portrayal of J. Marion Sims' Controversial Surgical Legacy," *The Journal of Urology* 185, no. 6 (June 2011): 2424–427.

27. Thomas Bulfinch, *Bulfinch's Mythology* (Random House, 1993), 224.

28. *Rabid*, directed by David Cronenberg (Cinépix Film Properties, 1977), https://www.amazon.com/gp/video/detail/0GDREY4RGY00JUC1RE42MN7X0K.

29. Priscilla Wald, "Cultures and Carriers: 'Typhoid Mary' and the Science of Social Control," *Social Text*, no. 52/53 (Autumn-Winter 1997): 181–214.

30. Judith Walzer Leavitt, "Typhoid Mary: Villain or Victim?" *NOVA*, August 2004, https://www.pbs.org/wgbh/nova/typhoid/mary.html.

31. Mary Mallon, "In Her Own Words," *NOVA*, uploaded August 2004, https://www.pbs.org/wgbh/nova/typhoid/letter.html.

32. *Rabid*, directed by Jen and Sylvia Soska (Back 40 Films, 2019), https://www.amazon.com/gp/video/detail/0QBTUDIYROC98PXGXOSWVHLFRN.

Chapter 5

1. *Jennifer's Body*, directed by Karyn Kusama (Fox Atomic, 2009), DVD.

2. *The Last House on the Left*, directed by Wes Craven (Sean S. Cunningham Films, 1972), https://watch.plex.tv/watch/movie/the-last-house-on-the-left.

3. Hole, "Jennifer's Body," by Courtney Love and Eric Erlandson, recorded October, 1993, track 5 on *Live Through This*, Geffen, 1994, vinyl LP.

4. John Kenneth Muir, *Horror Films of the 1970s*, Volume 1 (McFarland, 2008), 27–28.

5. *Revenge*, directed by Coralie Fargeat (M.E.S. Productions, 2017), https://www.shudder.com/movies/watch/revenge/2cef63838af05b94.

6. *M.F.A.*, directed by Natalia Leite (Villainess Productions, 2017), https://www.amazon.com/gp/video/detail/0RZFAO673AXFK6IYN583GTRKX0.

7. *The Woman*, directed by Lucky McKee (Moderncine, 2011), https://www.amazon.com/gp/video/detail/0IMRIYREOAVMZK7QKF3N4A76GA/.

8. *La Llorona*, directed by Jayro Bustamante (La Casa de Producción, 2019), https://www.shudder.com/movies/watch/la-llorona/0bdaa1df0ad05cc0.

9. Betty Leddey, "La Llorona in Southern Arizona," *Western Folklore* 7, no. 3 (July 1948): 272–77.

10. *Confessions*, directed by Tetsuya Nakashima (Toho, 2010), DVD.

11. Christopher Brown and Pam Hirsch, "Introduction: The Cinema of the Swimming Pool," in *The Cinema of the Swimming Pool* (International Academic Publishers, 2014), 12.

12. *Mermaid Legend*, directed by Toshiharu Ikeda (Art Theatre Guild, 1984), DVD.

13. Carol Clover, "Her Body, Himself: Gender in the Slasher Film," *Representations* 20 (October 1987): 209, 219.

14. Barbara Creed, *The Monstrous-Feminine*, Second edition (Routledge, 2024), Part II, chap. 9, Kindle.

Chapter 6

1. Barbara Creed, *The Monstrous-Feminine*, Second edition (Routledge, 2024), Part I, chap. 6, Kindle.

2. Bonnie Tsui, *Why We Swim* (Algonquin Books, 2020), 136–37.

3. Foxearth & District Local History Society, "The Swimming of Witches," accessed July 28, 2024, https://www.foxearth.org.uk/SwimmingOfWitches.html.

4. Hans Peter Broedel, *The Malleus Maleficarum and the Construction of Witchcraft* (Manchester University Press, 2003), 125.

5. Creed, *The Monstrous-Feminine*, Part I, chap. 6, Kindle.

6. *Ibid.*

7. *Carrie*, directed by Kimberly Peirce (Metro-Goldwyn-Mayer, 2013), DVD.

8. Creed, *The Monstrous-Feminine*, Part I, chap. 6, Kindle.

9. *Ibid.*

10. *Ibid.*

11. *The Rage: Carrie 2*, directed by Katt Shea (United Artists, 1999), VHS.

12. Alexandra West, *The 1990s Teen Horror Cycle: Final Girls and a New Hollywood Formula* (McFarland, 2018), 128.

13. Anita Sarkeesian, "Damsel in Distress: Part 1—Tropes vs Women in Video Games," uploaded March 7, 2013, video, 11:24, https://feministfrequency.com/video/damsel-in-distress-part-1/.

14. West, *The 1990s Teen Horror Cycle*, 130.

15. Creed, *The Monstrous-Feminine*, Part I, chap. 6, Kindle.

16. *Ibid.*

17. *The Craft*, directed by Andrew Fleming (Columbia Pictures, 1996), VHS.

18. Jeff Wiltse, *Contested Waters: A Social History of Swimming Pools in America* (The University of North Carolina Press, 2007), 124–25, 165.

19. Timothy M. Dasinger, et al., "Examining Minority Youth Swimmers' versus Non-Swimmers' Perceptions of Swimming Involvement," *International Journal of Aquatic Research and Education* 3, no. 3 (April 2020): Article 8.

20. *Hellbender*, directed by Toby Poser, John Adams, and Zelda Adams (Wonder Wheel Productions, 2021), https://www.shudder.com/movies/watch/hellbender/3c76506a2fbbb433.

21. Creed, *The Monstrous-Feminine*, Part I, chap. 2, Kindle.

22. *Suspiria*, directed by Dario Argento (Seda Spettacoli, 1977), VHS.

23. Creed, *The Monstrous-Feminine*, Part I, chap. 6, Kindle.

24. *Ibid.*, Part I, chap. 1, Kindle.

25. *Dumplings*, directed by Fruit Chan (Applause Pictures, 2004), https://tubitv.com/movies/620930/dumplings.

26. Sonya Bird, "A Cross-Cultural Look at Child-Stealing Witches," *Coyote Papers* 11 (2000): 1–23.

27. S.T. Joshi, ed., *Encyclopedia of the Vampire: The Living Dead in Myth, Legend, and Popular Culture* (Greenwood, 2011), 6.

28. *Paranormal Activity 2*, directed by Tod Williams (Blumhouse Productions, 2010), DVD.

29. Mark Fisher, *The Weird and the Eerie* (Repeater Books, 2016), 61.

Chapter 7

1. Jeff Wiltse, *Contested Waters: A Social History of Swimming Pools in America* (University of North Carolina Press, 2007), 3.

2. Alex Espinoza, *Cruising: An Intimate History of a Radical Pastime* (The Unnamed Press, 2019).

3. Jayne Caudwell, "Queering Indoor Swimming in the UK: Transgender and Non-binary Wellbeing," *Journal of Sport and Social Issues* 46, no. 4 (August, 2022): 338–62.

4. Harry M. Benshoff, *Monsters in the Closet: Homosexuality and the Horror Film* (Manchester University Press, 1997), 143–44.

5. Benshoff, *Monsters in the Closet*, 151.

6. Donald Spoto, *The Art of Alfred Hitchcock: Fifty Years of His Motion Pictures* (Doubleday, 1976), 188.

7. Melissa Block, "Accusations of 'grooming' are the latest political attack—with homophobic origins," NPR, May 11, 2022, https://www.npr.org/2022/05/11/1096623939/accusations-grooming-political-attack-homophobic-origins.

8. *Les Diaboliques*, directed by Henri-Georges Clouzot (Véra Films, 1955), https://watch.plex.tv/watch/movie/diabolique-1955.

9. *Diabolique*, directed by Jeremiah S. Chechik (Warner Bros. Pictures, 1996), https://www.amazon.com/gp/video/detail/0SGIDFT0UK9P8PFOKVSB87JRN4.

10. *Tombs of the Blind Dead*, directed by Amando de Ossorio (Plata Films S.A., 1972), https://watch.plex.tv/watch/movie/tombs-of-the-blind-dead.

11. John Kenneth Muir, *Horror Films of the 1970s*, Volume 1 (McFarland, 2008), 239.

12. Jamie Russell, *Book of the Dead: The Complete History of Zombie Cinema* (FAB Press, 2005), 89.

13. *Thelma*, directed by Joachim Trier (Motlys, 2017), https://tubitv.com/movies/589540/thelma.

14. Barbara Creed, *The Monstrous-Feminine*, Second edition (Routledge, 2024), Part I, chap. 6, Kindle.

15. *Ibid.*

16. Pew Research Center, "Cell Phone Ownership," March 19, 2012, https://www.pewresearch.org/internet/2012/03/19/cell-phone-ownership/.

17. Pew Research Center, "Teens and Internet, Device Access Fact Sheet," January 5, 2024, https://www.pewresearch.org/internet/fact-sheet/teens-and-internet-device-access-fact-sheet/.

18. Elia Abi-Jaoude, et al., "Smartphones, social media use and youth mental health," *Canadian Medical Association Journal* 192, no. 6 (February 10, 2020): https://doi.org/10.1503/cmaj.190434.

19. The Trevor Project, "2023 U.S. National Survey on the Mental Health of LGBTQ Young People," accessed July 29, 2024, https://www.thetrevorproject.org/survey-2023/.

20. *Assassination Nation*, directed by Sam Levinson (BRON Studios, 2018), https://tubitv.com/movies/100015799/assassination-nation.

Chapter 8

1. *A Nightmare on Elm Street Part 2: Freddy's Revenge*, directed by Jack Sholder (New Line Cinema, 1985), DVD.

2. Adam Scales, "'Something Is Trying to Get Inside My Body': A Gay Reception and Narrative Analysis of A Nightmare on Elm Street 2: Freddy's Revenge," *Networking Knowledge: Journal of the MeCCSA Postgraduate Network* 6, no. 4 (2014).

3. Michael Thorn, "Nightmare on Gay Street: Conflating Sexuality and Gender in the Discourse Surrounding the 'Gayest Horror Film Ever Made,'" *The Journal of Popular Culture* 55, no. 4 (2022).

4. Harry M. Benshoff, *Monsters in the Closet: Homosexuality and the Horror Film* (Manchester University Press, 1997), 143–44.

5. *Halloween Ends*, directed by David Gordon Green (Universal Pictures, 2022), DVD.

6. Barbara Creed, *The Monstrous-Feminine*, Second edition (Routledge, 2024), Part I, chap. 2, Kindle.

7. Carol Clover, "Her Body, Himself: Gender in the Slasher Film," *Representations* 20 (October, 1987): 209.

8. The Trevor Project, "2023 U.S. National Survey on the Mental Health of LGBTQ Young People," accessed July 29, 2024, https://www.thetrevorproject.org/survey-2023/.

9. Matt Pearce, "Florida girl, 12, found dead

after bullies said 'kill yourself,'" *Los Angeles Times*, September 12, 2013, https://www.latimes.com/nation/nationnow/la-na-nn-florida-cyberbullying-20130912-story.html.

10. Brody Levesque, "Zachary Kirchner was bullied and died: Mom sues Pa. school district," *Washington Blade*, February 23, 2023, https://www.washingtonblade.com/2023/02/23/zachary-kirchner-was-bullied-and-died-mom-sues-pa-school-district/.

11. *The Rocky Horror Picture Show*, directed by Jim Sharman (20th Century Fox, 1975), DVD.

12. *Bride of Frankenstein*, directed by James Whale (Universal Pictures, 1935), DVD.

13. Harry M. Benshoff, *Monsters in the Closet: Homosexuality and the Horror Film* (Manchester University Press, 1997), 220–21.

14. Julia Serano, *Sexed Up: How Society Sexualizes Us, and How We Can Fight Back* (Seal Press, 2022), chap. 8, Kindle.

15. *Footlight Parade*, directed by Lloyd Bacon and Busby Berkeley (Warner Bros. Pictures, 1933), DVD.

16. John M. Clum, *Something for the Boys: Musical Theater and Gay Culture* (St. Martin's Press, 1999), 6.

17. Benshoff, *Monsters in the Closet*, 37.

18. *The Cannibal Man*, directed by Eloy de la Iglesia (Atlas International Film, 1972), https://tubitv.com/movies/100002170/the-cannibal-man.

Chapter 9

1. Barbara Creed, *The Monstrous-Feminine*, Second edition (Routledge, 2024), Part I, chap. 5, Kindle.

2. *The Hunger*, directed by Tony Scott (Metro-Goldwyn-Mayer, 1983), VHS.

3. Creed, *The Monstrous-Feminine*, Part I, chap. 5, Kindle.

4. *The Velvet Vampire*, directed by Stephanie Rothman (New World Pictures, 1971), https://www.shudder.com/movies/watch/the-velvet-vampire/1a3f95d764dcdfdb.

5. *Let the Right One In*, directed by Tomas Alfredson (EFTI, 2008), https://www.amazon.com/gp/video/detail/0U8DDES6OSENT2FG544Y19DIVT.

6. *Let Me In*, directed by Matt Reeves (Hammer Film Productions, 2010), https://tubitv.com/movies/520923/let-me-in.

Chapter 10

1. Michael Mackenzie, *Gender, Genre and Sociocultural Change in the Giallo: 1970–1975* (Glasgow Theses Service, 2013), http://theses.gla.ac.uk/4730/, 13, 34, 141–42, 218.

2. *The Fourth Victim*, directed by Eugenio Martín (Filmayer, 1971), https://tubitv.com/movies/696546/the-fourth-victim.

3. Jamie Righetti, "Finding Feminism in the Women of Giallo," *Horror Homeroom*, February 16, 2016, https://www.horrorhomeroom.com/finding-feminism-in-the-women-of-giallo/.

4. *Naked You Die*, directed by Antonio Margheriti (Super International Pictures, 1968), https://watch.plex.tv/watch/movie/naked-you-die.

5. Scott A. Bonn, "Serial Killer Myth No. 5: All Victims are Female," *Psychology Today*, November 2, 2014, https://www.psychologytoday.com/us/blog/wicked-deeds/201411/serial-killer-myth-no-5-all-victims-are-female.

6. *The Prowler*, directed by Joseph Zito (Graduation, 1981), https://www.amazon.com/gp/video/detail/0ND6YIEJMVC6LZIVJW6ENXBBNU.

7. *The Slumber Party Massacre*, directed by Amy Holden Jones (Santa Fe Productions, 1982), DVD.

8. John Kenneth Muir, *Horror Films of the 1980s* (McFarland, 2007), 280.

9. Carol Clover, "Her Body, Himself: Gender in the Slasher Film," *Representations* 20 (October 1987), 219.

10. *Slumber Party Massacre II*, directed by Deborah Brock (Concorde Pictures, 1987), DVD.

11. Stu Hackel, "Sister Rosetta Tharpe: The Godmother of Rock'N'Roll," uDiscoverMusic.com, March 20, 2024, https://www.udiscovermusic.com/stories/sister-rosetta-tharpe-rocknroll-pioneer.

12. Benjamin H. Smith, "'The Go-Go's Is Richly Detailed, Warts-And-All History of Groundbreaking Female Rock Band," decider.com, July 31, 2020, https://decider.com/2020/07/31/the-go-gos-documentary-review/.

13. *Mortuary*, directed by Howard Avedis (Hickmar Productions, 1983), https://www.amazon.com/gp/video/detail/0SXLC2EYZ9HS0NYIQU1UYJNFAN.

14. *All the Boys Love Mandy Lane*, directed by Jonathan Levine (Occupant Films, 2006), DVD.

15. Vjosa Isai, "In Canada, a Judge Sentences an Incel Killer as a Terrorist," *New York Times*, November 28, 2023, https://www.nytimes.com/2023/11/28/world/canada/incel-killer-terrorist.html.

16. Adam Lankford and Jason R. Silva, "Sexually Frustrated Mass Shooters: A Study of Perpetrators, Profiles, Behaviors, and Victims," *Homicide Studies* 28, no. 2 (May 2024): 196–219.

17. *He Knows You're Alone*, directed by Armand Mastroianni (Metro-Goldwyn-Mayer, 1980), VHS.

18. *The Pool*, directed by Boris von Sychowski (Senator Film Produktion, 2001), VHS.

19. Clover, "Her Body, Himself," 209.

20. Larry McShane, et al., "Santa Barbara killer Elliot Rodger, son of Hollywood director, vowed to 'slaughter' women who rejected him," *New York Daily News*, May 27, 2014, https://www.nydailynews.com/2014/05/27/santa-barbara-killer-elliot-rodger-son-of-hollywood-director-vowed-to-slaughter-women-who-rejected-him/.

21. Elliot Rodger, "My Twisted World: The Story of Elliot Rodger," uploaded by *New York Daily News*, accessed July 29, 2024, https://www.document

cloud.org/documents/1173808-elliot-rodger-manifesto.

Part III

Introduction to Part III

1. Chris Wisniewski, "When Worlds Collide: An Interview with Lucrecia Martel," *Reverse Shot*, August 17, 2009, https://reverseshot.org/interviews/entry/938/interview_lucrecia_martel.
2. Jeff Wiltse, *Contested Waters: A Social History of Swimming Pools in America* (The University of North Carolina Press, 2007).
3. *The Twilight Zone*, season 5, episode 36, "The Bewitchin' Pool," directed by Joseph M. Newman, aired June 19, 1964, on CBS, DVD.
4. Christopher Brown and Pam Hirsch, "Introduction: The Cinema of the Swimming Pool," in *The Cinema of the Swimming Pool* (International Academic Publishers, 2014), 2.
5. Wiltse, *Contested Waters*.
6. Sarah Mervosh, "Woman Assaulted Black Boy After Telling Him He 'Did Not Belong' at Pool, Officials Say," *New York Times*, July 1, 2018, https://www.nytimes.com/2018/07/01/us/pool-patrol-paula.html.
7. Paula Rogo, "'Pool Patrol Paula' Fined $1000 After Pleading Guilty to Assault of Black South Carolina Teen," *Essence*, October 23, 2020, https://www.essence.com/news/pool-patrol-paula-fined-1000-guilty/.
8. *Traffik*, directed by Deon Taylor (Lionsgate, 2018), https://www.amazon.com/gp/video/detail/0S3PL527M8F3YCV1A4HK49OVCK.
9. Knolan C. Rawlins, "Reestablishing a Culture of Water Competency at an HBCU," *International Journal of Aquatic Research and Education* 11, no. 1 (August 2018): Article 5.

Chapter 11

1. Ryan Reft, "A Dive into the Deep End: The Importance of the Swimming Pools in Southern California," *PBS SoCal*, May 16, 2013, https://www.pbssocal.org/history-society/a-dive-into-the-deep-end-the-importance-of-the-swimming-pools-in-southern-california.
2. Daniell Cornell, "Exposed Desires: Poolside Reflections on Celebrity," in Daniell Cornell, ed., *Backyard Oasis: The Swimming Pool in Southern Californian Photography, 1945–82* (Palm Springs Art Museum: Prestel & Delmonico Books, 2012), 17.
3. Reft, "A Dive into the Deep End."
4. "A Deep Dive on L.A.'s Water Future," Chief Sustainability Office, Los Angeles County, March 9, 2020, https://ceo.lacounty.gov/2020/03/09/sustainability/a-deep-dive-on-l-a-s-water-future/.
5. Patt Morrison, "Does L.A. have an 'addiction to cults and cultists'? Sure seems like it," *Los Angeles Times*, June 14, 2022, https://www.latimes.com/california/story/2022-06-14/does-l-a-have-an-addiction-to-cults-and-cultists-sure-seems-like-it.
6. Carey McWilliams, "The Cults of California," *The Atlantic*, March 1946, https://www.theatlantic.com/magazine/archive/1946/03/the-cults-of-california/655250/.
7. *Sunset Boulevard*, directed by Billy Wilder (Paramount Pictures, 1950), DVD.
8. *Starry Eyes*, directed by Kevin Kölsch and Dennis Widmyer (Dark Sky Films, 2014), https://www.shudder.com/movies/watch/starry-eyes/5f3732ccd5469c29.
9. *The Neon Demon*, directed by Nicolas Winding Refn (Space Rocket Nation, 2016), https://www.amazon.com/gp/video/detail/0H3CQDC6UMANPNJF05C9ANDOJR.
10. S.T. Joshi, ed., *Encyclopedia of the Vampire: The Living Dead in Myth, Legend, and Popular Culture* (Greenwood, 2011), 6.
11. Barbara Creed, *The Monstrous-Feminine*, Second edition (Routledge, 2024) Part I, chap. 2, Kindle.
12. *MaXXXine*, directed by Ti West (A24, 2024).
13. *8MM*, directed by Joel Schumacher (Columbia Pictures, 1999), VHS.
14. Cornell, "Exposed Desires," 21, 25.
15. *The Apartment Complex*, directed by Tobe Hooper (Pacific Bay Entertainment, 1999), VHS.
16. *1BR*, directed by David Marmor (Malevolent Films, 2019), https://www.amazon.com/gp/video/detail/0NOT1BGA7HM41HUE0XA3AEG6UA.
17. Mark Travers, "3 Ways Cults 'Bait and Trap' Common People—According to a Psychologist," *Forbes*, April 26, 2024, https://www.forbes.com/sites/traversmark/2024/04/26/3-ways-cults-bait-and-trap-common-people-according-to-a-psychologist/.

Chapter 12

1. Jeffrey H. Anderson, "Classification of Urban, Suburban, and Rural Areas in the National Crime Victimization Survey," U.S. Department of Justice Bureau of Justice Statistics, December 2020, https://bjs.ojp.gov/content/pub/pdf/cusrancvs.pdf.
2. Jeff Wiltse, *Contested Waters: A Social History of Swimming Pools in America* (University of North Carolina Press, 2007), 193–4.
3. Kenneth T. Jackson, *Crabgrass Frontier: The Suburbanization of the United States* (Oxford University Press, 1985), 208, 241.
4. Ibid., 233.
5. Digital Public Library of America, "Children in Progressive-Era America," n.d., accessed July 17, 2024, https://dp.la/exhibitions/children-progressive-era/childhood-postwar-america/teenage-culture.
6. Glenn Kenney, "The rise and fall (and rise?) of teen horror films," *Salon*, May 3, 2010, https://www.salon.com/2010/05/03/teen_horror_films/.

7. Matt Lebovic, "How America's Jewish 'king of the suburbs' kept Blacks out of suburbia," *The Times of Israel*, February 16, 2021, https://www.timesofisrael.com/how-americas-jewish-king-of-the-suburbs-kept-blacks-out-of-suburbia/.

8. Alex Balashov, "Why even driving through suburbia is soul crushing," *Quartz*, June 10, 2016, https://qz.com/698928/why-suburbia-sucks.

9. *Society*, directed by Brian Yuzna (Society Productions Inc., 1989), https://watch.plex.tv/watch/movie/society.

10. *The Faculty*, directed by Robert Rodriguez (Los Hooligans Productions, 1998), VHS.

11. Amanda Reavy, "Economics daunting for schools to include swimming pools," *The State Journal-Register*, November 19, 2011, https://www.sj-r.com/story/news/education/2011/11/20/economics-daunting-for-schools-to/41731234007/.

12. National Center for Education Statistics, "Public School Revenue Sources," May 2024, https://nces.ed.gov/programs/coe/indicator/cma/public-school-revenue.

13. Alexandra West, *The 1990s Teen Horror Cycle: Final Girls and a New Hollywood Formula* (McFarland, 2018), 111.

14. *Idle Hands*, directed by Rodman Flender (Columbia Pictures, 1999), VHS.

15. *TerrorVision*, directed by Ted Nicolaou (Empire Pictures, 1986), DVD.

16. *Trick or Treat*, directed by Charles Martin Smith (DEG, 1986), DVD.

17. *C.H.U.D. II: Bud the Chud*, directed by David Irving (Vestron Pictures, 1989), https://tubitv.com/movies/321117/c-h-u-d-ii-bud-the-chud.

18. John Kenneth Muir, *Horror Films of the 1980s* (McFarland, 2007), 24.

19. *It Follows*, directed by David Robert Mitchell (Northern Lights Films, 2014), https://www.hulu.com/movie/6d9bda0a-5b6e-4c0e-b99b-52d51b5f78e6.

20. Peter Walsh, "In-Ground vs. Above-Ground Pools: Pros + Cons of Each," HGTV.com, n.d., accessed July 17, 2024, https://www.hgtv.com/outdoors/outdoor-remodel/in-ground-vs-above-ground-pools.

21. *Eegah!*, directed by Arch Hall, Sr. (Fairway International Pictures, 1962), https://www.amazon.com/gp/video/detail/0R2T79C88N1U1PHPE30EX1TDDL/.

22. Nick Cullather, "Bomb them Back to the Stone Age: An Etymology," *History News Network*, n.d., accessed July 17, 2024, https://www.historynewsnetwork.org/article/bomb-them-back-to-the-stone-age-an-etymology.

23. *Panic in Year Zero!*, directed by Ray Milland (American International Pictures, 1962), VHS.

24. Cullather, "Bomb Them Back to the Stone Age."

Chapter 13

1. Umberto Eco, "Ur-Fascism," *The New York Review of Books*, June 22, 1995.

2. *Ibid*.

3. *The Stepford Wives*, directed by Bryan Forbes (Palomar Pictures International, 1975), https://tubitv.com/movies/507433/the-stepford-wives.

4. Barbara Creed, *The Monstrous-Feminine*, Second edition (Routledge, 2024) Part I, chap. 1, Kindle.

5. *The Stepford Children*, directed by Alan J. Levi (Taft Entertainment Television, 1987), DVD.

6. Jay McInerney, "Yuppies in Eden," *New York Magazine*, September 22, 2008, https://nymag.com/anniversary/40th/50657/.

7. Eco, "Ur-Fascism."

8. *Don't Worry Darling*, directed by Olivia Wilde (New Line Cinema, 2022), DVD.

9. Regina Cole, "Don't Worry Darling: We Live at Canyon View Estates," *Forbes*, October 2, 2022, https://www.forbes.com/sites/reginacole/2022/10/02/dont-worry-darling-we-live-at-canyon-view-estates/.

10. Rachel Davies, "Midcentury-Modern Architecture: Everything You Should Know About the Funky and Functional Style," *Architectural Digest*, January 23, 2023, https://www.architecturaldigest.com/story/midcentury-modern-architecture-everything-you-should-know.

11. *Footlight Parade*, directed by Lloyd Bacon and Busby Berkeley (Warner Bros. Pictures, 1933), DVD.

12. Eco, "Ur-Fascism."

13. *John and the Hole*, directed by Pascual Sisto (3311 Productions, 2021), DVD.

Chapter 14

1. Shannon L. Walsh, *Eugenics and Physical Culture Performance in the Progressive Era* (Palgrave Macmillan, 2020), 10, 33.

2. Angela M. Smith, *Hideous Progeny: Disability, Eugenics, and Classic Horror Cinema* (Columbia University Press, 2011), 234.

3. *Ibid*., 10; Walsh, *Eugenics and Physical Culture*, 33.

4. Jeff Wiltse, *Contested Waters: A Social History of Swimming Pools in America* (University of North Carolina Press, 2007), 36–37.

5. Smith, *Hideous Progeny*, 27.

6. *A Cure for Wellness*, directed by Gore Verbinski (New Regency Productions, 2016), DVD.

7. Cindy S. Aron, *Working at Play: A History of Vacations in the United States* (Oxford University Press, 1999), 19.

8. Harry B. Weiss and Howard R. Kemble, *The Great American Water-Cure Craze: A History of Hydropathy in the United States* (The Past Times Press, 1967), 68.

9. "Partnership for a Drug-Free America—Diving Board," PSA/PIF Wiki, accessed January 17, 2024, https://pif.fandom.com/wiki/Partnership_for_a_Drug-Free_America_-_Swimming.

10. *A Nightmare on Elm Street: The Dream Child*, directed by Stephen Hopkins (New Line Cinema, 1989), DVD.

11. Barbara Creed, *The Monstrous-Feminine*, Second edition (Routledge, 2024), Part I, chap. 1, Kindle.
12. *The House on Sorority Row*, directed by Mark Rosman (VAE Productions, 1983), https://www.amazon.com/gp/video/detail/0ND548NWETAYRMI2VPTAQYZG79.
13. *Fever Dream*, directed by Claudia Llosa (Fabula, 2021), https://www.netflix.com/title/80233703.
14. *Don't Breathe 2*, directed by Rodo Sayagues (Ghost House Pictures, 2021), DVD.
15. Seth Hadley, "The Rhetorical Use of the Other: An Analysis of Symbolic Disability in Contemporary Horror Films," *MSU Graduate Theses* (2023): 3920.
16. Smith, *Hideous Progeny*, 36–37.
17. *Ibid.*, 3.
18. Walsh, *Eugenics and Physical Culture*, 35.

Chapter 15

1. John Kenneth Muir, *Horror Films of the 1990s* (McFarland, 2011), 23, 27.
2. Michael Flood, "False allegations of sexual and domestic violence: the facts," *XY Online*, April 15, 2022, https://xyonline.net/content/false-allegations-sexual-and-domestic-violence-facts.
3. "Getting Evicted for Calling the Police: Nuisance Ordinances and Their Impacts on Domestic Violence Survivors," National Housing Law Project, 2018, https://www.nhlp.org/wp-content/uploads/2018/06/Nuisance-Information-Sheet-for-Advocates-2018.pdf.
4. *Poison Ivy: The New Seduction*, directed by Kurt Voss (New Line Cinema, 1997), DVD.
5. *Swimfan*, directed by John Polson (20th Century Fox, 2002), DVD.
6. *Fear*, directed by James Foley (Universal Pictures, 1996), VHS.
7. Muir, *Horror Films of the 1990s*, 27.
8. Susan Benesch, "Vile Crime or Inalienable Right: Defining Incitement to Genocide," *Virginia Journal of International Law* 48, no. 3 (2008): 504.
9. *The Stepfather*, directed by Nelson McCormick (Screen Gems, 2009), DVD.
10. *The Glass House*, directed by Daniel Sackheim (Columbia Pictures, 2001), DVD.
11. *House on the Edge of the Park*, directed by Ruggero Deodato (F.D. Cinematografica, 1980), DVD.
12. Richard Mogg, *Analog Nightmares: The Shot on Video Horror Films of 1982–1995* (RickMoe Publishing, 2018), 175.
13. *Venus Flytrap*, directed by T. Michael (Campfire Video, 1987), DVD.
14. Mogg, *Analog Nightmares*, 175. I have taken care to avoid saying that *Venus Flytrap* was inspired by Deodato's movie, despite the apparent textual evidence. *Venus Flytrap*'s creators have claimed that they were not aware of the earlier film, and absent any contradicting statement, I choose to believe them.
15. "Moral Event Horizon," TVTropes.org, accessed July 30, 2024, https://tvtropes.org/pmwiki/pmwiki.php/Main/MoralEventHorizon.
16. Christopher J. Ferguson, "Psychologist: 'Affluenza' is Junk Science," *Time*, December 14, 2013, https://ideas.time.com/2013/12/14/psychologist-affluenza-is-junk-science/.
17. Manny Fernandez and John Schwartz, "Teenager's Sentence in Fatal Drunken-Driving Case Stirs 'Affluenza' Debate," *New York Times*, December 13, 2013, https://www.nytimes.com/2013/12/14/us/teenagers-sentence-in-fatal-drunken-driving-case-stirs-affluenza-debate.html.
18. Jeff Wiltse, *Contested Waters: A Social History of Swimming Pools in America* (University of North Carolina Press, 2007), 36.

Chapter 16

1. Statista Research Department, "Median sales price of new homes sold in the United States from 1965 to 2023," Statista.com, March 14, 2024, https://www.statista.com/statistics/199895/median-sales-prices-of-new-homes-sold-in-the-us-since-1965/.
2. "U.S. Inflation Calculator," CoinNews Media Group, accessed July 30, 2024, https://www.usinflationcalculator.com/.
3. "United States Median Household Income: 1950–1990," accessed July 30, 2024, https://web.stanford.edu/class/polisci120a/immigration/Median%20Household%20Income.pdf.
4. Jacob Channel, "Average Down Payments on Homes Across 50 Largest U.S. Metros Top $84,000," Lendingtree.com, October 23, 2023, https://www.lendingtree.com/home/mortgage/average-down-payments-study/.
5. Alejandra O'Connell-Domenech, "61 percent of renters worry they'll never own a home," *Changing America*, March 12, 2024, https://thehill.com/changing-america/sustainability/infrastructure/4526872-61-percent-of-renters-worry-theyll-never-own-a-home/.
6. Lily Katz, "16% of Home Listings Were Affordable for the Typical Household in 2023, Likely the Bottom for Housing Affordability," *Redfin News*, December 21, 2023, https://www.redfin.com/news/share-of-homes-affordable-new-2023/.
7. *Open House*, directed by Jag Mundhra (Intercontinental Releasing Corporation, 1987), DVD.
8. "The state of women in real estate: A look at the past, present, and future of our female-dominated field," Realtor.com, March 15, 2022, https://www.realtor.com/marketing/resources/state-of-women-in-real-estate/.
9. Grace Stetson, "The Untold History Behind Why Most Real Estate Agents Are Women," *Apartment Therapy*, March 30, 2019, https://www.apartmenttherapy.com/women-in-real-estate-history-268098.
10. Shawn G. Kennedy, "A Growing Leadership

Role for Women," *New York Times*, January 5, 1992, https://nytimes.com/1992/01/05/realestate/a-growing-leadership-role-for-women.html.

11. Stetson, "The Untold History."

12. Jeff Sommer, "Lessons from the '80s, When Volcker Reigned and Rates Were High," *New York Times*, August 5, 2022, https://www.nytimes.com/2022/08/05/business/inflation-investing-paul-volcker.html.

13. Stephen Rose and David Fasenfest, "Family Incomes in the 1980s: New Pressure on Wives, Husbands, and Young Adults," *Economic Policy Institute*, Working Paper No. 103, November 1988.

14. "The state of women in real estate," Realtor.com.

15. Stetson, "The Untold History."

16. *Halloween*, directed by Rob Zombie (Dimension Films, 2007), Bluray.

17. *Fright Night*, directed by Craig Gillespie (DreamWorks Pictures, 2011), DVD.

18. *Gremlins*, directed by Joe Dante (Amblin Entertainment, 1984), DVD.

19. John Kenneth Muir, John Kenneth Muir, *Horror Films of the 1980s* (McFarland, 2007), 392–93.

20. Hadley Meares, "How Gremlins Went from Fairy Stories to Warplanes to Hollywood Legend," *Atlas Obscura*, October 24, 2023, https://www.atlasobscura.com/articles/what-are-gremlins.

21. Muir, *Horror Films of the 1980s*, 393.

22. *Die Hard*, directed by John McTiernan (20th Century Fox, 1986), VHS.

23. Muir, *Horror Films of the 1980s*, 393.

24. Kristina Shull, "Hidden Transcripts," *Inquest*, September 14, 2022, https://inquest.org/hidden-transcripts/.

25. Alexander M. Stephens, "Making Migrants 'Criminal': The Mariel Boatlift, Miami, and U.S. Immigration Policy in the 1980s," *Anthurium* 17, no. 2 (2021): Article 4.

26. Shull, "Hidden Transcripts."

27. Kristina Shull, "'A Recession-Proof Industry': Reagan's Immigration Crisis and the Birth of the Neoliberal Security State," *Border Criminologies* (blog), April 30, 2015, https://blogs.law.ox.ac.uk/research-subject-groups/centre-criminology/centreborder-criminologies/blog/2015/04/%E2%80%98-recession-proof.

28. Leo R. Chavez, *The Latino Threat: Constructing Immigrants, Citizens, and the Nation* (Stanford University Press, 2008), 72.

29. Ibid.

30. "'Welfare Queen' Becomes Issue in Reagan Campaign," *New York Times*, February 15, 1976, https://www.nytimes.com/1976/02/15/archives/welfare--becomes-issue-in-reagan-campaign-hitting-a-nerve-now.html.

Chapter 17

1. *From Dusk Till Dawn*, directed by Robert Rodriguez (Dimension Films, 1996), VHS.

2. "Is there a psychological reason for hotels having swimming pools? Does this represent a survival instinct to want to be near water?" Quora.com, accessed July 30, 2024, https://www.quora.com/Is-there-a-psychological-reason-for-hotels-having-swimming-pools-Does-this-represent-a-survival-instinct-to-want-to-be-near-water.

3. Cindy S. Aron, *Working at Play: A History of Vacations in the United States* (Oxford University Press, 1999), 16–17.

4. Madeline Bilis, "Throwback Thursday: When the First Modern Hotel in America Opened in Boston," *Boston Magazine*, October 15, 2015, https://www.bostonmagazine.com/news/2015/10/15/tremont-house/.

5. Aron, *Working at Play*, 53.

6. John Margolies, *Home Away from Home: Motels in America* (Little, Brown, 1995), 9.

7. Aron, *Working at Play*, 4.

8. Saskia de Melker and Sam Weber, "Agrarian roots? Think again. Debunking the myth of summer vacation's origins," *PBS News*, September 7, 2014, https://www.pbs.org/newshour/education/debunking-myth-summer-vacation.

9. Ibid.

10. "Learn About Heat Islands," United States Environmental Protection Agency, August 28, 2023, https://www.epa.gov/heatislands/learn-about-heat-islands.

11. Aron, *Working at Play*, 49, 60.

12. Jeff Wiltse, *Contested Waters: A Social History of Swimming Pools in America* (University of North Carolina Press, 2007), 15.

13. James M. Pedersen, *Summer Versus School: The Possibilities of the Year-Round School* (Rowman & Littlefield, 2015), 4–7.

14. Margolies, *Home Away from Home*, 54.

15. Thrillist Editors, "The 20 Best Beach Towns in the U.S.," Thrillist.com, June 20, 2024, https://www.thrillist.com/travel/nation/best-beach-towns-in-the-usa.

16. Tom Fish, "25 Most Popular Beach Towns in America," *Newsweek*, April 15, 2021, https://www.newsweek.com/most-popular-beach-towns-america-1582230.

17. "Asbury Park, NJ," DataUSA.io, accessed July 30, 2024, https://datausa.io/profile/geo/asbury-park-nj.

18. Emily A. Shrider and John Creamer, "Poverty in the United States: 2022," United States Census Bureau, September 12, 2023, https://www.census.gov/library/publications/2023/demo/p60-280.html.

19. Matt McGrath, "Tourism's carbon impact three times larger than estimated," BBC News, May 7, 2018, https://www.bbc.com/news/science-environment-44005013.

20. *The Strangers: Prey at Night*, directed by Johannes Roberts (The Fyzz, 2018), DVD.

21. Mark Fisher, *The Weird and the Eerie* (Repeater Books, 2016), 61.

22. *The Strangers*, directed by Bryan Bertino (Rogue Pictures, 2008), DVD.

23. Kathryn J. Edin, et al., "One Overlooked Way to Fight Opioid Deaths? Give People Something to Do," Governing.com, September 11, 2023, https://www.governing.com/health/one-overlooked-way-to-fight-opioid-deaths-give-people-something-to-do.

24. *Bad Things*, directed by Stewart Thorndike (Baked Studios, 2023), https://www.shudder.com/movies/watch/bad-things/9275aca0731c9cb5.

25. *I Still Know What You Did Last Summer*, directed by Danny Cannon (Columbia Pictures, 1998), VHS.

26. *Death Valley*, directed by Dick Richards (Universal Pictures, 1982), https://watch.plex.tv/watch/movie/death-valley.

27. *Infinity Pool*, directed by Brandon Cronenberg (Film Forge, 2023), https://www.hulu.com/watch/4ff36610-ce17-4180-bcd5-f7e19da5e4cf.

Postscript

1. Jeva Lange, "The Climate Case for Pool Parties," *Heatmap*, April 16, 2023, https://heatmap.news/the-climate-case-for-pool-parties.

2. Mara Gay, "When It Comes to Swimming, 'Why Have Americans Been Left on Their Own?'" *New York Times*, July 27, 2023, https://www.nytimes.com/2023/07/27/opinion/drowning-public-pools-america.htm?.

Bibliography

Aron, Cindy S. *Working at Play: A History of Vacations in the United States*. Oxford University Press, 1999.

Benshoff, Harry M. *Monsters in the Closet: Homosexuality and the Horror Film*. Manchester University Press, 1997.

Brown, Christopher, and Pam Hirsch, eds. *The Cinema of the Swimming Pool*. International Academic Publishers, 2014.

Clover, Carol. "Her Body, Himself: Gender in the Slasher Film." *Representations* 20 (1987): 187–228. https://doi.org/10.2307/2928507/

Cornell, Daniell, ed. *Backyard Oasis: The Swimming Pool in Southern Californian Photography, 1945–82*. Palm Springs Art Museum: Prestel & Delmonico Books, 2012.

Creed, Barbara. *The Monstrous-Feminine*, Second edition. Routledge, 2024.

Eco, Umberto. "Ur-Fascism." *The New York Review of Books*, June 22, 1995, 12.

Fisher, Mark. *The Weird and the Eerie*. Repeater Books, 2016.

Hackett, John, and Seán Harrington, eds. *Beasts of the Deep: Sea Creatures and Popular Culture*. John Libbey, 2018.

International Journal of Aquatic Research and Education. Multiple volumes/issues.

Jackson, Kenneth T. *Crabgrass Frontier: The Suburbanization of the United States*. Oxford University Press, 1985.

Muir, John Kenneth. *Horror Films of the 1970s*. McFarland, 2008.

Muir, John Kenneth. *Horror Films of the 1980s*. McFarland, 2007.

Muir, John Kenneth. *Horror Films of the 1990s*. McFarland, 2011.

Smith, Angela M. *Hideous Progeny: Disability, Eugenics, and Classic Horror Cinema*. Columbia University Press, 2011.

Tsui, Bonnie. *Why We Swim*. Algonquin Books, 2020.

Van Leeuwen, Thomas A.P. *The Springboard in the Pond: An Intimate History of the Swimming Pool*. MIT Press, 1998.

Walsh, Shannon L. *Eugenics and Physical Culture Performance in the Progressive Era*. Palgrave Macmillan, 2020.

West, Alexandra. *The 1990s Teen Horror Cycle: Final Girls and a New Hollywood Formula*. McFarland, 2018.

Wiltse, Jeff. *Contested Waters: A Social History of Swimming Pools in America*. University of North Carolina Press, 2007.

Yuknavitch, Lidia. *The Chronology of Water: A Memoir*. Hawthorne Books, 2011.

Index

Numbers in **bold** indicate main entries.

above-ground swimming pool 166–167
adolescence 44, 53–54, 78–86, 92, 97, 101–103, 105–106, 131–132, 136, 155–156, 158, 166, 169, 208; *see also* bullying; pool party
affluenza 200–201
All the Boys Love Mandy Lane (2006) **134**
Alligator (1980) **22–23**, 59
American International Pictures 92
The Amityville Horror (book) 10
apartment buildings 14, 31, 37, 57–58, 68, 111–112, 152–154, 187–189
The Apartment Complex (1999) **152–154**, 157, 205, 226
aquaphobia 20, 40
architecture 151–152, 175–176, 197
Aron, Cindy S. 213–214
Ashe, Arthur 56
Asmodexia (2014) **46**
Assassination Nation (2018) **101–103**, 178
atavism 48–49, 51, 64, 156, 158; *see also* eugenics

Bad Things (2023) **217–219**, 222
Báthory, Elizabeth 87, 150
The Beach Boys 130
Benshoff, Harry 92, 100, 104, 106, 108–109, 111, 115, 116–117; *see also* monster queer
Berkeley, Busby 109–110, 177
Berry, Chuck 130
"The Bewitchin' Pool" (1964) **140–141**
Billy the Kid 221
Blood Rage (1987) **31–32**, 216
Bride of Frankenstein (1935) 109
Brown, Christopher 73, 141–142
bullying 1, 40, 81, 101, 106, 108, 118–121, 134; *see also* adolescence
Burnt Offerings (1976) **16–18**, 25, 75, 106

California 2, 145–154, 175
The Cannibal Man (1972) **111–113**, 140
cannibalism 33, 86–88, 109–110, 111–113, 150
Carrie (1976) 77–78, 79, 80, 100
Carrie (2013) **77–78**
Carroll, Lewis 176
Cat People (1942) **49–51**, 52–54, 61, 62, 65, 82, 84, 95, 120, 149
Cat People (1982) **51–53**, 54, 62
"Cat People shot" 51, 65, 67, 149–150
Century Magazine 214
Chandler, Raymond 24
Chavez, Leo R. 211–212
C.H.U.D. II: Bud the Chud (1989) **164–166**, 168, 169–170
classism 158, 185–186, 192–193, 195, 223
climate change 20, 25–26, 223, 226
Clover, Carol 75, 130, 136
Clum, John M. 110
Colossal (2016) **54–55**, 62, 122
Confessions (2010) **72–73**, 205
contagion *see* hygiene
Cornell, Daniell 145, 151–152
Couch, Ethan *see* affluenza
The Craft (1996) **81–82**, 84, 156
Crawl (2019) **25–26**
Creature from the Black Lagoon (1954) 20
Creed, Barbara 2–3, 45, 48, 49, 54, 75, 77–78, 80–81, 82, 84, 86, 99, 100, 107, 114–115, 119, 150, 160; *see also* monstrous-feminine
Cronenberg, David 20, 57–60
cults 145–146, 147–148, 151, 154
A Cure for Wellness (2016) **182–183**, 185, 187, 189, 190

Dante, Joe 20, 210
Death Valley (1982) **220–222**, 223, 226
Diabolique (1996) **95–97**
Les Diaboliques (1955) **93–96**, 116, 122, 124, 125, 185
Die Hard (1988) 211
disability 34–36, 100, 183, 185–190
diving 2, 56, 81–82
Don't Breathe 2 (2021) **187–189**, 194
Don't Worry Darling (2022) **175–178**, 179, 197
drowning 2, 72, 141, 193–194; deliberate 28, 36, 75, 79, 94–95, 123–124, 126, 132–133, 196–197
Dumplings (2004) **86–88**, 150, 183

Ebert, Roger 14
Eco, Umberto 171, 174, 177
Eegah (1962) **168–170**
8MM (1999) **151**, 153, 205
empty swimming pools 24, 46, 149–150, 153, 189, 206–207, 216, 219
entrapment in the swimming pool 25, 99–100
eugenics 48–49, 181–190; *see also* atavism

The Faculty (1998) **158–161**, 164, 171
fascism 171, 174, 177
Fear (1996) **194–195**, 198
Federal Housing Administration 155
feminine water symbolism 36, 45–46, 49, 54, 57, 90, 99, 134; *see also* sexualization of the swimming space; womb symbolism
Fever Dream (2021) **186–187**, 189, 190, 223, 226
final girl 7, 75, 104, 130, 184, 219; *see also* slasher film

247

Index

Fisher, Mark 23, 89, 216
Florida 23, 25, 211
Footlight Parade (1933) *see* Berkeley, Busby
47 Meters Down (2017) 23, **26–28**, 226
The Fourth Victim (1971) **123–125**
Freud, Sigmund 45
Fright Night (2011) **207–210**

Gaslight (film) 33–35
Gay, Mara 227
gender discrimination 32–33, 44, 52–53, 58, 59–60, 68, 70, 77, 79, 87, 102, 122–123, 131, 172–173, 174, 177–178, 192–193, 204–205; *see also* male fragility
gender nonconformity *see* queerness
Glass (2019) **40–41**
The Glass House (2001) **197–198**, 226
The Go-Go's 130–131
gothic 7, 86, 109, 146
Gremlins (1984) 1, **210–212**

Hadley, Seth 188
Halloween (2007) 2, **207–207**
Halloween Ends (2022) **106–108**, 119, 156
Harrington, Seán J. 30
He Knows You're Alone (1980) 128, 135
Hebdige, Dick 8
Hellbender (2021) **82–85**, 86, 114
Hirsch, Pam 73, 141–142
Hitchcock, Alfred 125
Hitler, Adolf 181
home invasion 198–202
home ownership 10, 203; *see also* real estate sales
homophobia *see* queerness
Hooper, Tobe 12–13, 152
hot tubs 60
hotels 28–29, 87, 213–215, 217–223; *see also* hotels; tourism
House (1985) 1, **9–12**, 21, 45, 140, 226
The House on Sorority Row (1983) **185–186**, 205, 226
The House on the Edge of the Park (1980) **198–202**, 226, 227
The Hunger (1983) **114–115**, 118, 183
hydrotherapy 10–11, 61, 183
hygiene 1, 11, 56–57, 61, 140, 142

I Still Know What You Did Last Summer (1998) **219–220**, 222, 223

I Was a Teenage Werewolf (1957) 156
Idle Hands (1999) 160
In My Skin (2002) 33, 117
incels 135
Infinity Pool (2023) **222–224**, 226
interlopers 191–198
Invasion of the Body Snatchers (1956) 158
It Follows (2014) **166–168**, 169

Jackson, Kenneth T. 155
Jaws (1975) 22–23
Jennifer's Body (2009) **63–65**, 82, 149, 160
"Joe Gillis shot" 146, 163, 197
John and the Hole (2021) **178–180**
Johnson, Magic 56

King, Stephen 10, 11, 160
King Kong (1933) 111
The Kiss (1988) **53–54**, 69, 75, 82
Kristeva, Julia 2–3, 84, 107, 156–157, 172

Lacks, Henrietta 58
The Ladies Club (1986) 65
Lady in the Water (2006) **37–41**
The Last House on the Left (1972) 64, 198
Led Zeppelin 164
Let Me In (2010) **120–121**
Let the Right One In (2008) **118–121**
Levittown 155–156
La Llorona (2019) **70–72**
Louganis, Greg 1, 56
Love, Courtney 64

Mackenzie, Michael 122, 126
male fragility 55, 116–117, 132–137; *see also* gender discrimination
male gaze 45, 65, 66, 70, 122, 129–130, 134, 149, 167, 174, 178; *see also* sexualization of the swimming space
Mallon, Mary 59–60
Margolies, John 214
Marlina the Murderer in Four Acts (2017) 65
MaXXXine (2024) **150–151**
McInerney, Jay 174
McWilliams, Carey 146
menstruation 33, 49, 53–54, 77–78, 79, 80, 82, 83, 86, 182–183
mental illness 35, 101, 124, 184
Mermaid Legend (1984) **73–76**, 78, 80
mermaids 48, 49, 58, 75, 80, 91

metamorphosis *see* shapeshifting
M.F.A. (2017) 65, **67–69**, 74–75
Migos 143
mirrors 10, 14, 30, 37–39, 46, 66–67, 146, 172, 176, 187
monster queer 92, 94, 105, 109–111, 115; *see also* Bensoff, Harry
monstrous-feminine 45, 49, 54, 77, 90, 121; *see also* Creed, Barbara
Mortuary (1983) **132–134**, 226
motherhood 46, 71–73, 84–90, 100, 114, 150, 160, 184; *see also* womb symbolism
Muir, John Kenneth 13, 37, 97, 129, 166, 191, 195, 210–211
My Bloody Valentine (1981) 128

Naked You Die (1968) **125–127**
Narcissus 15, 30, 38–39, 41
Naylor, Alex 51
The Neon Demon (2016) **148–150**, 183
Night Swim (2024) **10–12**, 75, 207
A Nightmare on Elm Street (2010) **7–8**, 10, 13, 133
A Nightmare on Elm Street: The Dream Child (1989) **183–185**
A Nightmare on Elm Street 2: Freddy's Revenge (1985) **104–106**, 107, 118, 156

ocean 6, 19, 27, 28
The Old Dark House (1932) 109
Olds, Sharon 45
IBR (2019) 154, 226
Open House (1987) **203–205**, 226

Panic in Year Zero! (1962) 169
Paranormal Activity 2 (2010) **88–90**, 216
Pet Sematary (book) 11
phallic symbolism 75, 108, 126, 129, 136
physical culture movement *see* Progressive era
Piranha (1978) **20–24**, 28, 59, 165, 227
Piranha 3DD (2012) 22
Poison Ivy: The New Seduction (1997) **192–193**, 194, 195, 205
Poltergeist (1982) **12–13**, 24, 25, 117, 140
Poltergeist III (1988) **13–16**, 30, 37, 44, 45
The Pool (2001) **135–137**, 209, 226
The Pool (2018) **23–25**, 45–46, 103, 226
pool party 14–15, 44, 53, 83,

104–105, 134, 135–136, 162–164, 168, 184, 192, 195; *see also* adolescence
"Pool Patrol Paula" 142
portals in swimming pools 7, 10, 15, 45, 100, 140–141, 184–185
Progressive era 181, 189, 200–201
Promising Young Woman (2020) 65
The Prowler (1981) **127–128**, 132, 227
public swimming pool 1, 2, 44, 64, 82, 91, 97, 167–168, 226, 227; history 11, 56, 141–142, 181

queerness 44, 48, 53, 56, 59, 91–121, 127, 150, 201, 202

Rabid (1977) **59–62**, 63, 66, 227
Rabid (2019) **60–62**, 63, 68
racism 2, 48, 81–82, 142–144, 155–156, 227
The Rage: Carrie 2 (1999) **78–81**, 82, 156, 226
rape-revenge *see* sexual assault
Reagan, Ronald 1, 174, 198, 200, 211–212, 226
real estate sales 13, 204–209; *see also* home ownership
reflections *see* mirrors
Revenge (2017) **65–67**, 68, 178
Roberts, Johannes 26, 215
The Rocky Horror Picture Show (1975) **109–111**, 113, 177
Rodger, Elliot 136–137
role reversal 51, 83, 85
Roosevelt, Theodore 181
Rope (1948) 92
Russell, Jamie 97

Sarkeesian, Anita 79
Sebby-Strempel, Stephanie *see* "Pool Patrol Paula"
self-harm 32–33, 81, 101, 147–148; *see also* suicide
sexism *see* gender discrimination
sexual assault 58, 60, 63–70, 75, 79, 97, 121, 122, 132, 150, 183–184, 198–202, 204
sexualization of the swimming space 44–45, 47, 60, 65–66, 80, 91, 129; *see also* feminine water symbolism; gender discrimination; male gaze

shapeshifting 48, 62, 68, 77, 83, 88, 91, 106, 148, 160
The Shining (1980) 218
Shivers (1975) **57–59**, 60, 62, 110, 227
Shock Waves (1977) **28–29**, 59, 159, 165, 226
Shull, Kristina 211
Shyamalan, M. Night 37–41, 45, 46
Sims, J. Marion 58
siren 58, 64
slasher film 7–8, 31–32, 75, 104–108, 122, 127–137, 183–186, 205–207, 219–220
The Slumber Party Massacre (1982) **128–130**, 149
Slumber Party Massacre II (1987) **130–132**
Smith, Angela M. 35, 189
social media 101–103
Society (1989) **157–158**, 162, 163, 171, 207
Split (2016 film) 39–40
Starry Eyes (2014) **147–148**, 149, 151, 152, 154
The Stepfather (2009) **195–197**
The Stepford Children (1987) **173–174**, 178
The Stepford Wives (1975) **171–173**, 175–178, 196, 226
Stetson, Grace 204
The Strangers: Prey at Night (2018) **215–217**, 218, 220
suburbs 31, 53–54, 103, 155–171, 179, 208
suicide 9, 30, 31, 35, 78, 99, 101–102, 106, 108, 115, 123, 134, 175, 206, 225; *see also* self-harm
Sunset Blvd. (1950) **146–147**, 151, 168, 226
Suspiria (1977) **85–86**, 87, 150
Swimfan (2002) **193–194**, 195, 196, 205
swimming 3, 27–28, 29, 47, 49, 64, 77, 82, 140, 142–144, 181; competitive 25–26, 56, 193, 195–196

"The Tale of the Dead Man's Float" (1995) **6–7**
Taste of Fear (1961) **34–36**, 125, 127, 185
teenagers *see* adolescence
TerrorVision (1986) **161–162**, 164
Tharpe, Sister Rosetta 130
Thelma (2017) **97–101**, 119, 125

"threesome murder" 92–93, 96, 105, 107–108, 115, 116–117, 120
Tombs of the Blind Dead (1972) **97**, 112, 227
tourism 22, 27–28, 215–217, 219–223; *see also* hotels; vacation
Traffik (2019) **142–144**
Tremont House 214
Trick or Treat (1986) **162–164**
Tsui, Bonnie 77
Typhoid Mary *see* Mallon, Mary

Unbreakable (2000) **38–41**, 55, 68

vacation 26–27, 213–224; *see also* hotels; tourism
vampires 114–121, 183, 207–210
Van Leeuwen, Thomas A.P. 46–47
The Velvet Vampire (1971) **115–118**, 119, 122, 178
Venus Flytrap (1987) **199–202**, 205, 216
Victorian era 11, 77
Vietnam War 9–10, 21
The Virgin Spring (1960) 65
"vulvic murder" 75, 94, 120, 124, 173

Wallace, Edgar 122
Walsh, Shannon L. 189
Walters, Barbara 56
water cure *see* hydrotherapy
West, Alexandra 79–80, 160
Whale, James 109
Wiltse, Jeff 11, 45, 56, 82, 140, 181
witches 54, 77–78, 80–88, 97–101, 114, 141, 156, 164
The Woman (2011) **69–70**, 196
A Woman's Torment (1977) 65
womb symbolism 32, 45–46, 49, 55, 58, 73, 80, 85, 88, 90, 97, 132, 150, 160, 183, 185; *see also* feminine water symbolism; motherhood
World War II 28, 49, 51, 152, 155, 204, 211
Wray, Faye 111

xenophobia 1, 27, 51, 210–212

YMCA 210–211
Yuknavitch, Lidia 9, 49

Zombie, Rob 2, 205–207

www.ingramcontent.com/pod-product-compliance
Lightning Source LLC
Chambersburg PA
CBHW060339010526
44117CB00017B/2890